MEDITERRANEAN SEA

Alexandria   Bilqas   Port Said

Sakha

Wadi al-Natrun   Cairo

SINAI

Fayyum

Beni Suef

NILE

The Monastery
of St. Antony

GULF OF SUEZ

St. Catherine's
Monastery

GULF OF AQABA

Minya

The Monastery
of St. Paul

Asyut

E G Y P T

RED
SEA

Sohag   Akhmim

Naqada

Luxor

Aswan

THE CHURCHES OF EGYPT

THE CHURCHES OF EGYPT

From the Journey of the Holy Family to the Present Day

Gawdat Gabra and Gertrud J.M. van Loon
with Darlene L. Brooks Hedstrom
Edited by Carolyn Ludwig

Photographs by Sherif Sonbol

A Ludwig Publishing Edition
The American University in Cairo Press
Cairo • New York

PAGES 1 AND 2:
Beam icon above the screen to the haykal *of the Archangel Gabriel,
probably dating to to ca. 1200. Two of the seven major feasts of
the Coptic Church are depicted: the Nativity and the Ascension.
The Church of the Holy Virgin, Harat Zuwayla, Cairo.*

First published in 2007 by
The American University in Cairo Press
113 Sharia Kasr el Aini, Cairo, Egypt
420 Fifth Avenue, New York, NY 10018
www.aucpress.com

Copyright © 2007 by Ludwig Publishing, Inc.

Published by arrangement with Ludwig Publishing, Inc.
419 North Larchmont Boulevard, #296, Los Angeles, CA 90004

The photographs on pages 92–97 by Araldo De Luca are copyright © Archivio White Star and are reproduced by
permission. The photograph on page 42 is by Hannah Sonbol. The photographs on pages 43 (main and left), 134
(top), and 140 (left) are by Carolyn Ludwig.

Dar el Kutub No. 3295/07
ISBN 978 977 416 106 3

Dar el Kutub Cataloging-in-Publication Data

Gabra, Gawdat
     The Churches of Egypt: From the Journey of the Holy Family to the Present Day / Gawdat Gabra,
  Gertrud J.M. van Loon; edited by Carolyn Ludwig.—Cairo: The American University in Cairo Press, 2007
     p.   cm.
     ISBN 977 416 106 8
     1. Jesus Christ—Family   2.Church history   I. van Loon, Gertrud J.M. (auth)   II.
     Ludwig, Carolyn (edit)   III. Title
     273.29

1 2 3 4 5 6 7 8 9 10 11 12   12 11 10 09 08 07

Designed by Morris Jackson
Printed in China

To my husband Bruce Ludwig
who makes every wish come true
Carolyn Ludwig

To the memory of
Otto Meinardus and Paul van Moorsel
for their pioneering work and their love and
dedication to the churches of Egypt
Gawdat Gabra and
Gertrud J.M. van Loon

Legend: Denominations of churches

Coptic
Orthodox

Greek
Orthodox

Roman
Catholic

Protestant

Armenian
Orthodox

Ruined
Churches

Contents

10   Preface *Carolyn Ludwig*

12   Introduction *Gawdat Gabra and Gertrud J.M. van Loon*

14   The History of Christianity in Egypt *Gawdat Gabra*

22   The Architecture of Coptic Churches *Darlene L. Brooks Hedstrom*

30   The Art of Coptic Churches *Gertrud J.M. van Loon*

Lower Egypt and Sinai

PORT SAID

40   The Cathedral of the Holy Virgin *(Mary Queen of the World)*

BILQAS

44   The Pilgrimage Center of St. Dimyana Monastery

ALEXANDRIA

48   The Coptic Patriarchal Church of St. Mark

52   The Church of St. Catherine

56   The Anglican Church of St. Mark

60   The Greek Orthodox Cathedral of St. Saba

WADI AL-NATRUN

64   The Monastery of al-Baramus *(Dayr al-Baramus)*

70   The Monastery of the Syrians *(Dayr al-Suryan)*

78   The Monastery of St. Pshoi *(Dayr Anba Bishoi)*

84   The Monastery of St. Macarius *(Dayr Anba Maqar)*

SAKHA

90   The Church of the Holy Virgin Mary

SINAI

92   St. Catherine's Monastery

Cairo

OLD CAIRO

100   The Church of St. Mercurius *(Abu Sayfayn)*

106   The Tomb of Ibrahim and Girgis al-Guhari

108   The Church of Sts. Sergius and Bacchus *(Abu Sarga)*

112   The Hanging Church *(al-Mu'allaqa)*

120   The Church of St. Barbara

122   The Greek Orthodox Church of St. George

124   Sleeping Mary Greek Orthodox Church *(Church of the Dormition)*

QASR AL-DUBARA

128   The Coptic Evangelical Church

RAMSES

130   The Armenian Cathedral of St. Gregory the Illuminator

MUSKI

132   The Franciscan Church of the Assumption *(Franciscan Center of Eastern Studies)*

HARAT ZUWAYLA

134   The Church of the Holy Virgin

FUMM AL-KHALIG

140   The Church of St. Menas

SHUBRA

146   The Catholic Cathedral of St. Mark

FAGGALA

150   The Jesuits' Holy Family Church
154   The Coptic Evangelical Church

ZAYTUN

156   The Church of the Holy Virgin

MATARIYA

160   The Jesuits' Holy Family Church
164   The Holy Family Tree

HELIOPOLIS

166   St. Cyril Melkite Catholic Church
170   The Basilica of Our Lady

AZBAKIYA

174   The Old Cathedral of St. Mark

ABBASIYA

178   Anba Ruways *(al-Khandaq)*
178   The Chapel of St. Athanasius
179   The Cathedral of St. Mark
182   The Church of the Holy Virgin Mary and St. Pshoi
183   The Church of the Holy Virgin Mary and Anba Ruways
184   The Church of Anba Ruways
184   The Shrine of St. Mark
186   The Church of St. Peter and St. Paul *(al-Butrusiya)*

MUQATTAM

188   The Cathedral of the Holy Virgin Mary and St. Simeon the Tanner

MAADI

194   The Church of the Holy Virgin

Upper Egypt

FAYYUM

202   The Monastery of the Archangel Gabriel *(Dayr al-Malak Ghubriyal/Dayr al-Naqlun)*

RED SEA

208   The Monastery of St. Antony *(Dayr Anba Antuniyus)*
220   The Monastery of St. Paul *(Dayr Anba Bula)*

BENI SUEF

230   The Church of St. Antony *(Dayr al-Maymun)*

MINYA

234 The Church of St. Theodore *(Dayr al-Sanquriya)*

238 The Church of the Holy Virgin *(Gabal al-Tayr/Dayr al-'Adra)*

242 The Monastery of Abu Fana *(Dayr Abu Fana)*

246 Al-Ashmunayn

ASYUT

248 The Monastery of al-Muharraq *(Dayr al-Muharraq)*

254 The Monastery of Durunka *(Dayr Durunka)*

256 The Cliff Churches of Dayr Rifa

262 The Monastery of al-Zawya *(Dayr al-Zawya)*

266 The Monastery of al-Ganadla *(Dayr al-Ganadla)*

AKHMIM

274 The Church of St. Mercurius *(Abu Sayfayn)*

SOHAG

278 The Red Monastery (of St. Pshai) *(al-Dayr al-Ahmar/Dayr Anba Bishai)*

284 The White Monastery (of St. Shenute) *(al-Dayr al-Abyad/Dayr Anba Shenute)*

NAQADA

290 The Monasteries of Naqada

290   The Monastery of the Cross *(Dayr al-Salib)*

292   The Monastery of St. Andrew *(Dayr Andra'us/Abu al-Lif)*

295   The Monastery of St. George *(Dayr Mari Girgis)*

296   The Monastery of St. Pisentius *(Dayr Anba Bisentiyus)*

297   The Monastery of St. Victor *(Dayr Mari Buqtur)*

299   The Monastery of the Archangel Michael *(Dayr al-Malak Mikha'il)*

LUXOR

300 Churches in Luxor Temple and Karnak Temple

ASWAN

304 The Monastery of St. Hatre *(Dayr Anba Hadra)*

308 The Monastery at Qubbat al-Hawwa *(Dayr Qubbat al-Hawwa)*

310 Glossary

311 Notes

315 Bibliographic References

319 Bibliography

325 Index

328 Acknowledgments

Preface

Carolyn Ludwig

*Icon from the
Church of the
Holy Virgin
in Sakha*

URING MY TRAVELS TO EGYPT over the last twenty-five years, I have come to appreciate the rich Christian heritage that is woven through this country's history along with the threads of its more famous pharaonic past. It is a heritage that dates back to the earliest days of Christianity, when the Holy Family fled to Egypt to escape the wrath of King Herod. Their sojourn here continues to be a defining narrative for Egyptian Christians, and has become an important part of Egyptian popular culture for Christians and Muslims alike.

I have been deeply moved by the humanity of the stories still told about these few years in the life of Christ, as well as by the devotion shown by both Egyptians and tourists in the churches and shrines dedicated to the memory of the Holy Family's journey through this remarkable country. I have also been moved by the humble simplicity of Egypt's early churches, which stand in stark contrast to the granite and marble, the gold inlays and bronze statues, of churches in Rome. Egyptian churches are built of brick and plaster, some with vaulted wooden ceilings like the hulls of ships. Their colors mirror the sand and clay of the vast desert landscape that surrounds them. Bright icons hang casually on wooden screens or inside domes above altars where they cannot easily be seen.

The brief reference to the Flight of the Holy Family in the Gospel of Matthew offers a glimpse into the three-and-a-half years they spent in Egypt, but most of the stories about this episode in Jesus's life are recorded in the various infancy narratives of the apocryphal texts. In 2000 the Coptic Orthodox Church, under the auspices of His Holiness Pope Shenouda III and his bishops, defined the route of the Holy Family's journey, with the first site marking their entrance into Egypt and the last marking their departure as they returned to Nazareth. The churches, shrines, and monasteries that I visited with Sherif Sonbol, who took the exquisite photographs in this book, generally follow this route.

Sonbol's photographs reveal the beauty of Egypt's ancient and more modern churches and monasteries, all of which testify to the determination of the Coptic Church for nearly two millennia to keep the Christian faith alive in Egypt, often in the face of adversity. Moreover, since early Egyptian monasticism is the root of both Western and Eastern monastic traditions, these sites are important monuments not only to Egypt's history, but also to the history of the Christian tradition worldwide.

The introductory chapters on the art and architecture of Coptic churches, by Gertrud J.M. van Loon and Darlene L. Brooks Hedstrom, explain how these sacred places developed over time. Many of the churches and monasteries survived successive waves of destruction and emerged stronger with each restoration—a wonderful testimony to the endurance and perseverance of the faithful in those

Now after they had left, an angel of the Lord appeared to Joseph in a dream and said, 'Get up, take the child and his mother, and flee to Egypt, and remain there until I tell you; for Herod is about to search for the child, to destroy him.' Then Joseph got up, took the child and his mother by night, and went to Egypt, and remained there until the death of Herod. This was to fulfil what had been spoken by the Lord through the prophet, 'Out of Egypt I have called my son.'
MATTHEW 2:13–15

communities. The chapter on the history of Christianity in Egypt, by Gawdat Gabra, underscores the resolve and leadership of Egypt's bishops, patriarchs, monks, and priests, who held their churches and congregations together over centuries of change, external threat, and internal strife.

Of the sites depicted in *The Churches of Egypt*, some are recognized landmarks on the Holy Family's journey, while others that have evolved along the same route, though not official Holy Family sites, enjoy considerable standing in popular Egyptian Christian tradition. At Matariya, for example, tradition holds that when Joseph drove his staff into the ground, water appeared for his family to drink. And when the Holy Family passed by Harat Zuwayla, Jesus drew water from a well, gave it to his mother, and blessed the site, saying that whosoever should believe and drink of these waters would be healed in Mary's name. Other sites, like the tomb of Ibrahim and Girgis al-Guhari, are historically important, but not necessarily tied to Holy Family traditions. While not itself a place of worship, the Guhari tomb is important to the story of the churches in Old Cairo: several churches in Egypt survived into the late eighteenth century because Ibrahim used his influence, as Egypt's chief scribe (then the equivalent of finance minister), to begin renovating churches and monasteries; Girgis, under Napoleon's reign, followed his brother's example. Whether or not their historical importance is officially acknowledged, however, all the sites in *The Churches of Egypt* attest to the centuries-long struggle to establish and maintain the Christian presence in Egypt.

This book also includes photographs of ancient and historically valuable icons, recently restored through the support of Dr. Zahi Hawass, Secretary General of the Supreme Council of Antiquities, and the efforts of Gerry Scott, Director of the American Research Center in Egypt (ARCE). Icons play an important spiritual role for Coptic Christians, portraying the lives and sacrifices, suffering and death, of Christian martyrs and saints. At the time of the ARCE restoration project, Sherif Sonbol and I were allowed to visit a site not yet open to the general public. I will never forget the feeling of climbing the scaffolding in the Red Monastery and coming suddenly face to face with these resplendent icons, only just freed from beneath centuries of black candle smoke. Their beauty and fragility overwhelmed us. Similarly, W. Raymond Johnson, Field Director of Chicago House in Egypt, allowed us to photograph on the sites of the Oriental Institute of Chicago University, and shared his wisdom.

In creating this book, we owe an enormous debt of gratitude to His Holiness Pope Shenouda III and other church leaders; they, like us, wish to thank the Egyptian people we encountered on our journey through the churches of Egypt for their generosity and gracious hospitality. Many thanks to the wonderful team of Gawdat Gabra, Gertrud van Loon and Darlene Brooks Hedstrom for contributing their knowledge to this project. We would also like to extend a special word of thanks to the American University of Cairo Press, which has published many important contributions to Egypt's Christian heritage in the last two decades, especially to Mark Linz, director, Neil Hewison, associate director for editorial programs, Nadia Naqib, managing editor, and Miriam Fahmi, production manager, for their interest, patience, and attention to detail in publishing this volume. We are also immensely grateful to Morris Jackson, not only for his talents, but for his dedication to this project and our first one together, *Jewels in Our Crown: Churches of Los Angeles*.

I hope that you will share my wonder at the simple beauty of these holy places, which have stood for so many years as the guardians of Egypt's Christian past and the gateways to its future.

Introduction

Gawdat Gabra and Gertrud J.M. van Loon

The lack of an up-to-date, well-illustrated book on Egyptian churches, including the most recent research and discoveries has been keenly felt in recent years. *The Churches of Egypt*, with over three hundred full-color photographs, is intended to fill this gap. Introductory chapters on the history of Christianity in Egypt, the architecture of the Coptic Church, and Coptic wall paintings enable readers to appreciate fully the immensely significant cultural, artistic, and architectural heritage of Egypt's Christians. Our hope is that the general reader, the scholar, and the student will all benefit from its text and illustrations.

The subtitle of the book requires some explanation. The Gospel of Matthew (Mt. 2:13–15) tells us that the Holy Family fled to Egypt to seek refuge from persecution in the Holy Land. The Scriptures, however, provide no information about the length of the sojourn or the places visited by the Holy Family. Nevertheless, there is no doubt that this story had a strong appeal to the Egyptians' imagination through the centuries. The Copts cherish the memory of the Flight of the Holy Family from its persecutor, Herod, in Palestine to safe refuge in their land, Egypt. The tradition of the sojourn of the Holy Family in Egypt is indeed fascinating. A wealth of wondrous tales and legends has been transmitted to us about that great event. Churches and monasteries have been built over the sacred ground where people believe the Holy Family sojourned. The places in Egypt associated with the Holy Family have gradually grown in number; some of them were added only during the last decade. The inclusion, therefore, of the Holy Family in the title of this book is an acknowledgment to the strength of the memory and emotional appeal of the presence of early Christianity in Egypt.

In fact, there is no evidence of Christian churches in Egypt prior to the fourth century. This does not mean, however, that the existence of churches before this period should be ruled out. According to some of our literary evidence, early Christians adapted caves, quarries, tombs, pharaonic cemeteries, and parts of temples for the practice of their faith. Furthermore, it is very likely that early churches were destroyed during the different waves of persecutions of Christians or replaced in later times by larger structures. Notwithstanding the lack of early evidence, Egypt's heritage of Christian church architecture, wall paintings, and icons is one of the richest in the Middle East and represents an important segment of the world's Christian heritage.

The most important historical sources for our knowledge of Egypt's early Christian churches and monasteries are *The History of the Patriarchs*, *The History of the Churches and Monasteries of Egypt*, and the list of monasteries compiled by the Muslim historian al-Maqrizi (d. 1442). Early western travelers in Egypt who described their visits and experiences are also a valuable source of information.

The History of the Patriarchs is a chronicle of the history of the Coptic Church from the first to the thirteenth century, organized in biographies of successive patriarchs; between the fourteenth and early twentieth century, brief supplementary information was added. The early compilers penned their contributions in Coptic, and from the eleventh century onward, the authors used Arabic.[1] *The History of the Churches and Monasteries of Egypt* was traditionally ascribed to Abu Salih al-Armani, but it is now generally attributed to the Coptic priest Abu al-Makarim. This topographical handbook in three volumes contains information on churches, monasteries, pilgrimages, and contemporary customs. Several authors, one of whom, Abu al-Makarim, compiled the basic text sometime between

1160 and 1187; later on, information was added from the late twelfth to the fourteenth century.[2] Al-Maqrizi wrote a study on Coptic history, listing monasteries and churches with short notes, providing valuable documentation for the existence and status of specific monasteries and churches during the early fifteenth century.[3]

The earliest accounts of pilgrims and travelers in Lower and Middle Egypt date to the fourth century. Upper Egypt was harder to conquer. One of the first Europeans to travel widely in Egypt was the Dominican father Johann Michael Wansleben (d. 1679), who is better known as Vansleb (the Gallic form of his name). The diary of his journey through Egypt during the years 1672–1673 is an important source because he paid special attention to Christian antiquities.[4] Similarly, the Jesuit father Claude Sicard (d. 1726) recorded his visits to churches and monasteries.[5] The artist, writer, and diplomat Dominique Vivant Denon (d. 1825) who witnessed the torching of churches near Sohag in 1798, belonged to the retinue of artists, scholars, and scientists of Napoleon's army.[6] Father Michel Marie Jullien S.J. (d. 1911) traveled extensively in Egypt; detailed reports of his visits to churches and monasteries were initially published in the Jesuit journal *Les missions catholiques* and later collected in several volumes.[7]

In writing this book we have benefited from the libraries of the Institute of Egyptology and Coptology in Münster, Germany, and Leiden University. We wish to acknowledge our debt to his Holiness Pope Shenouda III for his great interest in this volume, and to the abbots, priests, and pastors who graciously facilitated our work in their monasteries and churches. We would like to extend a special word of thanks to Sherif Sonbol, whose photographs beautifully capture the large selection of Egypt's Christian churches illustrated in this volume. Finally, our thanks go to Mrs. Carolyn Ludwig, without whose vision, dedication, and unending support this volume would not have been realized.

The History of Christianity in Egypt

Gawdat Gabra

THE TERM 'COPT' COMES DIRECTLY FROM THE ARABIC *QBT*, which appears to derive from the Greek *aigyptos* (Egypt)/*aigyptioi* (Egyptians), a phonetic corruption of the ancient Egyptian word Hikaptah, one of the names of Memphis. Initially, the word described a non-Arabic-speaking non-Muslim. By implication, a Copt was also a Christian, since Christianity was the predominant religion of the land at the time of the Arab conquest in 641.

When the majority of Egyptians gradually converted to Islam, they naturally ceased to be Christians (*aqbat*, sing. *qibti*). In that sense, the term 'Copt' and the adjective 'Coptic' are relatively elastic in a historical, ethnic, religious, cultural, and social sense. 'Coptic' often refers to matters relating to the Orthodox Church in Egypt, which in this case has nothing to do with other Orthodox Churches. The recent new phrase 'Oriental Orthodox Churches' distinguishes between the Eastern Orthodox churches, which are in communion with Constantinople, and the Orthodox churches of Egypt, Armenia, Ethiopia, Syria, and India, which reject the Council of Chalcedon (451). Moreover, the term Coptic is used also to designate Christians in Egypt without meaning that one is necessarily an Orthodox Christian. For example, the Coptic Evangelical churches of the Coptic Evangelical Synod of the Nile use the term Coptic to denote their ethnic identity as Egyptians. There is also the Coptic Catholic Church, which is in communion with Rome. The church of the Hellenic Greeks in Egypt is known as the Greek Orthodox Church. Today, the Christians of Egypt represent the largest Christian community in the Middle East, which unofficial sources estimate at nine million or more, and the Coptic Church can confidently state it is one of the oldest in the world.

Earliest Christianity is not archaeologically visible in Egypt. Nevertheless, the New Testament provides a few hints of a Christian presence in Egypt (Acts 2:10, 6:9, 18:24). The Copts also take pride in the tradition handed down by Eusebius, the fourth-century church historian, that St. Mark the Evangelist preached the Gospel in Alexandria and was the first to establish churches there. In his writings, Eusebius is clearly passing on previously existing traditions of the association of St. Mark with earliest Christianity in Egypt, which may be traceable to the second century, if not earlier. Other than this, there is very little information about the history of Christianity in Egypt during the first two centuries.

The new religion spread gradually into Egypt, as evidenced by the establishment of the Catechetical School of Alexandria in about 180 and the appointment of three bishops by Demetrius, the Patriarch of Alexandria (188–230). The Catechetical School of Alexandria, an important theological school, was led by great scholars, teachers, and writers of the late second and third century, such as Pantaenus, Clement, Origen, and Dionysus. In Roman times the Greek language continued to be the official and cultural language of the country, whereas Latin was used only in the army.

In 202, the Roman emperor Septimius Severus visited Egypt, and his special veneration for the pagan god Serapis may have initiated the first phase of persecutions of Christians in the country. It was under these first persecutions that Origen's father, Leonides, was beheaded. The Egyptian Christians suffered another wider persecution during the reign of Emperor Decius (249–251). In 250 he issued a universal order to sacrifice to the gods. Each citizen had to prove that he made offerings to them. Many Egyptians preferred to die than deny Christ, while others escaped to the desert or capitulated to the emperor's demand. This wave of persecution continued under Emperor Valerianus (253–260). Patriarch Dionysius and some of his companions were banished to Libya. Thousands suffered worse fates.

The most severe and systematic wave of persecution of the Egyptian Church started during the reign of Emperor Diocletian (284–305) and continued under Emperor Maximinus Daia (305–313). We do not have any reliable data for the number of martyrs from Diocletian's reign. Church sources speak of hundreds of thousands, but some scholars estimate the number of victims at between 2,500 and 3,000. Peter I, the Patriarch of Alexandria, was martyred on 25 November 311 during the Great Persecution and given the title 'Seal of the Martyrs.' The severity of the Great Persecution prompted the Copts to use the Era of the Martyrs as the point of reference for their calendar, with year one beginning with the accession of Diocletian to the throne in 284 (that is, First Year of Martyrs—abbreviated to AM 1). Only with the Edict of Milan in 313, issued by the emperor Constantine I, did the Great Persecution finally end. The commemoration and veneration of martyrs as saints by the Copts is one significant factor that led to the survival of Christianity in Egypt and is a hallmark of contemporary Coptic faith.

During and after the persecutions, Alexandria continued to serve as a center for Christian education and theological training. Emperor Constantine I (306–337) favored Christianity, which therefore flourished in Alexandria. In approximately 320, Alexander, Patriarch of Alexandria (312–326), assembled one hundred bishops in a synod. In the second half of the fourth century, the majority of the inhabitants of Alexandria were Christians. By the early fifth century about 80 percent of the Egyptian population was Christian.

The patriarchs of Alexandria played a significant role in the theological controversies and the formulation of Christian doctrine during the fourth and fifth centuries. Patriarch Alexander I and his young deacon Athanasius, who later became the most important Coptic patriarch, fought against the heresy of Arius. Arius (256–336), a presbyter of Alexandria and an eloquent speaker, began, in approximately 318, a controversy over the nature of Christ's relation to the Father that differed from Alexander's orthodox position. Arius and his followers, taught that Christ, the Son was not eternal with the Father: he had originated by the creative act of God, the Father's will. Thus, the Arians stressed Christ's creaturely nature and dependence on God's nature and will. By contrast, Alexander's position expressed the orthodox belief that Christ and the Father shared a common nature or essence. Arius's teachings were ultimately condemned by the Council of Nicea in 325.

In 330 , Constantinople (Byzantium) became the new eastern capital of the Roman empire, thus rivaling Alexandria's political and theological supremacy. During the rule of Patriarch Athanasius (328–373) nationalist feeling increased among the Egyptians, a trend that was subsequently strengthened by the theological controversies of the fifth century. Patriarch Athanasius was a hero of orthodoxy, the chief protagonist in the struggle against the Arians. He spent twenty of the forty-six years of his patriarchy in periods of exile imposed by the imperial authorities. In his second exile, which lasted three years in Rome, he was accompanied by a number of Egyptian monks. During his exile Athanasius introduced the Egyptian monastic system to the West. He was the first Alexandrian patriarch who knew the Coptic language.

In 392, emperor Theodosius I passed an edict forbidding paganism throughout the empire. The church historian Socrates (380–450) informs us that Emperor Theodosius granted Patriarch Theophilus's request that the temples be destroyed. According to Coptic tradition, the aged Patriarch Athanasius expressed to his secretary Theophilus, the future patriarch, his wish that the Serapeum be closed. Theophilus (385–412) took this opportunity to limit both pagans and heretics within the church. The Alexandrian mob destroyed the Serapeum, which was a huge complex of buildings that included a temple to the god Serapis, lecture halls, a library, and shrines for other gods.

Theophilus's successor, Patriarch Cyril I (412–444), spent five years at the Monastery of St. Macarius in Wadi al-Natrun and counted monks among his supporters. Intolerance of paganism continued under Cyril's patriarchy. In 415 Hypatia, a female philosopher and leader of the Neoplatonist school, was brutally murdered in Alexandria by a Christian mob thought to include monks from Wadi al-Natrun.

After the orthodox struggles with the Arians in the early fourth century, theologians continued to argue about the unity or duality of Christ with God the Father. Nestorius, Patriarch of Constantinople (d. ca. 451) supported his chaplain, Anastasius (328–373), who had preached against the application of the word Theotokos (God-bearer) to the Virgin Mary, thus questioning her divine motherhood on the grounds that she was the mother of only the humanity of Christ. Cyril opposed the theology of Nestorius in the Council of Ephesus in 431. The Holy Virgin was declared Theotokos, and Nestorius was condemned and exiled first to the Kharga Oasis and then to Akhmim in Upper Egypt. Cyril's writings reflect his great qualities as a theologian, and his theology prevailed in the church until his death in 444. Patriarch Dioscorus I succeeded Cyril the Great in the See of St. Mark. The Alexandrian See reached its apogee through the efforts of Athanasius and Cyril.

In around 448 Eutyches, an archimandrite of a monastery in Constantinople with great influence in the Byzantine court, denied the human nature of Christ. He declared that before the Incarnation, the divine and human natures of Christ were united, while after the Incarnation, Christ was fully divine. In 449 Patriarch Dioscorus presided over the Council of Ephesus (431), which had been summoned by Emperor Theodosius II (408–450). Eutyches was vindicated, and Flavian was deposed from the See of Constantinople. The theology of Eutychus was later rejected, however, by the Church of Alexandria. The death of Emperor Theodosius II in 450 led to the reversal of the theological policy.

Emperor Marcian (450–467) convoked an ecumenical council at Chalcedon, on the Asiatic coast opposite Constantinople, in 451. The decisions of the Council of Ephesus (449) were repudiated, and Eutyches was condemned and exiled; he died in obscurity in 454. The Council made the See of Constantinople second only to Rome. The nature of Christ was defined as twofold, divine and human, and united unconfused, unchangeably, indivisibly, and inseparably.

The Egyptians believed that the doctrine accepted at the Council of Chalcedon (451) would destroy the essential unity of the person of Christ. Patriarch Dioscorus did not accept the Chalcedonian decisions and was exiled to the island of Gangra in Paphlagonia. Alexandria's leading position in the Christian Church had been lost. An irresolvable schism resulted in the church after the Council of Chalcedon. The dispute over the nature of Christ led to bloodshed and caused an irreparable rift between the church in Egypt and the rest of the Christian world. The Egyptian or Coptic Church became a national church united behind the Patriarch of Alexandria. The emperors of the Byzantine Empire wanted to fill the See of Alexandria with men loyal to Constantinople (Melkite Christians) who would provide them with imperial, political, and military support. The Copts recognized only their patriarch, who often had to leave Alexandria in order to lead his church, which was far from the Byzantine authorities.

The fourth and fifth centuries also witnessed the birth and spread of Egyptian monasticism, a distinctive spiritual discipline with great influence on Christianity. It is one of Egypt's most important contributions to civilization. In the third century, the Egyptian desert had become a refuge for farmers who were forced to abandon their land under the pressure of debts caused by excessive taxation. Moreover, Christians had fled urban environments and villages to occupy tombs and caves on the desert margin to escape the Decian persecution (251). Some discovered that life in the desert areas was more suitable for religious practice and meditation. We know very little about the first monks other than the absence of rules by which they had to live.

St. Antony, "the father of the monks," was born in Coma in Upper Egypt in 251. Following the Lord's command, "sell all your possessions and give to the poor, and come follow me, and you will have treasure in heaven" (Mt 19:21), he sold his possessions when he was around twenty years old and practiced a solitary life outside the village. Between approximately 285 and 313 he lived in complete solitude in a deserted fortress at Pispir (the present-day Monastery of al-Maymun). We are told that St. Antony came with his disciples to Alexandria to encourage the confessors at the time of persecution. Finally by 313 he had moved to the 'interior desert' at the Red Sea, the site of the present day Monastery of St. Antony. Toward the end of St Antony's life the number of ascetics increased. The influential *Life of Antony*, written by Patriarch Athanasius shortly after the saint's death, had a great impact on the spread of monasticism in the West. Antony, who died in 356, was a popular saint in Europe in the Middle Ages. During the rule of Patriarch Athanasius (328–373) nationalist feeling increased among the Egyptians, a trend that was subsequently strengthened by the theological controversies of the fifth century.

In about 320, St. Pachomius established the first community at Tabennisi, in the district of Nag' Hammadi, in Upper Egypt. He founded coenobitic or communal monasticism, which was based on precise rules. These rules governed all aspects of monastic life: monks lived together in houses, each with a steward assigned special duties. Offices rotated every three weeks. There were set times for prayer, Mass, work, meals, and sleep. Pachomius ruled over nine monasteries for men and two for women. In 404 St. Jerome rendered the Pachomian Rule into Latin from an intermediate Greek translation of the Coptic original. Thus Pachomius's rule would influence the Western monastic rules of St. Basil (ca. 330–379) and St. Benedict of Nursia (ca. 480–550). After John Cassian visited Egypt in the late fourth century, he founded the monasteries of St. Victor for men and St. Salvador for women in Marseilles. The Western monastic tradition, in particular the Benedictine order, owes much to Coptic monastic traditions.

Another center of fourth-century monastic life was in the region west of the Delta. Here in Scetis (Wadi al-Natrun), Nitria, and Kellia, many colonies of monks gathered to live in communities surrounding an elder monastic. Literary sources tell of Amun, Macarius the Great, and many other hermits. Around 330 Amun went to the inner mountain of Nitria, about 100 kilometers south of Alexandria. Disciples gathered around Amun and a form of semi-anchorism flourished. Monks lived alone in independent cells five days a week and on Saturday and Sunday came together in the church, where they participated in the eucharistic liturgy and took part in a common meal (agape). Within a few years Nitria became too crowded, and Amun and St. Antony together founded Kellia, or the Cells, about sixteen kilometers south of Nitria. Hundreds of monk cells with interesting architecture and wall paintings have been discovered in Kellia. Unfortunately, these were nearly obliterated by the encroachment of modern cultivation, except for a number of wall paintings and some fine examples of pottery that are preserved in Cairo's Coptic Museum.

St. Macarius (ca. 300–390) founded a colony of monks in Wadi al-Natrun around 330. By the time of his death there were four flourishing monasteries there: the monastery of the Romans (al-Baramus), Pshoi, Macarius, and John the Little. The latter ceased to exist in the fifteenth century, but the three other monasteries have been continuously occupied since the fourth century. The monastery of the Syrians was built in the sixth century. When security deteriorated in the ninth century, all four monasteries had to be protected by enclosure walls, which are still visible today.

Many monasteries and hermitages were built in Upper Egypt. Two of the most important monasteries are those of St. Shenute and St. Pshoi, known as the White and Red monasteries near Sohag in Upper Egypt. One of the greatest figures of monasticism is Shenute, who was the Abbot of the White Monastery between 385 and 465. He was also a great preacher who struggled against paganism in the region of Panopolis. An indication of his importance as a leader of orthodoxy is the fact that he accompanied Patriarch Cyril to the Council of Ephesus in 431. Shenute was an authoritarian, a zealot, and a philanthropist whose monastery received thousands of refugees in hard times.

According to Palladius (ca. 363–431), monk, bishop, and historian, there were 5,000 monks in Nitria and 600 in Kellia toward 390. At the beginning of the fifth century, St. Jerome reported that 50,000 Pachomian monks attended the annual meeting. We are told that 2,200 monks and 1,800 nuns were under Shenute in the region of the White Monastery. Before the Arab conquest of Egypt in 641, hundreds of monasteries and colonies of hermits were established and flourished all over Egypt. Many of them began to decline and gradually deteriorated or were abandoned after 705, when a poll tax was imposed on the monks for the first time.

The monks played an important role in the history of Christianity in Egypt. Patriarch Athanasius was the first to encourage Egyptian monks to be ordained bishops, and many of the patriarchs and bishops of the Coptic Church were chosen from among the monks. Indeed, since the eighth century, most of the patriarchs of the Alexandrian See have been elected from among the monks of Wadi al-Natrun. In addition to providing ecclesiastic authority, monasteries have actively preserved Christian history. Monastic libraries throughout Egypt contain valuable Greek, Old Nubian, Ethiopian, Syriac, Armenian, Coptic, and even Arabic manuscripts. They bear witness to the multiethnic character of some of Egypt's monastic communities. The artistic heritage of these monasteries is beyond estimation.

The last ten years of Byzantine rule in Egypt were among the fullest in Egyptian history. Byzantine authorities attempted to reconcile the Copts after the ten-year Persian occupation ended in 629, but their efforts failed and the situation deteriorated. In 631 Emperor Heraclius sent Cyrus—known also as al-Muqawqas—to Alexandria as an imperial prefect to control Egypt and continue as a loyal patriarch to the Empire. When he could not persuade the Copts to deny their doctrine, Cyrus chased the Coptic Patriarch Benjamin into exile in Upper Egypt between 631 and 644, and even attacked monasteries in his hunt for the leaders of the Coptic Church.

It is a wonder that the Coptic Church survived the many waves of persecution. It not only survived, but has had a direct influence on other churches in Africa. For example, in 362 Patriarch Athanasius sent a bishop to Philae in Nubia. We know that these two churches enjoyed good relations until at least the time of Patriarch Gabriel IV (1370–1380), who consecrated a bishop for the Nubians. And beginning in the fourth century it was established tradition that an Egyptian monk be sent to head the Ethiopian Church—a tradition that was abandoned only in 1948.

The Byzantine wave of persecution did not last long. The Arab conquest of Egypt in 641 had far-reaching consequences for Egypt's history in general and for the Coptic Church in particular. The attitude of the Muslims toward the 'People of the Book,' or dhimmis, ensured the protection of the Copts' possessions and churches, but the building of new churches was prohibited. Non-Muslims were not allowed to bear arms and were obliged to pay an additional tax known as the *jizya*, or poll tax. The principal concern of Islamic rule was the smooth levy of taxation irrespective of any consideration. Therefore, the Arabs did not make any sectarian distinction between 'Monophysite' and 'Melkite' Christians, and the Copts enjoyed doctrinal freedom. During the first few decades of the Arab occupation, educated Copts filled most of the high administrative positions in the country, but in later centuries higher office was restricted only to Muslims.

The succeeding centuries witnessed a sometimes radically exploitative policy by the Arab occupants toward the Egyptian Christian population. When the taxation became unbearable, Copts revolted. Sources refer to nine revolts against Arab authorities between 696 and 832, all of which were suppressed. It seems that the ferocious repression of the last one, known as the Bashmurite revolt, resulted in the conversion of a considerable part of the Coptic population. It is therefore not surprising that not long after the crushing of the Bashmurite rebellion in 832 the Copts had to obey the orders of the Abbasid caliph al-Mutawakkil (847–861). He required for the first time that all Copts wear distinctive dress and be forbidden to ride horses.

In addition to the poll tax and arbitrary financial burdens, a number of factors played a significant role in the Islamization of Egypt. First, a number of Arab tribes settled in various regions of Egypt, especially in the Delta. Second, despite employing Copts in posts of authority during the early decades of Arab rule, the government's administration began to employ only Arabs and Muslims. Third, the Church's economy and institutions, especially the monasteries, were systematically weakened. Fourth, the social status of the Copts was deliberately lowered. Monks and clergy were humiliated, and even bishops and patriarchs were sometimes imprisoned and shackled.

The Tulunids (869–905), the Ikhshids (935–969), and the Fatimids (969–1171) were in general tolerant Muslim rulers. Under the Shi'a Fatimid caliphs, the Copts were employed in the most important positions and allowed to carry the highest honors. The only exception was Caliph al-Hakim (996–1021) who ordered the destruction of monasteries and churches and the dismissal of the Copts from government office. Copts were compelled to wear wooden crosses suspended from their necks, each weighing at least five pounds, and other distinctive dress.

Patriarch Christodoulus (1047–1077) moved the patriarchal seat from Alexandria to al-Mu'allaqa Church in Old Cairo to be near the government. The advent of the Crusades brought new problems for the Christians in the region. Crusaders did not distinguish between the 'Monophysites' and the Muslims in Egypt and considered the Copts heretics. Syrian Christians fled to join their coreligionists in Egypt. Crusader victories resulted in reprisals against the Copts, for Muslim rulers did not distinguish between the two groups of Christians.

When Salah al-Din (Saladin) came to power, he dismissed the Copts from government office and reinforced the distinctive dress code of the Christians. The famous St. Mark Cathedral in Alexandria was pulled down on the pretext that the Crusaders might fortify it should they seize Alexandria. With his victory over the Crusaders and the capture of Jerusalem in 1187, Salah al-Din changed his intolerant attitude toward the Copts. The Ayyubid sultans (1171–1250) were also relatively tolerant. The Mamluks, or slave dynasty, ruled Egypt from 1250 to 1517. They were slaves of a special kind, brought mainly from the region of the Caspian and Black seas, sold as young boys, converted to Islam, and trained as soldiers in Egypt.

During the Mamluk period, the status and number of Copts continued to decline, and by the time of the Ottoman conquest of Egypt their situation was very precarious. They were often dismissed from government office and frequently had to wear distinctive and demeaning dress. On one day in 1321, fanatic groups looted, destroyed, and burned over sixty of the main churches and monasteries throughout Egypt. Apparently, the churches were attacked simultaneously after the Friday prayer, and the authorities were taken by surprise. The Arab historian al-Maqrizi (1364–1442) reported that in the year 1321, "the attacks of the Muslims against Christians increased to the extent that Christians ceased to walk in the streets and many of them converted to Islam. Jews were spared during this period. If a Christian wanted to leave his home he had to borrow the yellow turban of a Jew and wear it in order to be safe from the mob in the streets." In 1517 the Ottomans wrested control from Mamluks, but the Mamluk leaders continued as provincial beys under Ottoman governors into the early nineteenth century. The Ottoman sultans in Istanbul were interested only in Egypt's revenues. The impoverishment of the entire population of Egypt, Christians and Muslims alike, reached previously unparalleled levels during that dark period. The life of the Copts was less miserable, however, during Ottoman times than under the Mamluks. One of the reasons behind the sustained existence of the Copts is their success in financial administration. Ibn Khaldun (1322–1406), a great medieval Islamic scholar, says: "It is a custom of [the Turks] that the Wazir be appointed from among the Copts in charge of the office of bookkeeping and tax collection, because in Egypt they have been familiar with these matters since ancient times."

Copts rendered their services to the Mamluk beys and some of them occupied significant positions in the administration, such as Ibrahim al-Guhari (d. 1795), who was a finance minister. His influence was so great that he was able to restore many Coptic monasteries and churches, and to construct new churches as well.

The French expedition under Napoleon, despite its brevity (1798–1801), is considered a turning point in Egypt's modernization. Muhammad 'Ali (1805–1849) and most of his descendants were relatively tolerant toward the Copts. During the nineteenth century, the Ottomans revoked the traditional poll tax, the *jizya*, imposed on the dhimmis in 1855, and the Coptic population began to flourish. This revival of Coptic Christianity was visible in the cultural movement within the Coptic Church under the pontificate of Patriarch Cyril IV the Reformer (1854–1861).

The multicultural character of Christianity, which is deeply rooted in Egypt, is reflected in many ways. For example, some monasteries and monastic colonies in the Egyptian deserts received European, Syrian, Armenian, Nubian, and Ethiopian monks and visitors in Byzantine and medieval times. A considerable number of the saints commemorated in the Arabic synaxarion of the Copts are not Egyptians. Many Coptic churches are dedicated to non-Egyptian saints such as Mercurius (Abu Sayfayn), Sergius, George, and Barbara. In 1219 St. Francis of Assisi met the Ayyubid sultan al-Malik al-Kamil (1218–1238) near the city of Damietta during one of the Crusades. He preached the message of Christ to the sultan, but without success. The existence of European traders and missionaries in Alexandria in the fourteenth and fifteenth centuries increased interest in more contact between Rome and the Copts. The efforts to reunite the Copts with Rome during the Council of Ferrara–Florence (1438–1445) and its acceptance by the Coptic Patriarch John XI was rejected by the majority of Copts and therefore failed. Other attempts were made during the pontificate of the Coptic Patriarchs Gabriel VII (1559–1565), John XIV (1570–1585), Gabriel VIII (1586–1601), Matthew IV (1660–1675), and John XVI to attract the Coptic Church to Roman obedience, but without success. Apparently, the Copts preferred a union in love and rejected a strict legal subjection to Rome.

The advent of the Catholic missions in the Ottoman period led to the establishment of mission schools that offered some young Copts a European education long before the modern reform or the Coptic Renaissance under Patriarch Cyril IV (1854–1861). In 1824 Pope Leo XII of Rome consecrated Abraham Khashur as bishop for the Catholic Copts, and a Catholic patriarchate was established in Alexandria in 1895. Its establishment contributed greatly to the growth of the Coptic Catholic Church in Egypt, which comprises a variety of Catholic communities. The largest of these are the Coptic Catholics, joined by the Greek Melkites, the Armenian Catholics, the Syrian Catholics, the Chaldeans, the Maronites, and the Latins.

Protestant missionary activities eventually began in Egypt through the efforts of the Presbyterian Church of North America in 1854. In 1863 the Egyptian Presbytery founded a theological school to prepare the national Evangelical pastors, and in 1926 a new building for the theological seminary of the Evangelical Coptic Church was founded in Cairo. In the late 1980s there were 340 pastors serving the Evangelical churches all over Egypt that belong to the Synod of the Nile. It is to be noted that foreign missionaries, both Catholic and Protestant, came to Egypt to bring the Gospel to Muslims, but they ended up proselytizing the Orthodox Copts through modern education, humanitarian efforts, and medical work. The newly formed Catholic and Protestant minorities contributed to some extent to the awakening of the Coptic Orthodox Church from centuries of sluggishness under Mamluk and Ottoman rule.

In 1973 Pope Shenouda III visited Rome, where he issued with Pope Paul IV a joint statement of Christology. Five years later, Pope Shenouda organized a meeting, at the Monastery of St. Pshoi in Wadi al-Natrun, with the Greek Orthodox Patriarch of Alexandria, the Syrian Orthodox Patriarch of Antioch, the Greek Orthodox Patriarch of Antioch, and the Armenian Catholicon. They confirmed their Christological agreement: "We confirm our right understanding of the Person of Christ, who is God from God, the only Son of the Father, who became truly man and has fully accepted our human nature, and made it one with His divinity without mingling, nor confusion, nor alternation. His divinity never departed from His humanity, even for a single moment nor the twinkling of an eye."

In 1988 there was a meeting between the Coptic Evangelical Community Council and Coptic Orthodox theologians upon the invitation of Pope Shenouda, which led to theological dialogue between the two churches.

Egyptian Christianity is as old as Christianity itself. Its contributions to world civilization in general and Christian heritage in particular are beyond estimation.

The Architecture of Coptic Churches

Darlene L. Brooks Hedstrom

THE CHRISTIANS OF EGYPT OFTEN FOUND THEMSELVES facing the monumental architecture of the pharaonic past. The grand limestone and colorful granite temple complexes of the ancient gods were still active in the first centuries under the patronage of the Roman emperors; paganism was certainly not overshadowed by the rise of Christianity in Egypt. The foreign pharaohs sought to refurbish and add to these ancient monuments to solidify their names in history and to earn the eternal favor of the ancient Egyptian gods. With the vibrancy of the old cults, it was difficult for the Christians of the first centuries to imagine that one day Egypt would be home to one of the largest pilgrimage centers in the Mediterranean world and that Christian monasticism would be born in the deserts that held the tombs of the long-forgotten pharaohs.

Initially, there was no place for early Christians to practice their religion, except in their homes. Christians in Egypt, as elsewhere in the empire, were not allowed to practice their religion freely. The house meetings therefore provided a safe environment for observing their traditions and creating a community. Their church was to be the body of believers and they continued to gather, as they had in the time of first apostles, in the homes of those who could afford to host the gatherings.

By the second century, the *Didache* recounts that Christians were gathering for a thanksgiving meal, possibly the Eucharist, and a communal meal.[8] The homes were eventually remodeled to accommodate larger gatherings of Christians and to provide the proper furniture for the celebration of a sacred meal, baptism, and worship. The earliest example of a house–church, *domus ecclesiae*, dating to 256, was found at Dura Europa in Syria. This house church demonstrates the natural evolution of a communal space into sacred space and includes the basic components of what would become indicative of church architecture throughout the Byzantine Empire.[9] Unfortunately, few parallels exist for Christian architecture until the fourth century, when the first monumental constructions were sponsored by Emperor Constantine and his mother Helena. With imperial support, they built churches that would rival the size and splendor of the old pagan temples and marked the landscape with visible sacred spaces for creating a new form of religious architecture.

Given the late start to church building in the empire, it is not surprising that the earliest churches in Egypt do not date before the late fourth and early fifth centuries; however, written sources from the fourth century do suggest that churches were being used earlier in Egypt, although no physical remains have been found.[10] The earliest layouts of churches in Egypt and the Byzantine Empire include a nave, or *naos*, where the laity would gather; a sanctuary, complete with an altar table and seating for the clergy, the *synthronon*; and barriers that separate the two spaces. Additional elements, such as a baptistery, clerestory, a narthex, a crypt for the honored dead, and side rooms for the preparation of the Eucharist, appear in a variety of forms, depending upon the period and the needs of community. Even the method of constructing a timber- or brick-domed roof would influence church design in the later medieval periods.

In Egypt, church architecture bears particular features which set these spaces of worship apart from their Greek counterparts in the broader Byzantine Empire. With the evolution of church architecture in Egypt, there are distinctive features that reflect particular needs and theological beliefs regarding the space in which one worshiped and gathered for the synaxis, the gathering for the liturgy or celebration of the Eucharist. Even the manner in which churches were painted with

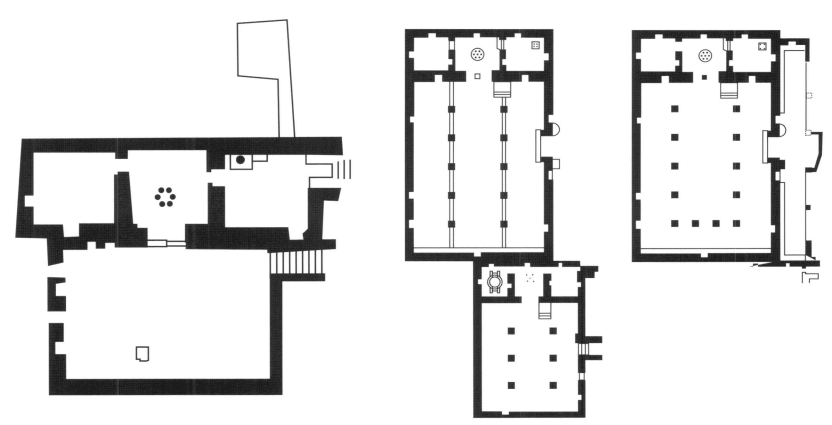

Fig. 1. North church at Kellia

Fig. 2. West and East churches at Kellia

scenes from the Biblical and monastic world would distinguish Egyptian churches from other Christian churches.

The first Egyptian churches, dating to the late fourth and early fifth centuries, include examples found at the famous monastic sites of Kellia and Wadi al-Natrun. In both locations, excavations have revealed one-room structures with sanctuaries in the eastern end of the building. At Qusur 'Isa and Qasr al-Waheida, churches were built with an early basilica form (figs. 1 and 2). The buildings included two rows of columns that created bays in the small nave, which was often entered from the south. The square sanctuary housed the altar table and the space was flanked on either side by chambers that were entered from the sanctuary. In a few cases, these rooms were used as the location for the baptistery. As the monastic communities expanded in the sixth and seventh centuries, so did the churches. The new churches were larger and had a full colonnade that created an ambulatory around the nave. While the sanctuaries were relatively similar in size to the first churches, the naves were substantially larger, reflecting a need for more space for the growing communities.

In the fifth century new churches were mostly built to follow what would be later recognized as the Christian basilica. The architects had copied a Roman model of secular and public architecture to provide a space for the gathering of large crowds. As the examples from Kellia demonstrated in the changing size of the nave, the church could be expanded without jeopardizing the sanctity of the sanctuary and altar. The ability to increase the width and length of the nave allowed for the sanctuary space to remain relatively small and secluded, while the community area could satisfy the needs of the laity. The shape of the sanctuary would vary between following the Roman model of an apsidal space, often with a *synthronon* seat, and a squared sanctuary.

Four churches provide examples of the variety present in fifth-century Egyptian church architecture. Each contains architectural features that make it a unique form, and each reflects the influence of some Roman and Egyptian models of monumental architecture. The monastic site at Faw Qibli, ancient Pbow, was home to a monastic community that followed the rules of St. Pachomius.[11] Excavations in the 1970s have provided evidence of two church constructions of five-aisled basilicas from the fifth century and a third church from the sixth century (fig. 3). The churches reflect the basic rectangular shape of Ptolemaic temples while also adopting the interior of the

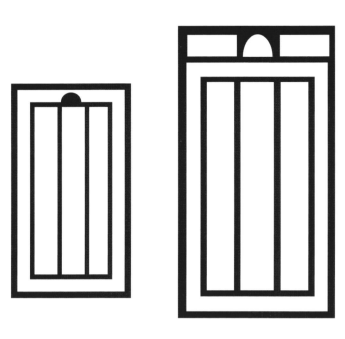

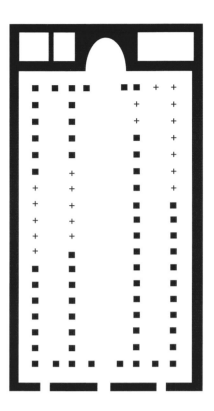

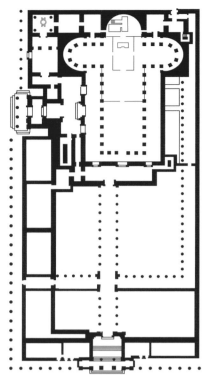

Fig. 3. Faw Qibli

Fig. 4. Great Basilica, al-Ashmunayn

Roman basilica with reused Roman columns and the apsidal, almost horseshoe-shaped sanctuary in the eastern end. The presence of four rows of columns nearly equidistant from one another means that the nave was almost as narrow as the aisles. The five-aisled church would not become a regular feature of Coptic churches in later periods, but it was adopted in the fifth and sixth centuries and is present at other sites such as at Armant, Antinoopolis, and Madinat Madi.

In contrast to the linear churches at Faw Qibli, the second example of early Egyptian architecture is the Great Basilica at al-Ashmunayn, ancient Hermopolis Magna. The church illustrates the more experimental phase of early church basilicas that included a massive transept (fig. 4). In the case of the Great Basilica, the transept in the north and south ended in semi-circular arms. The styling of the transept was new in Egyptian architecture and was exclusively found within the realm of more urban ecclesiastical environments. It was a form that was more popular outside Egypt and therefore is thought to be more of a Byzantine layout than a Coptic plan. A similar church plan was discovered recently from the site of al-Hawariya, ancient Marea, on the coast, west of Alexandria. Unlike the church at al-Ashmunayn, the al-Hawariya church lacks a western return aisle and does not have sanctuary rooms to the north and south of the central, eastern apse.

The basilica at al-Ashmunayn was built on top of the remains of a Ptolemaic temple. The two-aisled basilica had an entrance on both the north and west sides of the nave. The western entrance led from a narrow narthex to a *tribelon*, or three-arched doorway, that opened to the nave.[12] As with the church at Faw Qibli, the columns reflect Hellenistic tastes on the interior of the church with the use of Corinthian capitals for the columns. The church was part of a larger complex of rooms, one of which contained a baptistery, and a large courtyard that was likely used for assemblies.

A second church, the South Church at al-Ashmunayn, was far more modest in scale and bears the sign of the more traditional layout of Egyptian churches (fig. 5). It was also built near the remains of a pharaonic temple built originally by Ramesses II and later restored by Emperor Nero. The church has a western return aisle and was a two-aisled basilica with a simple eastern apse. The small rooms on the south side of the church included a water-delivery system for a baptistery and a staircase that led to an underground chamber for holding relics. The presence of two very different

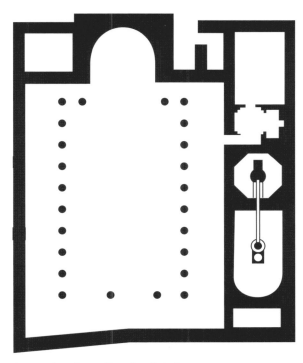

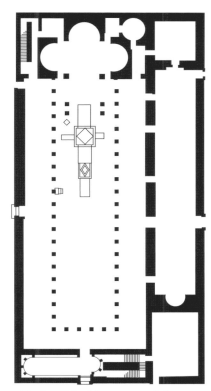

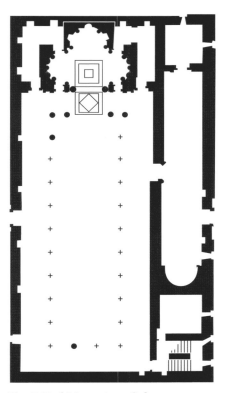

Fig. 5. Southern Church, al-Ashmunayn   *Fig 6. White Monastery, Sohag*   *Fig. 7. Red Monastery, Sohag*

churches in the same city suggests that one was likely the ecclesiastical center for the district, while the smaller church may have served the needs of a smaller congregation. The basilica transept would not be adopted until after the seventh century.

A third and equally grand example of church architecture from the mid-fifth century is found not in the urban setting, but in a monastery in the southern region of Sohag. The White Monastery of St. Shenute included a large limestone basilica whose exterior mirrored the cavetto cornices along the exterior walls of pharaonic temples. Although pharaonic blocks were reused in the construction of the church, the church does not appear to be built over an older pagan temple. It is striking that from the exterior the church evokes Egypt's past, while the interior clearly exhibits a uniquely Christian layout, with a trilobe or triconch sanctuary with niches and side rooms extending its north and south (fig. 6).

The interior of the church is a basilica form with monumental entrances on the north, west, and south sides. Although most of the columns are now lost, the bases of the columns indicate that the nave was divided by two aisles and a return aisle on the western side. The church was entered on two sides by narthexes and two doorways on the northern wall; the western narthex was small, although it ended in the north and south with a small colonnaded apse and a stairway leading to the upper gallery. The southern narthex spanned almost the entire length of the church and also had an apse on the western end. Evidence is still visible of the ambon, or pulpit, in the nave. The interior of the church also includes several highly decorative niches which would become a common feature of Egyptian church architecture in later periods.

About three kilometers to the north is the Red Monastery. Together, the Red and White Monasteries formed part of the White Monastery Federation of St. Shenute in the fifth century. While much is known about the White Monastery due to the extensive collection of Coptic manuscripts written by its abbot, St. Shenute,[13] little is known of the Red Monastery. The church of the Red Monastery is smaller in scale than the White Monastery and was made of red brick, rather than white limestone (fig. 7). It also lacks the elaborate western narthex entrance and bears entrances only on the north and south sides. The southern narthex is more linear than that of the White Monastery. On the exterior and interior it would seem that the Red Monastery church is

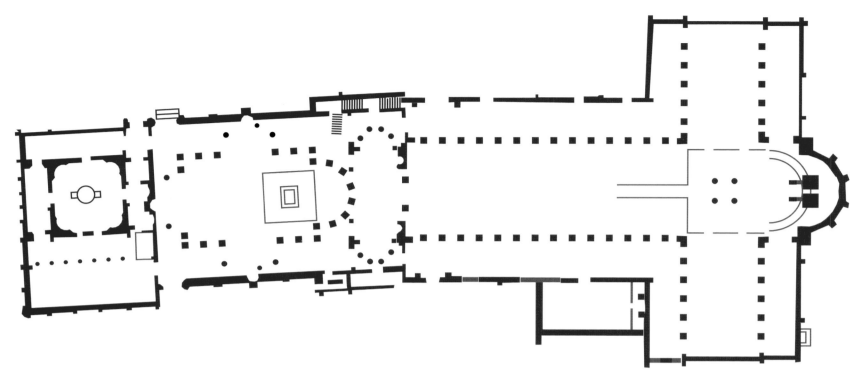

Fig. 8. Basilica and baptistery at Abu Mina

merely a copy of the White Monastery; however, on closer inspection the trilobe sanctuary is far more elaborate and all the architectural features are painted, including the niches and columns that flank the spaces. The paintings of this trilobe sanctuary are the object of a large conservation effort and, once finished, the sanctuary will be one of the few entirely painted spaces preserved from the late antique world. The paintings also reflect a Coptic style that demonstrates the richness of the Egyptian tradition independent of Byzantine models. Other triconch churches are found at Dendara and Dakhla Oasis (the Monastery of Abu Matta).

The final example of fifth-century architecture is considered the largest pilgrimage center of the late antique Mediterranean world. The site of Abu Mina, seventy kilometers southwest of Alexandria, was the center of a large cultic sanctuary dedicated to the memory of St. Menas, a third-century martyr. The popularity of the saint and the rituals surrounding his life would be a catalyst for the expansion of the center into a full urban pilgrimage center, one of the largest in the Christian late antique world.[14] The city's center was a massive church complex that included the largest basilica in Egypt in the fifth century (fig. 8). The model for this basilica is thought to be the Constantinian Basilica of the Holy Apostles in Constantinople, due to the imperial transept basilica form.[15] The quality of the masonry and materials used also suggests that the building was inspired by imperial craftsmen.

In the fifth century, a new basilica church was erected over the earlier *martyrion*. The basilica was an addition and later remodeling of a much smaller and earlier *martyrion*. The new church contained an eastern apse and, on the western end, a baptistery. Despite this construction, the expansion was not sufficient to meet the needs of the pilgrims and therefore additional aisles were added to the church. In the sixth century, the basilica was replaced by a tetraconch church made up of four semicircular apses (fig. 9). This unique structure would be found only at the pilgrimage center in Egypt and would physically highlight the importance of the St. Menas cult and its importance in the region. The tetraconch church is perhaps modeled after Syrian and Greek originals.[16]

All of these churches represent structures of the late fourth, fifth, and early sixth centuries built specifically for Christian worship. Spiritual needs and financial resources guided the design and

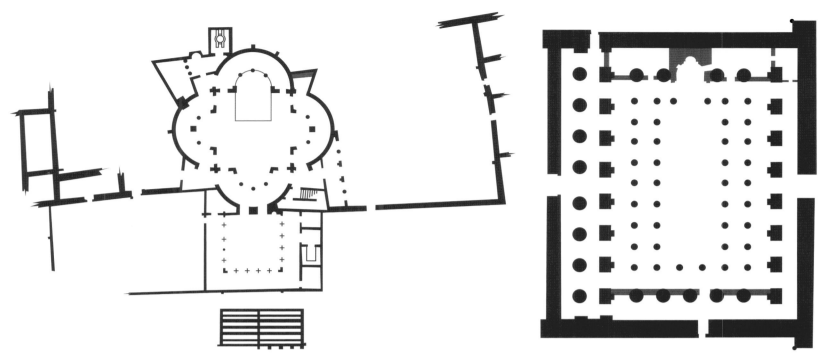

Fig. 9. Tetraconch Church at Abu Mina   Fig. 10. Madinat Habu

layout of the churches such that larger monasteries and cities had more elaborate churches, and smaller communities opted for simpler church designs. However, in some cases, Christians were able to modify already existing structures to create spaces for worship. Several pharaonic temples were used for Christian worship, but only select areas of the temples were altered for Christian use. At Madinat Habu, in Thebes, a church was built in the fifth century inside the walls of the old mortuary temple of Ramesses III from the Nineteenth Dynasty (fig. 10). The church was a five-aisled basilica in plan and incorporated the pharaonic colonnades into the return aisle. An apse was added in the eastern end of the courtyard. The architects needed to remove one of the eastern pillars and this was the only structural change that required the removal of any elements of the ancient temple. By placing crosses on the walls and painting images of saints on the columns, the space was converted into a church that could be used by the inhabitants of the town of Djeme.

In other cases, Christians built churches alongside or inside the large temple complexes. One example is found at the Ptolemaic site of Dendara where a small triconch church, similar to that of the grand churches at the White and Red Monasteries in Sohag, was built, and follows the layout of the basilica church with side aisles and a western narthex. This early sixth century church has a rather elaborate narthex with apses at each end and a triple entrance into the nave. Like the church at Madinat Habu, the church at Dendara demonstrates that Christians were eventually free to assume the rights to pagan temple lands and were able to build churches within and among these structures without needing to remove the massive pharaonic temples. By placing churches within the pagan precincts, the Christians were able to claim that land as sacred for Christ.

The seventh century marks a significant change in the interior layout of Coptic churches. While the basilica form was maintained, the introduction of a new feature, the *khurus*, created a greater physical division between the congregation and the clergy. The *khurus* is frequently a wall that hides the sanctuary from direct view, except for one entrance. The wall would later be pierced, in some examples, by two other entrances that would give access to the side chambers that made up part of the tripartite sanctuary. One of the first appearances of a *khurus* built within a new church is found in the large monastic church at the Monastery of Jeremiah (fig. 11). The *khurus* was used frequently in the monasteries of Wadi al-Natrun: the Monastery of al-Baramus, the Monastery of St. Pshoi, the

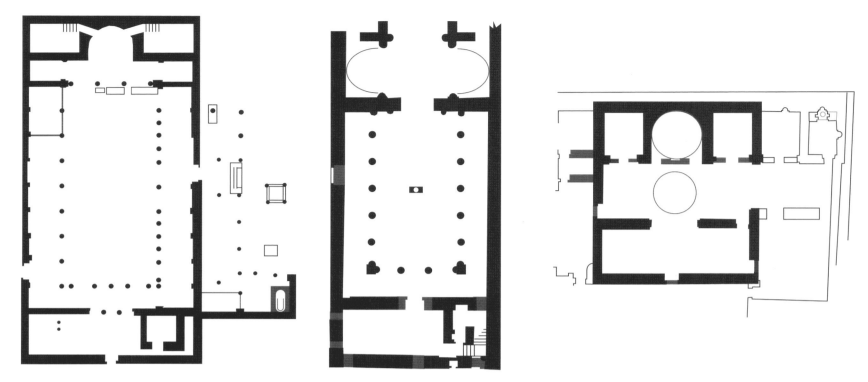

Fig. 11. Monastery of St. Jeremiah, Saqqara

Fig. 12. The Church of the Virgin at the Monastery of the Syrians

Fig. 13. Church at the Monastery of the Martyrs

Monastery of the Syrians, and the Monastery of St. Macarius. In particular, the Church of the Virgin at the Monastery of the Syrians includes a fully developed single-entrance *khurus* covered with wooden doors (fig. 12). The basilica plan is still in use, with an entrance on the north and a narthex on the west end. As found in other Coptic churches, the walls are pierced with niches along all the interior walls and the upper levels decorated with wall paintings. The practice of using the *khurus* can be found throughout the medieval period until its eventual abandonment in the Mamluk period.

By the tenth and eleventh centuries, in the Fatimid period, Egyptian churches had evolved from the basilican plan to either the domed octagon or the domed oblong plan. Part of the shift in design can be attributed to the preference to roof buildings throughout Egypt with domes rather than timber. The use of mud and fired bricks was far more affordable than the use of timber. This shift from five-aisled to three-aisled plans and then to a grid pattern of domed spaces created more intimate spaces that did not have clerestories or galleries, as was once common in the sixth century.

The domed oblong plan is best exhibited in the monastic complex of the Monastery of St. Hatre in Aswan. The church, built in the eleventh century, includes a *khurus* that connected the sanctuary to two smaller domed bays which made up the nave.[17] The side aisles were added at a later point and create elongated chambers that open onto the nave bays and have two entrances to the *khurus*.

Another domed oblong plan is that of the Fatimid-period Church of St. Antony in the Monastery of St. Antony by the Red Sea. The first sacred building in the area was originally a chapel that may have commemorated the burial of St. Antony, one of the forerunners of Egyptian monasticism. Like the Monastery of St. Hatre, the Church of St. Antony has a tripartite sanctuary, a *khurus*, and two domed bays that comprise the nave. However, the Church of St. Antony is unique in that it contains a dated painted program by the hand of Theodore from 1232/1233.[18] This dating provides an opportunity to examine in detail the form of the church and its evolution. An extension to the chapel was added after the tenth century, although exactly when is not clear; based upon its axis of orientation, the new church was likely built at the same time as the keep of the monastery. The final phase of the church, with its tripartite sanctuary, each part containing altars, was possibly built in the thirteenth century. Its current form reflects the last major significant alteration to the church.[19]

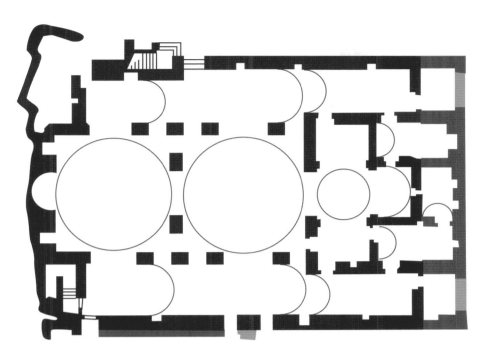

*Fig. 14. The Monastery
of St. Hatre*

The domed octagon is seen prominently in the churches in Akhmim, such as the church at the Monastery of the Martyrs (Dayr al-Shuhada) (fig. 13). These churches reflect the preference of the late medieval Christians who adopted this plan in the sixteenth century. The churches of this period represent the last phase of the use of the *khurus*.[20] The medieval churches are divided by columns that then carry the weight of the domes and the naves are therefore usually divided into large bays. The church at the Monastery of the Martyrs exhibits the shift to the more intimate interiors with low walls and domed roofs that would be indicative of the late medieval church.

Church architecture in Egypt evolved from the plan of a secular Roman basilica to that of an exclusively Christian plan that incorporated architectural elements, such as the *khurus*, to reflect the needs and practices of the Christian communities. The manner in which these structures were then decorated with images of saints and scenes of Biblical heroes demonstrates that these spaces were always sacred spaces, regardless of how many galleries or chapels the church contained. We know little about the architects who were responsible for these grand structures, but they were perhaps guided by the belief that God had inspired them just as St. Apollo was directed by Christ in how to build his *martyrion* to commemorate the life of his companion, Apa Phib. The evolution of church architecture reflects the richness of the history of Christianity in Egypt, including the importance of monastic communities.

The Art of Coptic Churches

Gertrud J.M. van Loon

"WE WENT TO THE CHURCH while the elders of the monastery went with us. There were pictures of monks on the wall of the place, representing our monastic fathers: Antony the Great and Apa Pachom and Apa Paule and Apa Makarios.[21] These were on one side and the archbishops of the see were on another: St. Markos and Apa Petros and Apa Athanasius and Liberios, mounted on the Cherub, St. Kyrillos and Dioskoros.[22] These were painted on the other wall.

"I testify to you that at the moment my father Apa Benjamin entered the church and went toward them in order to salute them, they exhaled a perfumed oil and all of them called out in a heavenly tongue: 'Holy you are, O King, O Lord, together with your saints!' and [we] saw the Cherub, on which Athanasius and Liberios were mounted, spread out his wings as if he were flying up on high, so that the wall shook to and fro from joy. And the Angel of the Sanctuary shouted: 'Worthy, worthy, worthy, o archbishop, he who will with fear celebrate holy Mass today!'"

This vision of Patriarch Benjamin (626–665), told by his scribe and successor Agathon,[23] tells us two important things: First, images of saints and bishops were painted in the church, most probably in the nave, because immediately upon entering the church, Benjamin went to greet them. Second, they were not just images: At the entry of the patriarch, they came to life and praised God. A miracle happened.

In Egypt, a church is not simply regarded as a place of worship; it is a mystical place. Functionally speaking, a church is a building designed for people to gather in prayer and for various liturgical ceremonies, especially the celebration of the Eucharist, the consecration of bread and wine in commemoration of Christ's sacrifice. Therefore, the church building is a holy place and was (and is) consecrated before being brought into use. Liturgically speaking, the eastern part is of major importance: the consecration of bread and wine takes place in the altar room; the reading of the Gospels, prayers, and hymns takes place in the space directly in front of it, the *khurus*, which was designed especially for this function in the seventh century. The nave is the spot where the lay people or the monks congregate to partake in the celebration, pray, and sing, but it does not play a direct role in the liturgy.

From early Christian times onward, the various parts of the building were charged with a symbolic meaning. When Patriarch Benjamin consecrated the church in the Monastery of St. Macarius in Wadi al-Natrun, the hand of God took over the anointment of the altar. Witnessing this miracle, Benjamin uttered the words, "How dreadful is this place! This is none other but the house of God and this is the gate of Heaven" (Gen. 28:17).[24]

As the "House of God," the church contains several layers of symbolic images. The altar room represents first the Holy of Holies of the Old Testament Tabernacle, a tent constructed by Moses to house the Law, the covenant between God and his people. The tribes of Israel took this movable sanctuary with them during their wanderings in the desert on their way from Egypt to the Promised Land (the Books of Exodus and Numbers). Second, the altar room is a symbol of the Holy of Holies of the Temple in Jerusalem, built by King Solomon as a permanent house of worship. Finally, it symbolizes Jerusalem, both the earthly city where Christ died and the heavenly Jerusalem, the paradise of the end of times. In this line of thought, the *khurus* in front of the altar room symbolizes the holy place in front of the Holy of Holies where the Old Testament priests dwelled, as well as paradise, the place where the souls of the righteous await the Last Judgment in order to ascend into heaven.[25] The symbolic meaning of the spaces is not always clear or binding. Holy place or paradise can also signify the *khurus* and the nave. Only the altar room is always exclusively the Holy of Holies, the heavenly Jerusalem. Simultaneously, the church itself can be compared to paradise. In a hymn sung at the end of the consecration of a church, she is compared to "the Paradise of God."[26]

When the priest, standing in the tradition of Old Testament priests as Melchizedek, Aaron, and Zacharias, consecrates bread and wine, it is felt to be part of the heavenly liturgy: the heavens open and Christ and his heavenly host come down in order to partake in the earthly ritual.[27] At that moment, heaven and earth are one and priests are as "earthly angels and heavenly men"[28] symbolically assisting in the heavenly liturgy. It is obvious that in a setting like this miracles happen.

These ideas, a timespan of past, present, and future, merging and overlapping in symbolic meaning and ritual, are mainly expressed in ecclesiastical treatises and encyclopedias of the tenth to fourteenth century.[29] They have undoubtedly much older roots, as the literary witnesses cited above testify,[30] and, from early times onward, the symbolic meaning and the liturgical ceremonies performed determined the decoration of the various parts of the building.

Church decoration before the year 1000

Completely decorated churches dating from before the year 1000 have not been found so far. Until recently, two large monastic complexes known from excavations at the beginning of the twentieth century, the Monastery of St. Jeremiah in the Saqqara necropolis and the Monastery of St. Apollo in Bawit (Middle Egypt), were mainly responsible for our knowledge of painting in monastic cells, chapels, and churches.[31] However, one hundred years ago excavation techniques were limited. In conjunction with incomplete (photographic) documentation and concise reports, this means that a systematic study of the wall paintings and finds in churches and other buildings is not possible. Almost all of the murals found in these monasteries, generally dated to the sixth to eighth century, have disappeared; a few were saved and are at present on display in the Coptic Museum in Cairo and the Louvre in Paris. Extensive restoration campaigns in, for example, the church of the Monastery of St. Pshai (the so-called Red Monastery) near Sohag,[32] the Old Church of St. Antony in the Monastery of St. Antony near the Red Sea,[33] the Church of the Virgin in the Monastery of the Syrians in Wadi al-Natrun (see pages 278–83, 208–19, 70–77),[34] as well as new excavations in Bawit, re-excavating the North Church,[35] yield important new data on church decoration while modern techniques permit a more secure dating.

In combination with the results of the excavations of other churches during the past years and a reassessment of older documentation, a decorative program that illustrates and underlines the symbolic meaning comes to light.

First of all, an intense love for colorful decorative designs immediately catches the eye: borders and panels were used to accentuate or imitate architectural features, and walls were adorned with painted imitations of textiles (curtains) or allover decorative patterns. Also, architectural sculpture in wood or stone was painted.

The lower part of the walls in the church was painted with panels showing an imitation of *opus sectile* (a pattern of inlaid stones), a painted curtain, or a space-filling decorative design (floral or geometrical). In the nave, the upper part was filled with figurative paintings (Virgin and Child, angels, prophets, standing or equestrian saints, scenes from the Old or the New Testament) or crosses, sometimes with flanking animals or under canopies (for example the oldest layers in the quarry church of the Monastery of al-Ganadla and the Old Church of St. Antony, or in the church of the Monastery of St. Pshai near Sohag (see pages 266–73, 208–19, 278–83). This system, a dado with a geometrical pattern and a figurative frieze above, has a long history in late antique Egypt, where it could be found in temple and tomb decoration and in private houses.[36]

In most churches of the early period, the decoration of the altar room has not survived. In the South Church of Bawit and the quarry church of Wadi Sarga (Middle Egypt, both dated to the sixth to eighth century), the Communion of the Apostles was painted on the east wall or in the conch of the apse. The scene looks like a depiction of the Last Supper, with one main difference: Christ has descended from heaven and is standing behind an altar as a priest during Mass, distributing bread and wine to his disciples. The historical image has become a liturgical image, uniting heaven and earth.[37]

The interior of the semi-domes of the trilobed sanctuary of the Church of St. Pshai in the Monastery of St. Pshai, the so-called Red Monastery near Sohag (first half of the sixth century (see pages 278–83) has been repainted four times. Recent research dates the fourth layer to around 800.[38] It is clear that the subjects, in more or less detail, remained the same. The eastern semi-dome is decorated with an apocalyptic vision of Christ enthroned riding on a chariot of fire, surrounded by the Four Living Creatures[39] and flanked by (arch)angels (in an earlier layer accompanied by apostles). The background shows stars. The final layer of the northern semi-dome is painted with a complicated architectural framework. In the center, the enthroned Virgin nurses her son, surrounded by prophets (with scrolls), angels, Joseph, and Salomé the midwife.[40] The southern semi-dome shows a similar architectural framework with Christ enthroned, surrounded by St. John the Baptist and his father Zacharias, angels, the four evangelists, and patriarchs. Inscriptions identify the saints and biblical personages.

These three intricate compositions are undoubtedly related to paintings that, in a simplified arrangement, were found in large numbers in the eastern niches of cells and chapels in Bawit and Saqqara, and that were to become the predominant representation for the eastern niche of the altar room: In the upper zone Christ enthroned (often in a *mandorla*), surrounded by the Four Living Creatures and riding on a chariot of fire. The background consists of a starry sky with sun and moon and often angels. It must be noted that at this time in Egypt the Four Living Creatures—the man or angel, the lion, the ox, and the eagle—do not represent the four Evangelists as they do in Western art but are solely seen as adoring angelic beings around the throne of God.[41] The Virgin Mary occupies the lower zone. She is depicted as an *orant* or enthroned with Child and surrounded by the apostles, sometimes accompanied by local saints.

This double composition symbolizes at the same time the past, the present, and the future: It is a vision of the Ascension, in which Christ is carried to heaven on a chariot-throne surrounded by angels, as described in various Coptic texts. Furthermore, it refers to Christ's Kingship following his Ascension (the present) while simultaneously, it refers to His second coming on the Day of Judgment, foretold in his Ascension (Acts 2:11).[42] The sun and moon together are symbols of cosmic and eternal power. Hymns praise Mary as "the Chariot of the Cherubim": she carried Christ as the chariot carries Him in heaven. His divinity and humanity are made manifest.[43] In a poem attributed to St. Ephrem the Syrian (d. 373), Mary sings to her son: "The very chariot stops amazed that I carry its Master; . . . Your radiance rests on my knees, the throne of Your majesty is held in my arms. Instead of the chariot wheels, my fingers clasp you."[44]

Khurus decoration is seldom preserved. An exception is the *khurus* of the Church of the Virgin in the Monastery of the Syrians, where several levels of paintings have come to light. Imitation stone panels and decorative borders were painted in the lower zone, with patriarchs and saints (among others, medical and equestrian saints) above (eighth century).[45] In December 2006, the restoration team removed the thirteenth-century painting of the Dormition of the Virgin in the northern half-dome. A theme unique for Egypt came to light: a magnificent image of the Virgin enthroned with Child surrounded by the Magi and shepherds. Research on the date of this mural is in progress. The southern half-dome still carries the thirteenth-century painting of the Annunciation and the Nativity.[46]

Vaults and domes were most probably painted but their decoration is rarely preserved. Exceptions are the cassette pattern and crosses in medallions on the ceiling of the quarry church of the Monastery of al-Ganadla and the geometrical pattern with busts in the cave of the Monastery of St. Hatre (see pages 268, 307). Sometimes, a pattern can be reconstructed from fragments found during excavations. The *khurus* dome of the Monastery of the Syrians was covered with paintings, but only a few fragments remain (among others, throne fragments).[47]

In the altar room, all decoration was directed to the ceremonies that took place . In the nave, the place where the people or monks gathered, saints and martyrs—the forerunners and champions of faith—were frequently depicted. It is noteworthy that nearly all churches with murals preserved are monastic churches, and monastic life clearly influenced the choice of saints depicted. The "fathers of the monks" are prominently present. Equestrian saints had, apart from being sanctified, another much valued quality: as mounted soldiers who were conquering enemies of faith, they were venerated for their protection against evil. In this function they are often seen as guardians of entrances or the sanctuary. Apart from a theological view, images in churches also had a didactic reason: they were painted to "give instruction concerning every good thing, especially purity," as Shenute of Atripe (d. ca. 465) wrote.[48] Inscriptions in the murals give the names of the persons depicted, and sometimes also the names of donors, painters, and plasterers, but unfortunately rarely dates.

Stone sculpture (often reused pieces blended with elements made to order) consists mainly of capitals, door frames, and niche heads. Horizontal borders set in long walls (South Church, Bawit) could be executed in wood or stone. Wooden corbels, door beams, and doors were often sculpted. It was nearly all architectural sculpture, decorative designs enhancing the architecture and the spatial layout of the building, sometimes including reliefs of Christ, the Virgin, saints, and scenes from the Old and the New Testaments. Almost certainly, all sculpture was once painted, as can be observed in the sanctuary of the Church of St. Pshai near Sohag and the quarry church of the Monastery of al-Ganadla (see pages 278–83, 266–73). A number of pieces preserved from various monuments still retain traces of original coloring.

Church furniture in wood or stone is seldom preserved. Exceptional works of art are the two sets of tenth-century wooden doors in the Church of the Virgin in the Monastery of the Syrians (Dayr al-Suryan). The panels of the doors are decorated with ivory inlays showing geometrical designs and Saints (see pages 70–77). The Coptic Museum houses a wooden a wooden altar from the fifth century.[49]

Churches from 1000 to 1400

The Old Church of the Monastery of St. Antony near the Red Sea (see pages 208–19) is one of the rare churches with a largely preserved decorative program. A recent restoration campaign returned the murals to their former splendor and revealed many unknown details.[50] Inscriptions date the murals to the years 1232–1233 and mention the painter Theodore, who most probably worked with a team. The program (with some earlier remains and later additions) confirms the choice of themes from earlier centuries. In the eastern niche in the central altar room (*haykal* in Arabic), Christ enthroned is surrounded by the Four Living Creatures, sun, moon, and angels. In the lower register, the Virgin Mary with Child is accompanied by the archangels Michael and Gabriel. New elements of the altar room program are Old Testament scenes: Abraham, willing to sacrifice his son Isaac (Gen. 22:1–19), Jephthah sacrificing his daughter (Judg. 11:30–40), the meeting of Abraham and Melchizedek, offering bread and wine (Gen.14:18–20), and Isaiah, his lips being purified by a coal from the heavenly altar (Is. 6:1–7). They prefigure Christ's sacrifice which is replaced, in turn, by the bloodless sacrifice of the Eucharist. Above these scenes, an image of heaven as described in the Book of Revelation (4–5) is given: A frieze with the Twenty-Four Priests[51] runs all around the walls. In the center of the dome, Christ is depicted in majesty, surrounded by angels and seraphim/cherubim. On the soffit of the arch to the *haykal*, six prophets are painted. Their prophesies are a link between the Old and the New Testaments.

In the *khurus*, equestrian saints, the three Hebrews in the fiery furnace (Dan. 3:1–97), and the three patriarchs Abraham, Isaac, and Jacob in Paradise are represented. The eastern part of the nave contains a frieze of standing saints (mainly monks) and the Virgin Mary, while the western part is decorated with a frieze of equestrian saints.[52] The domes above the nave are bare. Decorative borders and patterns play an important part in the murals: they are used to edge scenes and saints, fill left-over spaces, and are found on clothing and furniture.

With variations, and not as well preserved, this *haykal* program can be found in other churches of this period. The Old Testament scenes can, for example, be seen in the Church of the Virgin in the Monastery of al-Baramus and the Church of St. Macarius (*haykal* of St. Mark) in the Monastery of St. Macarius in Wadi al-Natrun (see pages 64–69, 84–89). Christ enthroned (or in combination with the Virgin in the lower register) in the eastern niche or semi-dome of the altar room, is seen in most places where (fragments of) paintings are preserved (see, for example, the Church of the Archangel Gabriel in Fayyum, the churches of the Sohag monasteries, and the church of the Monastery of St. Hatre in Aswan (see pages 202–207, 278–89, 304–307).[53]

The murals preserved in the *khurus* and nave of the Church of the Archangel Gabriel in Fayyum (see pages 202–207) show saints and a fragment of a composition with Christ and an apostle, equestrian saints, a standing monk, the Virgin and Child, and angels.[54] Apart from the Old Church of St. Antony, dome and ceiling decoration is seldom preserved.

Architectural sculpture as found in the early churches has disappeared, but the motifs are preserved in painting. Wooden sculpture is present in the splendid high doors closing *haykal* and *khurus* in, for example, the old churches of the Monastery of St. Macarius, the Monastery of al-Baramus, and the Monastery of St. Pshoi (Wadi al-Natrun) and in the elaborated, finely carved designs of the haykal and khurus screens in the churches of Cairo, inlaid with ebony, ivory, and bone. The techniques and the patterns are influenced by Islamic decorative designs although combined with Christian images.[55] Screens were also used to divide the nave into a men's and a women's section.

In the Cairene churches, the latter type of screen was often still preserved until around 1900, when a large-scale modernization destroyed the original layout of nave interiors.

Style of wall paintings

The first impression of the majority of paintings found in Bawit and Saqqara is a feeling of direct contact: the figures depicted frontally watch you with wide-open eyes and large pupils. Even when their bodies are angled away, the head is mostly painted in a frontal position. On reflection, these persons are not really looking at you, but beyond you, to a world you are unable to see. Faces in profile are rare, but a three-quarter pose (the lower part of the body shown from the side while the upper part is depicted frontally) is frequently shown.

A second impression is the lack of depth in figures and compositions. Persons are clearly outlined with heavy contours, the folds of their clothes sharply defined, looking like a row of paper dolls. In a number of paintings, however, a subtle play of colors and thin lines to model faces can be observed within the clear outline. The apse from Room 6 in Bawit, showing Christ enthroned in the upper register and the Virgin Mary with Child accompanied by apostles and local saints below, is a good example of this flat, rather heavy style and mesmerizing eyes.[56] At the same time, the lively faces (in profile) of the Four Living Creatures and the angels around the frontally depicted and stiff Christ enthroned seem to belong to another world, a heritage from late antique painting.

Although Christ, the Virgin and Child, angels, and portraits of saints and holy monks are almost always shown in this strictly frontal pose, the Hellenistic world, as well as influences from farther east (Sassanian art) can be frequently seen in hunting scenes, narrative scenes, secondary characters, and background. In the profusion of decorative borders and patterns, the Mediterranean world's heritage of Greco-Roman art is evident. These elements show that different styles of painting can go together and a more classical approach with depth, movement, and expression exists side by side with a formal and frontal approach, sometimes in the same room or even in a single composition. This emerging frontality demonstrates that the intention of images had changed. Instead of a true-to-life rendering of Christ, Mary, angels, biblical personages, and saints, they were painted larger than life: they are not, or are no longer, part of a real world, but of a world to come.

The number of paintings known from documentation, preserved in museums, or discovered during recent excavations or restoration campaigns is obviously only a fragment of what once existed. In this corpus, the general lines sketched above are clear. As a consequence, a more 'classical' style does not necessarily mean an earlier date. As an additional element, the ability and talent of the painter make a huge difference in style and quality. In Egyptian Christian painting, dating on the basis of style is tricky and full of traps. A more secure chronology can only be obtained from modern excavation technology or the luck of finding dated inscriptions.

From about 1000 onward, the classical style is found no more. The lack of depth in the treatment of figures and compositions, the heavy outlines, and the love for decorative borders and designs continued, but other influences also leave their mark. The paintings in the Old Church of St. Antony show inspiration from different traditions. They are part of "a shared visual culture" of twelfth- and thirteenth-century eastern Mediterranean art. The painter Theodore and his team worked in an Egyptian Christian style, but influences from Islamic, (Cypriotic) Byzantine, and perhaps 'Crusader art'[57] as well as aspects of everyday life in a Muslim society can be pointed out.[58]

Similar observations can be made in the Wadi al-Natrun churches. In the octagon of the haykal of St. Mark in the Monastery of St. Macarius, the composition of the Dream of Jacob (Gen. 28:10–22)[59] and Job, his wife and his friends (Job 2:7–13 and Job 3–41),[60] are classical Byzantine designs, while the ornamentation of furniture in the paintings and the decorative panels below[61] betray Islamic influence. In the Church of the Virgin in the Monastery of al-Baramus, the Byzantine Dodekaorton, a series of twelve liturgical feasts, inspired the series of scenes in the nave.[62] The thirteenth-century paintings in the three semi-domes of the Church of the Virgin in the Monastery of the Syrians show influences from Byzantium and Crusader art (via Syria and Lebanon).[63]

The Islamic influence is especially visible in ornamental design, for example in the painted decoration of the *khurus* ceiling of the Old Church of St. Antony or the beautifully carved and inlayed twelfth to thirteenth century wooden screens in the churches of Wadi al-Natrun and Old Cairo. Without the architectural setting and Christian elements like a cross, it is impossible to distinguish a screen made for a Muslim or a Christian.[64]

In thought and ideas, Egyptian Christian art was rooted firmly in local tradition and theological views. The composition and the style of murals and church furniture, however, betray a participation of painters and donors in the world of their time, even if they must be considered as followers of trends rather than leaders.

After 1400

Curiously, there are hardly any wall paintings preserved after 1400. Over the centuries, restoration campaigns, sometimes influenced by liturgical needs, replaced, removed, or added interior elements in the existing churches. Older paintings were restored or 'refreshed,' at times altering their style or composition but, from around 1400 until the present, wall painting as chief decorative medium is hardly found.

The subterranean Church of St. Paul in the Monastery of St. Paul near the Red Sea (see pages 220–29) houses a rare example of an almost complete eighteenth-century decorative program. Patriarch John XVI (1676–1718) added the northern part of the church, the oldest part consisting of the hermitage of St. Paul. A monk of the monastery decorated the new part and parts of the old church with paintings.[65] However, the monk did not invent the iconographical program: it echoes earlier programs, known for example from the Old Church of the neighboring Monastery of St. Antony: Equestrian saints at the entrance (the staircase), an enthroned Christ surrounded by the Four Living Creatures, and the eye-studded wings of the Cherubim with angels and the Twenty-Four Priests in the dome of the new *haykal* and rows of saints, archangels, and the Three Hebrews in the Fiery Furnace in the nave. Fragments of murals from the thirteenth and fourteenth centuries are preserved in the *haykal* of St. Antony in this church and visible in parts of the nave.[66]

In the sixteenth century, an Ethiopian monk painted standing and equestrian saints in keep chapels of the Monastery of St. Macarius (see page 87). Nevertheless, the main medium became painting on wood: panels fixed to the walls of a haykal showing a design that originally was executed directly on the walls. Well-preserved examples can be seen in the central haykal (eighteenth century, restored in the nineteenth century) and upstairs chapel of the Church of Mar Mina in Fumm al-Khalig (Cairo, see pages 140–45). The wall panels were painted with icon-painting techniques. They reflect all characteristics of contemporary icon painting in Egypt and the same masters and workshops executed them.

Icons

Texts demonstrate that from an early date, images or pictures had a place in church decoration. It is often difficult to interpret this source material. Frequently, it is not clear what kind of image is meant. Even if the word 'icon' is used, it might designate an image on different media: wood, papyrus, paper, textile, or wall painting. In this section, 'icon' will be used for a representation of a holy person on a portable wooden panel. If otherwise, it will be clearly indicated.[67]

Saints (female and male, monks or horsemen), archangels, and the Virgin and Child were types that were most suited for personal devotion and belong to the oldest icons known. In the late twelfth and early thirteenth centuries, a beam icon showing the principal feasts of the church was placed on the altar screen, in later times replaced with large icons of Christ, Mary, and St. John the Baptist (Deesis) accompanied by apostles or evangelists (Great Deesis). Icons could also be placed on top of the nave division screens, as can still be seen in the Church of St. Mercurius in Old Cairo: since the screens have been removed, the rows of eighteenth-century icons are suspended in the air. Modern division screens with icons on top were recently installed in the Church of the Virgin in the Monastery of al-Baramus (Wadi al-Natrun; see page 66).

Icons were greeted, kissed, and venerated. The saints depicted could bleed and weep for injustice, troubles, and grief, perform miracles, protect people from illness and demons, and grant fertility to barren women. However, textual sources make clear that the saint depicted is an intercessor: it is always God who is venerated through the saint, and it is God who weeps for the world and grants the petitions made.[68] Icons also play a role in the liturgy. They are censed and are carried in procession on feast days, or are displayed on the feasts of the saint depicted. For personal devotion, a precious old icon or a modern printed image makes no difference to the Orthodox believer. What matters is the representation of the saint depicted and the intercession of the saint.

A small number of icons survive from the sixth to seventh century, such as Christ and St. Menas (Paris, Louvre), St. Theodore, and the Archangel Gabriel (Cairo, Egyptian Museum and Coptic Museum), all found in Bawit.[69] The style of these panels reflects a similar treatment of figures as found in wall paintings of that period.

There is a curious, unexplainable gap from the ninth to the twelfth century, from which apparently no icons survive. As a result of restoration projects, a small corpus of icons from the thirteenth century to ca. 1500 was identified, mainly in the churches of Old Cairo.[70] More treasures of this era might be hidden in the churches and monasteries all over Egypt. At first glance, these icons look very Byzantine, with their gilded background and saints in Byzantine vestments. Closer study reveals the use of local wood for the panel and typical Egyptian compositions, saints, iconography, and inscriptions in Coptic, Greek, and Arabic. Painters were often Byzantine trained, but working locally.

Some sixteenth or seventeenth century icons are preserved, but the grand corpus of surviving icons dates to the eighteenth and nineteenth centuries when icons were not only painted on wooden panels but also on canvas or even paper. Several icon painters are known by name. Most famous were Ibrahim al-Nasikh and Yuhanna al-Armani (Abraham the scribe and John of Armenia), who frequently signed their work together (eighteenth century) and A[na]stasi al-Qudsi al-Rumi (Anastasius the Greek from Jerusalem, nineteenth century).

Ibrahim was a Copt, but the names of Yuhanna and A[na]stasi betray their provenance. They all brought with them their heritage and their style, and the iconography reflects a fusion of local tradition, influences from religious painting in Western Europe and various Middle Eastern communities, and Islamic art.

These artists not only painted icons but also decorated ciboria (canopies sheltering the altar) and chalice thrones. A fair number of eighteenth to nineteenth century ciboria are preserved in the old churches of Cairo (the three examples in the Hanging Church might even date to the fifteenth century). The interior reflects the older dome program: Christ in Glory surrounded by heavenly hosts. The exterior, the spandrels of the arches, show Old Testament prefigurations of the Eucharist and New Testament scenes.[71] The Ark or "Throne of the Chalice" (Arabic, *Kursi al-ka's*), a small wooden casket in which the prepared chalice is kept until Holy Communion, was equally painted with saints and fitting scenes.[72] The style of these ciboria and chalice thrones reflects contemporary icon painting in Egypt.

Epilogue

Although the artistic media changed over the centuries and influences and interaction in the artistic milieu brought about changes in the composition and/or choice of themes, the ideas behind church decoration have remained the same until the present day. The subjects chosen underscore the symbolic meaning and function of the building. Together, buildings, images, and ceremonies evoke a picture of past, present, and future. For the contemporary man or woman, being part of the ritual, surrounded by the saints painted on the walls and/or present in the icons, the light of candles and oil lamps, the long recitation of psalms and hymns, and the smell and smoke of incense, enhanced the feeling of being transformed, being transplanted to a heavenly sphere—a paradise on earth.

For a Western visitor these feelings and words, so familiar in Coptic literature and liturgy and still perfectly recognizable for Egyptian Christians today, may sound odd and hard to grasp. I thought so too. During one of my first visits to the Monastery of St. Antony, I was invited to attend the morning office in the Old Church. It was before the restoration. The paintings were still blackened by soot and grime and only recognizable if one knew the subjects. I was sitting at the back of the nave, leaning against the wall. The monks were praying and reciting. Candles were burning and the small church was filled with the smoke of incense. At that moment, I suddenly had a feeling of being moved in time and space. For centuries, generations of monks had sung God's praise in this small church, surrounded by the same champions of faith on the walls and in icons, in similar words. It felt like being part of eternity, if only for an instant. It is indeed a magical place.

Lower Egypt and Sinai

PORT SAID

40   The Cathedral of the Holy Virgin

        (Mary Queen of the World)

BILQAS

44   The Pilgrimage Center of St. Dimyana Monastery

ALEXANDRIA

48   The Coptic Patriarchal Church of St. Mark

52   The Church of St. Catherine

56   The Anglican Church of St. Mark

60   The Greek Orthodox Cathedral of St. Saba

WADI AL-NATRUN

64   The Monastery of al-Baramus

        (Dayr al-Baramus)

70   The Monastery of the Syrians

        (Dayr al-Suryan)

78   The Monastery of St. Pshoi

        (Dayr Anba Bishoi)

84   The Monastery of St. Macarius

        (Dayr Anba Maqar)

SAKHA

90   The Church of the Holy Virgin Mary

SINAI

92   St. Catherine's Monastery

The Cathedral of the Holy Virgin

THE CATHEDRAL OF THE HOLY VIRGIN (Mary, Queen of the World) is the largest church in Port Said and one of the most majestic sanctuaries in Egypt. It is located on 23rd of July Street in the eastern district (the European Quarter) in Port Said.

On April 10, 1927, the first bishop of the newly established Suez Canal Catholic Metropolitan arrived in Port Said. The cathedral's foundation stone was laid on February 11, 1934, and the building was completed in 1937. Artist Madame Frimone started the work on the cathedral's paintings in 1937 and completed them after the Second World War in 1947. The cathedral bells were used for the first time on February 26, 1938.

The southern part of the cathedral is occupied by an altar whose ceiling is decorated with the symbols of the zodiac. The zodiac is painted in some medieval Christian buildings in Europe. For example, Christ is depicted in the center of a zodiac pattern on a gateway at Vézelay. This may symbolize the universal character of Christ's mission. The church's magnificent wall paintings depict 207 saints, including the Holy Trinity, angels, prophets, the apostles, martyrs, founders of the monastic orders, and holy queens. There are three marble statues behind the altar: the Virgin Mary "Queen of the World" carrying a globe (middle), St. Bernadette (left), and St. Catherine (right). The door of the tabernacle is decorated with a scene of the Virgin and Child.

After the Suez Canal Crisis and the Anglo-French attack on Port Said in 1956, the Catholic community of Europeans left Port Said. Eventually, the Coptic Orthodox community bought the church. In 1985, on the 24th of the Coptic month Bashons, Anba Tadrus, the Coptic Bishop of Port Said, celebrated Mass in the cathedral. The sanctuary is dedicated to the Holy Virgin Mary. Its wooden screen is surmounted by the scene of the Last Supper flanked by twelve icons representing the apostles.

Exterior view of the Cathedral of the Holy Virgin (Mary, Queen of the World).

Carved marble statue of St. Bernadette behind a wrought-iron screen.

The original
Catholic tabernacle
with a painting of
the Virgin Mary
and Jesus. It is
found in the
northeast corner
of the sanctuary.

Nearby, encased in
glass on the life-
size Crucifixion,
is believed to be
a stone from
Golgotha.

LEFT:
Catholic and Coptic
altars showing the
Coptic seating.

The Pilgrimage Center of St. Dimyana Monastery

THE PILGRIMAGE CENTER OF ST. DIMYANA MONASTERY is situated near the town of Bilqas, which lies in the northeast region of the Nile Delta about 45 kilometers from the city of al-Mansura. A Monastery of Jimyana (Dimyana) is mentioned by the historian al-Maqrizi (d. 1442), although the expansion of the cult of St. Dimyana is traced to the sixteenth century. St. Dimyana is one of the most venerated female saints in Egypt. She was the only daughter of Marcus, governor of the district of Parallus and Za'faran in the northern Delta. When she heard that her father had accepted to offer incense and libation to the idols of Emperor Diocletian (284–305), she rebuked him. She was tortured with her forty virgin companions over several days and they were martyred. Today, the convent of St. Dimyana is one of the most important pilgrimage sites in Egypt. Each year hundreds of thousands of pilgrims travel to the site on January 20 (the commemoration of the martyrdom of St. Dimyana) and on May 21 (the commemoration of the consecration of her church).

The monastery contains several churches. The oldest church features four domed bays. The eastern bay serves as a sanctuary in which an earlier altar of fired bricks was discovered in 1974. The church dates from the Ottoman period, very possibly from the sixteenth century. The other churches are modern. Of special interest is the shrine of St. Dimyana, which was built in the last century. It was constructed as a four-pillar church with a high dome. On the occasion of the two-thousand-year celebration of the Holy Family's Flight into Egypt in 2000, the shrine of St. Dimyana was completely renovated. It is worthy of note that a number of nuns of St. Dimyana Monastery produce beautiful icons that decorate many Coptic churches in Egypt and abroad.

OPPOSITE:
The oldest church of the monastery features four domed bays.

ABOVE:
The Flight into Egypt: Window created by the nuns of the convent of St. Dimyana.

RIGHT:
Modern Icon of Christ holding the Gospel and the Cross.

Old church (sixteenth century).

Pilgrimage church with the shrine of St. Dimyana.

47

The Coptic Patriarchal Church of St. Mark

THE CHURCH IS LOCATED ON COPTIC CHURCH STREET off Saad Zaghloul Street. In 1819 Patriarch Peter VII (al-Gawli) consecrated this church, which replaced an older one. It was renovated in the reign of Patriarch Demetrius II in 1870 and adorned with a beautiful marble iconostasis that was decorated with more than thirty icons. The cathedral was reconstructed between 1950 and 1952, and was consecrated on November 9, 1952. The nineteenth-century marble iconostasis was dismantled and reused in the new building with its original icons, which date to the same period.

The cathedrals' three sanctuaries are dedicated to St. Mark (center), St. Michael (north), and St. George (south). Above the three sanctuaries there is a scene representing the Last Supper. The reused nineteenth-century iconostasis betrays a preference for Greek-style icons. They include Christ, St. Mark, St Antony, and St. George (right); Virgin and Child, St. Dimyana, St. Paul the Theban, and St. Michael (left). The iconostasis is surmounted by the icons of the twelve apostles and other saints. The huge vault of the cathedral is supported by two rows of seven columns with modified Corinthian capitals. The cathedral's western part was enlarged between 1985 and 1990, and an upper gallery was added. The cathedral's belfries have been strengthened and house new bells from Italy.

Mosaic of the Archangel Michael and carved-marble spiral staircase leading to the gallery.

The Coptic Patriarchal Church of St. Mark's façade with belfries housing bells from Italy.

Interior view toward the sanctuary. The tan-rose section is the original church. The white section begins the later addition.

The Church of St. Catherine

Sᴵᴛᵁᴀᴛᴇᴅ ON ST. CATHERINE STREET, this church is one of the most picturesque churches in Egypt. St. Catherine of Alexandria, also known as St. Catherine of the Wheel, was a virgin who was martyred in Alexandria in the fourth century because of her Christian faith. She was tortured, tied to a wheel, and beheaded. She was highly venerated in medieval times, especially in France during the Crusades. The church was built on a plot which was given by Muhammad 'Ali in 1835. Fr. Serafino da Bacceno designed the cathedral and it was consecrated by Archbishop Perpetuo Guasco on November 25, 1850. The cathedral boasts the largest organ in Egypt. It was brought from Italy and installed in the church in 1927.

On entering the church, one admires the ceiling, which is decorated by large medallions enclosing portraits of the saints Cyril, Antony, and Athanasius. The four spandrels of the dome are occupied by the four evangelists. One of the side altars shows the statue of St. Francis of Assisi flanked by statues of King Louis IX and St. Elizabeth. It is noteworthy that there is another statue of St. Francis of Assisi adorning the façade of the cathedral. The magnificent wooden pulpit is decorated with sculptures representing the life and martyrdom of St. Catherine of Alexandria. The upper part of the apse is decorated with a portrait of St. Clara. A large painting of St. Catherine, which is dated to 1948, hangs from the apse. The back of the altar is occupied by the tomb of Vittorio Emenuelle di Savoia (1869–1947); it is said that King Farouk attended his funerary procession.

St. Francis of Assisi flanked by the King Louis IX and St. Elizabeth.

One of the stations of the cross. Jesus falls for the third time.

OPPOSITE:
The Church of St. Catherine, Alexandria: exterior view approaching from the driveway.

Ceiling including portraits of Sts. Cyril, Antony, Athanasius.

Interior view: apse with a large painting of St. Catherine (1847), St. Clara (above).

Pulpit: Christ and angels appear to St. Catherine in prison.

Pulpit: The martyrdom of St. Catherine

54

ALEXANDRIA

The Anglican Church of St. Mark

THIS SPECTACULAR CHURCH IS LOCATED IN TAHRIR SQUARE (al-Manshiya). Muhammad 'Ali offered the land for the church to the Anglican community in the early nineteenth century. The church foundation stone was laid in 1839, but because of some difficulties, construction was delayed for fifteen years. In April 1855 it was finally consecrated by Bishop Samuel Cobat. On entering the church there is a small baptistery supported by four graceful columns. The reredos, located behind the altar, features a central panel with the crucifixion, two panels depicting St. David and St. Andrew to the left, and two panels with St. Patrick and St. George to the right. The apse has five stained glass windows that show Christ flanked by the four evangelists. An elaborately executed wooden pulpit stands to the left near the apse with a central figure of Christ in the front. The church boasts a large organ.

Exterior view of the Anglican Church of St. Mark from the road on Tahrir Square.

RIGHT:
Christ raises his right hand in benediction.

FOLLOWING PAGES:
Interior view toward the altar.

The Greek Orthodox Cathedral of St. Saba

THE CATHEDRAL OF ST. SABA is situated on Greek Patriarchate Street. St. Saba (439–532) was a native of Mutalaska in Cappadocia, Turkey. In 478 he founded a monastic settlement in Wadi al-Nar between Jerusalem and the Dead Sea. He was a strong supporter of the doctrines promulgated at the Council of Chalcedon (451). The Melkite Partiarch Eutychus (Sa'id ibn al-Batriq: 877–940) states that in the seventh year of the Caliphate of Hisham (724–743) Cosmas occupied the See of Alexandria for twenty-eight years, and the Christian Melkites prayed in those days in the church of St. Saba. The Monastery of St. Saba was a patriarchal residence for many years. It had been renovated several times in the reign of the patriarchs Loakeim (1486–1567), Parthenios I (1678–1688), Matthaios the Cantor (1746–1765), Lerotheos I (1825–1854), Sophronios IV (1890–1899), and Photios (1900–1925).

Red-granite altar of St. Catherine at the northeast corner of the nave.

OPPOSITE:
Nave and wooden iconostasis.

The large bell which lies in the outer court is a gift of H.B. Alexis, Patriarch of Moscow and all Russia. Fourteen steps lead down to the church of St. Saba, which is two meters below the level of the street. The church's entrance is in the north wall. The ceiling of the nave is supported by six ancient columns of red granite. The church's *ambon* features a spiral staircase winding around a granite column. Modern metallic icons adorn the wooden iconostasis. To the right of the sanctuary's door is an icon of Christ, to the left the Virgin and Child. The altar of St. Catherine, which features crosses and conches, stands at the northeast corner of the nave. Eighteenth-century icons decorate the church's western wall. Two icons represent the Assumption of the Virgin Mary and St. Mark the Evangelist in the land of Egypt, with the Nile, the pyramids, and the lighthouse of Pharos in the background. There is a chapel dedicated to St. Mark behind the church of St. Saba.

Outer court and bell tower two meters below street level.

Nave looking toward the ambon, showing two of the red granite columns.

The Monastery of al-Baramus

The Archangel Michael, painted on a pillar in the Church of the Virgin.

The name Baramus contains the Coptic *romaios*, 'the one of the Roman(s).' According to Coptic tradition, these Romans are the fourth-century princes Maximus and Domitius, sons of the Emperor Valentinian I. They lived in Wadi al-Natrun under the spiritual guidance of St. Macarius the Great who, after their death, had a church built in their memory.

The present Monastery of al-Baramus is in fact a double monastery of the original monastery dedicated to the royal brothers, which was already in ruins in the eighteenth century.[73] Double monasteries were founded in the sixth century by monks who were opposed to the doctrine of the Gaianite heresy, which stated that Christ was incorruptible and thereby denied his Incarnation. As a consequence, the Virgin Mary lost her position as *Theotokos*, the God-bearer. Monks adhering to the traditional views founded new establishments, often dedicated to the Mother of God.

Historical evidence for the monastery's past is meager. It certainly shared the vicissitudes of fortune of the other monastic establishments in Wadi al-Natrun. Over the centuries, Berber raids caused considerable damage and, following attacks, churches, utility buildings, and cells had to be renovated and reconstructed. In the ninth century, walls and keeps were built to provide greater safety. The historical events and the plague of the fourteenth century had a large impact on the number of monks. A decline of monastic life in Wadi al-Natrun set in, and was only reversed at the beginning of the twentieth century.

The Church of the Virgin in the Monastery of al-Baramus is the oldest existing church in Wadi al-Natrun and still contains elements from the late sixth century. It was built on a basilican plan with a return-aisle and a tripartite sanctuary. A *khurus* was added in the seventh century. Later phases of rebuilding affected the roof (vaults and domes have replaced the wooden roof) and interior (remodeling of various parts) but not the size of the church.

During the most recent restoration (1979–1992), wall paintings were discovered in the nave, and in the central and southern altar rooms (thirteenth century). The walls above the colonnades of the nave were decorated with a series of twelve feasts of which fragments of the Annunciation, the Visitation, the Nativity, the Baptism of Christ, the Entry into Jerusalem (south wall), and Pentecost (north wall) have survived. In the central altar room, three apostles are painted on either side of the niche. The upper part shows the lower part of Abraham's Sacrifice (left) and the meeting of Abraham and Melchizedek (right). A later master painted the double composition in the niche (Christ enthroned above and the Virgin enthroned with Child accompanied by two archangels below). On the walls of the southern altar room, a series of fourteen saints was painted.

As with the other monasteries in Wadi al-Natrun, the Monastery of al-Baramus is now thriving. Outside the old walls, a guest house and retreat houses have been built. Water pumps have been installed, bringing about the development of vegetable gardens, orchards, and a farm.

OPPOSITE:
The monastery of al-Baramus, founded in the sixth century.

FOLLOWING PAGES —
LEFT:
The Church of the Virgin is the oldest existing church in Wadi al-Natrun with some elements from the sixth century still there, looking from the khurus *to the nave. Modern screens with icons partition the nave.*

RIGHT:
View from the nave to the central altar room. The six-meter-high wooden doors with delicately sculptured panels in front of the altar room date to the twelfth century. To the left, a wooden ambon *(pulpit).*

*South wall of the
nave: the Annunciation
and the Visitation
(thirteenth century).*

LEFT:

*The east wall of the central altar room. In
the niche, Christ enthroned and the Virgin
with Child and archangels. To the left, the
lower part of Abraham's Sacrifice; to the
right the Meeting of Abraham and
Melchizedek. Six apostles are painted below.*

*South wall of the
nave: the Entry
into Jerusalem.*

The Monastery of the Syrians

The Monastery of the Syrians from the northeast.

OPPOSITE:
Moses of Nisibis's doors to the central altar room. The panels are inlaid with ivory (first half of the tenth century).

THE MONASTERY OF THE MOTHER OF GOD OF THE SYRIANS, as it has become known, was established in the sixth century, as a double monastery of the Monastery of St. Pshoi. According to tradition, a certain Marutha from Tigrit (Takrit, in present-day Iraq) bought the monastery for his countrymen. Recent scholarship, however, holds the view that an actual purchase did not take place. The monastery was never entirely Syrian but can be seen as a mixed community where Syrian and Coptic monks lived together, each at times constituting a majority or minority. The Monastery of the Syrians is first attested in the ninth century and a strong Syrian presence was evident until the eleventh century. In the seventeenth century it probably became a Coptic monastery again.

The most important person in the history of the monastery is the abbot Moses of Nisibis (first half of the tenth century), who refurbished the Church of the Holy Virgin and enriched the library with a large number of Syriac manuscripts. Syriac inscriptions on the wooden folding doors of the altar room and the *khurus* tell that he commissioned these doors. The unique stucco decoration in the central altar room and the Chapel of the Martyrs next to the entrance of the church might be attributed to his abbacy, although a ninth-century date also seems possible. The stucco shows close similarities to stuccowork from Samarra (Iraq).

The Church of the Holy Virgin (seventh century) still retains most of its original features, nave, side-aisles with a western return aisle, and a *khurus*: this is the first example preserved where a *khurus* was planned from the start. The altar rooms were rebuilt at a later date, but before the stucco decoration.

Until 1988, three wall paintings in the church were visible, executed in three half-domes, two on either end of the *khurus* and the third on the western end of the nave (dated to the thirteenth century). A fire at the western end of the church caused large parts of the plaster to fall. The older layer below revealed a magnificent Annunciation and initiated a campaign of restoration of the church. Up until now, four layers of painting and inscriptions in Syriac, Coptic, and Arabic have been discovered, dating to the seventh through the thirteenth centuries. These new data have yielded important information on the history of the monastery and the history of wall painting in Egyptian churches. The continuing work in the church will undoubtedly hold new surprises.[74]

Panels from the doors to the khurus *(top left) and to the central altar room (right and bottom) with the Virgin Mary on the latter panel.*

OPPOSITE:
Khurus, *the entrance to the southern altar room. Above the entrance are two equestrian saints; on the half-column, the Virgin enthroned with Child (eighth century).*

FOLLOWING PAGES — LEFT:
The northern part of the khurus, *with the two sets of doors. The painting in the half-dome represents the Dormition of the Virgin (thirteenth century). At present, this painting has been taken down, revealing an Adoration of the Virgin and Child by the Magi and shepherds. Standing saints (eighth century) were discovered on the walls.*

FOLLOWING PAGES — RIGHT:
The central altar room with stucco decoration.

The western part of the nave, with, in the half-dome, the painting of the Annunciation with four prophets, each holding a scroll with an appropriate citation from his prophecy (eighth century).

76

Nave, south wall:
The three patriarchs
Abraham, Isaac, and
Jacob in Paradise
(ca. 1000). The small
naked figures in their
laps and climbing
trees represent the
souls of the blessed,
eating fruit from the
trees of paradise.

77

The Monastery of St. Pshoi

The Church of St. Pshoi, view to the central altar room.

RIGHT:
The khurus. *On both sides of the doors to the central altar room are modern paintings of the Virgin with Child, Christ, Saint John the Baptist, apostles, and saints. On the left, next to the entrance to the side chapel dedicated to Patriarch Benjamin II (1327–1339) is a reliquary with the relics of St. Pshoi and his friend St. Paul of Tamweh.*

SAINT PSHOI WAS A FOURTH-CENTURY ANCHORITE living in Wadi al-Natrun. After a Berber raid, he fled to a place near the city of Antinoë (Middle Egypt) where he died at the beginning of the fifth century. In the ninth century, his relics were brought back to the monastery that was named after him.

Although historical information is scarce, the Monastery of St. Pshoi undoubtedly belongs to the oldest monastic settlements in Wadi al-Natrun. It must therefore have suffered from the numerous Berber raids, resulting in renovations and the reconstruction of churches, cells, and utility buildings and, in the ninth century, the building of the first walls and a tower for refuge. Apart from an extensive restoration of the church and buildings by Patriarch Benjamin II (d. 1339), little more is known from the following centuries.

The Church of St. Pshoi, in the southern part of the old enclosure, most probably dates to the rebuilding of the monastery after the raids of 830–849. Originally, it was built on a basilican plan, with a deep *khurus* and an altar room with narrow side chambers. Afterward, the southern side chamber was enlarged and used as an altar room. Still at a later date, a small church dedicated to the equestrian saint Iskhirun was added along the south wall and an adjoining chapel was constructed in the northeastern corner, at present dedicated to Patriarch Benjamin II. During the restoration under his patriarchate, the vaults of the roofs were replaced. Remarkable are the high doors to the central altar room with their beautifully sculptured panels (twelfth century). In 1989, twelfth-century wall paintings were discovered in the Chapel of Benjamin. Saints, angels, (some of) the Twenty-Four Priests, and the Three Hebrews in the Fiery Furnace (Dan. 3:1:97) could be identified.

Beginning in the seventeenth century, Western visitors reported repeatedly that the number of monks living in the monastery was dwindling. At present, however, it is a flourishing community and one of the busiest in Wadi al-Natrun. Before his election, his holiness Patriarch Anba Shenouda III was a monk here and a patriarchal residence has been built outside the old walls. A large farm with cattle and gardens has been developed.

The corridor between the Church of St. Pshoi and the ancient refectory to the west of the church.

The churches of the monastery, both old and new.

OPPOSITE:
*The keep with
drawbridge. It is
the largest and finest
tower in Wadi al-
Natrun. Building
dates vary between
the eleventh and
thirteenth century.*

RIGHT:
The well in the keep.

The Monastery of St. Macarius

The Church of the
Forty-Nine Martyrs,
rebuilt by Mu'allim
Ibrahim al-Guhari
(eighteenth century),
with the keep in the
background. Ibrahim
al-Guhari (d. 1795)
was one of the Guhari
brothers buried in
Old Cairo (see pages
106–107).

OPPOSITE:
The tomb of the Forty-
Nine Martyrs, monks
slain in the third
Berber raid on the
monasteries of Wadi
al-Natrun in 444.

THE FOUNDING FATHER OF THE MONASTERY, ST. MACARIUS (Anba Maqar, ca. 300–390) was one of the first hermits in Wadi al-Natrun. According to his *vita*, a cherub took him by the hand and showed him the place where he should build cells and a church. This site must have been somewhere in the neighborhood of the present Monastery of St. Macarius.

Until the fourteenth century, when the decline of monastic life in Wadi al-Natrun set in, the *History of the Patriarchs* testifies to the important role of the monastery in ecclesiastical affairs such as the election and consecration of patriarchs. Traditionally, the new patriarch celebrated his first Mass in the Church of St. Macarius, retreated to the monastery during Lent, and consecrated the Chrism.[75] More than thirty patriarchs were monks from this monastery.

The monastic community has a similar history of destruction, renovation, rebuilding, and fortification as the other monasteries in the Wadi al-Natrun. The main church, dedicated to St. Macarius, is only part of the large church complex as it once existed. There used to be four altar rooms, each with its own nave while two of these also had side aisles. This unusual building was the outcome of a complicated building history spanning several centuries.

At present, the church consists of three altar rooms with two rectangular rooms in front, spanning the whole width of the church, the *khurus*, and the nave. The northernmost altar room (previously dedicated to St. Mark, now to St. John the Baptist) was built in the twelfth century and simultaneously painted with standing saints and subjects from the Old and New Testaments. The adjoining altar room, dedicated to St. Macarius, is better known as the sanctuary of Patriarch Benjamin, who restored the church in the seventh century. The paintings preserved were executed in the ninth century and show Christ enthroned and his apostles, equestrian saints, the Twenty-Four Priests of the Apocalypse, and scenes from the New Testament on the soffit of the entrance arch. In the nineteenth century, the church was rapidly falling into ruin and the two southern altar rooms had fallen down. Building activities at the beginning of the twentieth century preserved the two northern altar rooms; the remains of the naves were dismantled. The present southern altar room, dedicated to the Three Hebrews in the Fiery Furnace, was reconstructed in modern times.

In 1969, the monastery, at that time nearly deserted, was re-inhabited by a group of monks under the spiritual guidance of Father Matta al-Miskin (d. 2006). A thorough restoration and modernization project of the monastic buildings and churches was carried out. Moreover, a printing press was installed and pioneering agricultural activities resulted in a large farm.

The high priest Aaron (right) and his brother Moses, receiving the Tablets of the Law (east part of octagon). A deesis (Christ accompanied by his mother Mary and St. John the Baptist, both interceding for mankind) is painted below.

OPPOSITE:
The Church of St. Macarius, haykal of St. Mark/ St. John the Baptist: the dome (rebuilt at the beginning of the twentieth century) with twelfth-century paintings in the octagon.

Seraph on the pendentive of the dome of the central haykal, dedicated to St. Macarius/ Patriarch Benjamin.

The Church of St. Macarius, haykal of Benjamin. Paintings on the west wall: Christ enthroned accompanied by the archangels Michael and Gabriel and the apostles.

The northern part of the west wall: apostles and (at the far right) St. Stephen. Two equestrian saints, St. Claudius and St. Menas, are depicted below.

St. Onophrius, St. John, and St. Samuel in the Chapel of the Hermits, one of the chapels in the keep. In the early sixteenth century, the Ethiopian monk Takla decorated the keep chapels.

The southwestern corner: St. John the Baptist and one of the Twenty-Four Priests.

The Church of the Holy Virgin Mary

THE TOWN OF SAKHA lies about 130 kilometers north of Cairo in the Nile Delta. Sakha is known as one of the Delta sites that was blessed by the Holy Family: when Jesus touched a stone with his foot, water sprouted forth, and his foot left an imprint. According to Abu al-Makarim / Abu Salih, people came and put oil on the footprint and considered themselves blessed. Due to fear that Muslims might take the stone, it was hidden in a monastery called 'Bekha Isus.' Some scholars believe that 'Bekha' could be a corrupted word for 'Sakha.'

In April 1984, workers were digging a hole for sewage near the Church of the Holy Virgin and found a stone with the footprint of a child. Copts of Sakha believe that it is the footprint of Jesus. The stone is now on display in the church in a glass case that pilgrims touch to be blessed. On the 24th day of the Coptic month Bashons, corresponding to the June 1, the commemoration of the Entry of the Holy Family into Egypt, the stone is carried by the clergy in a liturgical procession around the church. The church is modern and has three domes which cover the sanctuaries at its eastern part. The wooden screen of the central sanctuary, which is dedicated to the Virgin, features an inlaid panel dating back to AM 1587 / AD 1872.

Stone with footprint believed to be of child Jesus. This photograph was taken on a rare occasion when the glass case was open.

Exterior view with the belfry and domes.

Interior view of the Church of the Holy Virgin Mary.

St. Catherine's Monastery

Text by Carolyn Ludwig
Photographs by Araldo De Luca

ST. CATHERINE'S MONASTERY, at the foot of Gebel Musa in the Sinai desert, was built in the sixth century by the Byzantine emperor Justinian (527–565). It is one of the earliest remote Christian monasteries, and the oldest still used for its original purpose.

Anchorites had settled at the foot of the mountain by the fourth century on the site of what they believed was the original Burning Bush, which convinced them that they had found the Biblical Mount Sinai. The monks built a church next to the bush, and a tower to which they could retreat when nomadic raiders attacked. The monastery was built around these structures. It has retained its Eastern Orthodox culture and doctrine since it was founded.

The monastery became associated with St. Catherine of Alexandria in the ninth century. Legend has it that after her death, St. Catherine's remains were transported by angels to the top of Mount Sinai (or, according to the monks of Sinai, to the adjacent Gebel Katarina), where they were found in around 800. Her cult eventually spread throughout Europe, bringing fame, wealth, and pilgrims to the monastery. By the twelfth century, the monks had moved her relics to the church, and the monastery had taken her name.

Today the monastery's chief treasures are its library and collection of icons. The monastery is home to over two thousand icons, said to constitute the largest and oldest collection in the world. The library at St. Catherine's houses more than 5,000 ancient manuscripts and scrolls in at least twelve languages, and over 5,000 early printed books.

The Church of St. Catherine remains the most important building in the monastery. Two rows of granite columns separate the nave and side aisles and nine chapels encircle the basilica, which is hung with silver chandeliers and gilded icons. A beautiful mosaic depicting the Transfiguration of Christ graces the apse. Separating the apse from the nave is an eighteenth-century iconostasis with large depictions of Jesus, Mary, John the Baptist, and St. Catherine surrounded by smaller icons and intricately carved gilded wood. Behind the apse is the Chapel of the Burning Bush, decorated with Damascene tiles and silver ornaments, and bearing a silver plaque to show the bush's original location. On the other side of the wall, outside the chapel, is a living shrub that the monks say is the Burning Bush itself, transplanted in the tenth century after the chapel was built over it.

An impressive example of Greek church architecture, the Basilica of St. Catherine was built in the sixth century. The eighteenth-century iconostasis separates the sanctuary and apse. St. Catherine's relics are stored in a marble reliquary in the basilica.

The fortified monastery and church was built by Byzantine emperor Justinian in AD 537. Not until the tenth century was the monastery dedicated to the virgin martyr St. Catherine.

Icon of Moses and the Burning Bush is painted on the basilica's iconostasis. It depicts Moses watering his flock and seeing the Burning Bush; on the top of the mountain he receives the Tablets of the Law. The body of St. Catherine is taken to the top of the mountain by two angels.

The most important manuscript in the library of the monastery is the Codex Syriacus.

In another icon, Moses receives the Tablets of the Law on the peak of Mount Sinai, while below he kneels before the Burning Bush, inside which the Virgin and Child appear. St. Catherine witnesses the scene from the side.

OPPOSITE:
Chapels, dedicated to various saints, line the sides of the basilica. The first chapel on the left is dedicated to St. Marina.

LEFT:
The interior of the Chapel of the Burning Bush is covered in bright blue-and-white tiles and decorated with precious icons and sacred ornaments in silver. The precise spot where the bush is believed to have stood is indicated by a silver plaque.

RIGHT:
Outside the basilica in the area behind the Chapel of the Burning Bush is a bush surrounded by a high stone wall. It is believed to be the site where Moses stood.

Cairo

OLD CAIRO

100   The Church of St. Mercurius *(Abu Sayfayn)*

106   The Tomb of Ibrahim and Girgis al-Guhari

108   The Church of Sts. Sergius and Bacchus *(Abu Sarga)*

112   The Hanging Church *(al-Mu'allaqa)*

120   The Church of St. Barbara

122   The Greek Orthodox Church of St. George

124   Sleeping Mary Greek Orthodox Church *(Church of the Dormition)*

QASR AL-DUBARA

128   The Coptic Evangelical Church

RAMSES

130   The Armenian Cathedral of St. Gregory the Illuminator

MUSKI

132   The Franciscan Church of the Assumption *(Franciscan Center of Eastern Studies)*

HARAT ZUWAYLA

134   The Church of the Holy Virgin

FUMM AL-KHALIG

140   The Church of St. Menas

SHUBRA

146   The Catholic Cathedral of St. Mark

FAGGALA

150   The Jesuits' Holy Family Church

154   The Coptic Evangelical Church

ZAYTUN

156   The Church of the Holy Virgin

MATARIYA

160   The Jesuits' Holy Family Church

164   The Holy Family Tree

HELIOPOLIS

166   St. Cyril Melkite Catholic Church

170   The Basilica of Our Lady

AZBAKIYA

174   The Old Cathedral of St. Mark

ABBASIYA

178   Anba Ruways *(al-Khandaq)*

178   The Chapel of St. Athanasius

179   The Cathedral of St. Mark

182   The Church of the Holy Virgin Mary and St. Pshoi

183   The Church of the Holy Virgin Mary and Anba Ruways

184   The Church of Anba Ruways

185   The Shrine of St. Mark

186   The Church of St. Peter and St. Paul *(al-Butrusiya)*

MUQATTAM

188   The Cathedral of the Holy Virgin Mary and St. Simeon the Tanner

MAADI

194   The Church of the Holy Virgin

The Church of St. Mercurius

The interior of the ciborium of the main altar (eighteenth century, painted by the icon painter Yuhanna al-Armani). Christ is surrounded by the Four Living Creatures and the composition is carried by angels.

THE CHURCH OF ST. MERCURIUS is part of a complex of three churches and a convent, also dedicated to St. Mercurius (Abu Sayfayn). St. Mercurius, "the Father of the Two Swords," was a commander in the army of the Emperor Decius (249–251). On the eve of an important battle, he received his second sword from an angel, and the next day he destroyed the enemy. As a Christian, he refused to sacrifice to pagan gods and was subsequently tortured and beheaded. In the fourth century, in answer to St. Basil of Caesarea's prayers, he miraculously appeared on the battlefield to slay Emperor Julian the Apostate (d. 363). He is one of the most beloved military saints in Egypt, and he is usually depicted on horseback, slaying the emperor.

This church in his honor was probably built in the sixth century as a basilican church with a return aisle, a large apse and side chambers, and possibly galleries. A *khurus* was built in afterward. At the time of Patriarch Abraham (d. 978), the church was ruined and was used as a storehouse for sugarcane. The patriarch received permission to rebuild the church as a reward for the Miracle of the Mountain: in showing the Caliph that faith can literally move a mountain, he shifted the Muqattam Mountain.[76]

When Abraham restored the church, pillars replaced the columns of the nave and galleries were rebuilt or added. During a riot in 1168, the church was pillaged and largely burned down. The restoration started shortly afterward and the church was solemnly reopened in 1175. At this stage, the dome above the present *haykal* and the half-domes in the nave were built. The half-domes reduced the width of nave and thereby also the width of the wooden roof. *The History of the Churches and Monasteries of Egypt* (ca. twelfth century) reported that private donors of wealthy Coptic families donated money for construction and furnishings. Three chapels to the north of the main church, accessible via a small courtyard, were also rebuilt at that time.[77]

A small crypt in the north aisle is dedicated to St. Barsuma the Naked who dwelled here for more than twenty years in the company of a dangerous serpent. Because it was forbidden to live in churches, the authorities arrested him and sent him to a monastery near Helwan, where he died in 1317. The Church of St. Mercurius is one of the most important churches of Cairo. From the middle of the twelfth century until around 1300, the patriarchs resided alternately, sometimes even simultaneously, at the Hanging Church and the Church of St. Mercurius. Two thirteenth-century patriarchs and virtually all patriarchs from the seventeenth and eighteenth centuries were buried here. In the gallery chapels, wall paintings from the twelfth-century restoration are preserved. The church houses a valuable collection of icons, dating from the thirteenth century to the present.

The main haykal. *At the back, the marble steps of the synthronon and a combination of tiles, mural painting, and wooden panels fixed to the walls, painted by Ibrahim al-Nasikh (eighteenth century: Christ enthroned in the center) and A[na]stasi al-Qudsi al-Rumi (nineteenth century: the twelve apostles and Christ carried by two angels).*

The altar screen of the central haykal *with a row of feast icons on top. Christ and the Virgin Mary are painted on the columns flanking the entrance.*

Icon of St. Mercurius in its original setting, a reliquary (mid-eighteenth century).

The Twenty-Four Priests
of the Apocalypse
(thirteenth century).
The priests, swinging
their censers, belong
to the heavenly court,
worshiping God
continuously. They are
seen as intercessors for
mankind, the incense
symbolizing the prayers
of the saints.

St. Philip converting
the Ethiopian eunuch
(Acts 8:26–39;
thirteenth century).
The conversion of
the eunuch made
St. Philip, a deacon
appointed by the
apostles, the saint
who introduced
Christianity into
Ethiopia.

OPPOSITE:
St. Shenute (d. ca.
465), abbot of the
Monastery of St.
Shenute (White
Monastery) near
Sohag and St. Besa,
his disciple and
successor (A[na]stasi
al-Qudsi al-Rumi,
nineteenth century).

The Tomb of Ibrahim and Girgis al-Guhari

The Tomb of Ibrahim and Girgis al-Guhari, newly renovated by the Supreme Council of Antiquities under the direction of Dr. Zahi Hawass, is located near the Coptic Church of St. George in Old Cairo. Ibrahim al-Guhari (d. 1795) is one of the most significant Coptic personalities. He contributed to the beginning of the renaissance of the Coptic Church in the eighteenth century. Mamluk Ibrahim Bey appointed him Chief Scribe, a position that was the equivalent of finance minister for all of Egypt. Al-Guhari used his financial and political influence in the Egyptian state and succeeded in restoring many monasteries and churches. Due to his position, he was able to obtain permission to build new churches. His brother Girgis (d. 1810) was also an influential Coptic official who witnessed the birth of modern Egypt. He served as director of the Egyptian administration of taxes and finances under both Napoleon Bonaparte and Muhammad 'Ali. He greatly served the Coptic Church and continued the mission of his brother Ibrahim. Without the Guhari brothers, it is possible that the churches of Old Cairo as we know them would not exist.

The superstructure of the tomb is roofed over with decorative timbering and contains a beautiful *mashrabiya*. The attractive lectern is adorned with geometric designs. There is a tombstone beneath the *mashrabiya* decorated on the top with a Coptic cross and inscribed below with the names of Ibrahim and Girgis al-Guhari and the dates of their deaths in Coptic and Arabic.

Tomb of Girgis and Ibrahim al-Guhari: interior of the superstructure.

Tomb of Girgis and Ibrahim al-Guhari: exterior view with mashrabiya and tombstone.

The Church of Sts. Sergius and Bacchus

THE CHURCH OF STS. SERGIUS AND BACCHUS (*Abu Sarga*) was founded in the late seventh century by Athanasius, scribe (*katib*)[s] of 'Abd al-Aziz ibn Marwan, governor of Egypt from 685 to 705. Athanasius came from Edessa (Syria) where St. Sergius suffered martyrdom, a few days after his friend Bacchus was martyred.

Athanasius built a basilican church with a western return aisle, an apse with two side chambers, and galleries above the side aisles. The marble columns (and one of granite) separating the nave and side aisles have reused late-antique capitals. The ravages of time led to restorations and rebuilding. Although in general the initial plan has been preserved, only a few building elements are original. Almost immediately after the church was consecrated, it became an Episcopal church. From the seventh until the twelfth century, a number of patriarchs were elected in the church, and although clear evidence is lacking, patriarchs were most probably also consecrated here.

The Church of Sts. Sergius and Bacchus became an important pilgrimage site. According to tradition, the crypt of the church is one of the places where the Holy Family stayed before traveling to Upper Egypt or back to Palestine. The oldest sources mentioning this resting place date to the twelfth or thirteenth century. Western pilgrims from the thirteenth and fourteenth centuries onward reported that they visited this *locus sanctus*. For them, the dwelling place of the Holy Family was the chief attraction, and the church is often simply called 'the Church of the Cave.' The architecture of the crypt can, most probably, be dated to this period. From the fourteenth to the eighteenth century, Franciscan fathers (who owned a hospice near the Church of Sts. Sergius and Bacchus) had the privilege of celebrating the liturgy in the crypt. For years it was inaccessible, completely flooded because of the high groundwater level of Old Cairo. A successful drainage and restoration project, recently completed, has made it possible to visit this beloved pilgrimage site again.

The restoration project yielded a surprise: in the apse of the southern altar room, part of a wall painting of Christ enthroned, surrounded by the Four Living Creatures, the sun and moon, and the archangels Michael and Gabriel was discovered. It might be dated to around 1200.

The interior of the church. The monolithic columns separating the nave from the side oasiles are white marble except for one in red granite. Paintings of military saints are still faintly visible on the columns.

Fourteenth-century wooden panels showing the Nativity and the equestrian saints Theodore and George. They are incorporated in the modern altar screens on both sides of the fourteenth or fifteenth century screen veiling the central haykal.

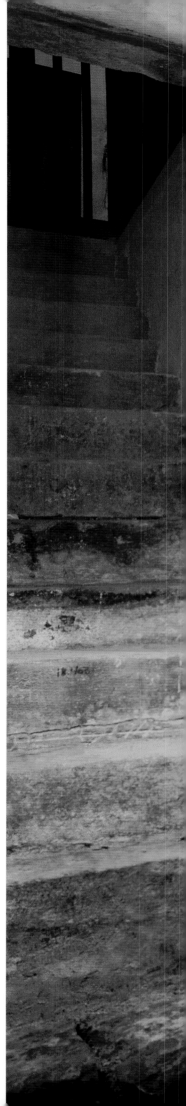

The crypt beneath the central altar room is a traditional resting place of the Holy Family. It looks like a small church with columns dividing the space into three bays and niches in the east, north, and south wall.

The Hanging Church

THE CHURCH OF THE HOLY VIRGIN was built on the remains of one of the gates of the Roman fortress, Babylon. This high position earned her the name 'the Hanging' or 'the Suspended' (al-Mu'allaqa) Church. Medieval Western pilgrims referred to the church as "the Church of the Steps" (the high stairway to the entrance) or "the Church of the Column." The latter name is connected with the miracle of moving the Muqattam Mountain. Prior to the miracle, Patriarch Abraham (d. 978) fasted for three days and nights in the Hanging Church. On the third day, the Virgin appeared to him, according to some sources near a column, and told him what to do.

The location of the church on top of a fortress gate makes a building date before the Arab conquest improbable. Originally, it seems to have been built on a basilican plan with a nave and side aisles with galleries, and an apse with side chambers. Over a tower in the southeastern corner, a small church was constructed, connected to the main church by a colonnade. An upper floor was added to the small church around 1100, serving as a cell for the patriarch. Excluding periods of exchange with churches in the Delta or other churches in town, the Hanging Church served as the patriarchal residence from Patriarch Abraham until around 1300. From the eleventh to the fourteenth century, it played an important role in ecclesiastical life: patriarchs were elected, consecrated, and buried in the church, synods convened, and occasionally the Holy Chrism was consecrated here.

During the centuries, the church did not escape pillage, looting, and destruction, and subsequent restorations were carried out. However, an extensive nineteenth-century renovation thoroughly altered its appearance. The western end was rebuilt and a small courtyard was added. Inside, a four-aisled church emerged while the galleries disappeared. The colonnade to the small church was closed, thereby turning it into a side chapel dedicated to the thirteenth-century Ethiopian St. Takla Haymanot. The 1992 earthquake caused considerable damage, and the most recent restorations have not yet been completed. Among the treasures of the church are a marble ambon, wooden altar screens of outstanding quality, wall paintings in the Chapel of Takla Haymanot, icons, and the ciboria crowning the three altars in the main church.

The interiors of the domes of the three altar ciboria (fifteenth century?). Four angels are carrying a circular composition of Christ Pantocrator.

The courtyard with the entrance to the church. Instead of domes the church has a wooden roof. Its position on top of the Roman gate does not allow for the weight of the domes.

Details of wooden screens in the church. Top: Each cross of this allover cruciform pattern is filled with ebony and has an ivory border. Below, left and center: geometrical inlays of ebony and finely carved ivory or bone make up a rosette pattern. Below, right: the wood is inlaid with translucent ivory.

Icon of St. Mark, according to tradition the founder of the Coptic Church (fourteenth century), in a setting of reused pieces of woodwork dating from the twelfth to fourteenth century.

Chapel of Takla Haymanot, wall painting of the Nativity (thirteenth century).

RIGHT:
A reused marble plaque in the staircase of the ambon, dating to the sixth to seventh century with two different crosses: a Resurrection cross (right) and a cross in a wreath under a canopy.

OPPOSITE:
The interior of the church, with the ambon to the left. The platform of the ambon probably dates to the fourteenth century.

OVERLEAF:
The southern part of the Babylon fortress. The gate with the cross gives access to the Hanging Church; to the left are the ruins of a tower and the Coptic Museum.

The Church of St. Barbara

Athanasius of Edessa, scribe *(katib)* of amir 'Abd al-Aziz ibn Marwan (685–705) founded a second church in Old Cairo, known as the Church of St. Barbara. Because of their similar architecture, Sts. Sergius and Bacchus and St. Barbara are often considered 'twin churches' or 'sister churches.'

Originally, the church was dedicated to St. Cyrus (Abu Qir/Apa Kir) or St. Cyrus and St. John, brothers, physicians, and martyrs venerated for healing. The first mention of St. Barbara in relation to this church is found in a thirteenth-century manuscript of the Coptic Synaxarion (Calendar of Saints), which states that the relics of St. Barbara were preserved in the Church of St. Cyrus in Old Cairo. Western pilgrims reported on the Church of St. Barbara from the thirteenth century onward. By then, it was one of the most important churches in Cairo.

Barbara was the daughter of a nobleman, Dioscoros, who built a tower with two windows in order to keep her safe and in seclusion. When Barbara had a window added to honor the holy Trinity, her father found out that she had become a Christian and handed her over to the magistrate. She suffered martyrdom together with St. Juliana, who saw her sufferings and wept, whereupon she too was tortured and killed.

Like the Church of Sts. Sergius and Bacchus, this church was built on a basilican plan with a tripartite sanctuary and upper floor galleries. However, the building suffered considerable damage over the centuries and subsequent reconstructions and restorations affected the original structure. At the beginning of the twentieth century, the church was restored and modernized again; the *khurus* screen and the screens dividing the women's and men's sections in the nave of the church were removed. The beam icon of the *khurus* screen, once spanning the width of the nave and part of an eighteenth-century restoration and refurbishing, is on display (in four parts) on the south wall of the church. A precious thirteenth-century icon of the Virgin and Child is preserved in the north aisle. Treasures that once belonged to the Church of St. Barbara are now exhibited in the Coptic Museum, for example, a wooden door (fourth/fifth century, found between two walls during the latter restoration) and a unique eleventh-century wooden altar screen.[79]

A small church at the northeastern end of the church is still dedicated to the Saints Cyrus and John.

The interior of the church with, to the left, a marble ambon of similar design to that in the Hanging Church (end of thirteenth century).

The eighteenth-century beam icon of sixteen feasts, originally placed on top of the former khurus screen. Starting in the upper left-hand corner, the Annunciation, the Nativity, the Presentation in the Temple, the Baptism of Christ, the Wedding of Cana, the Transfiguration, the Raising of Lazarus, the Entry into Jerusalem, the Last Supper, the Crucifixion, the Descent from the Cross, the Harrowing of Hell, Christ meeting one of the women in the garden ("Noli me tangere"), the doubting Thomas, the Ascension, and Pentecost.

The Greek Orthodox Church of St. George

The Greek Orthodox Church of St. George was constructed over the northern tower of the former river gate of the Babylon fortress. The Arab historian Ibn Duqmaq (1349–1407) assigned the church to the Melkites and mentioned its association with a convent. According to al-Maqrizi (1364–1442) there was a Nilometer near the convent. In the late fifteenth century, the Metropolitan of Smyrna Daniel stated that the church was under the control of the Monophysite Copts, but apparently they did not occupy the church for any length of time, since it was restored under the Melkite Patriarch of Alexandria, Joachim (1487–1567). In 1672 Johann Wansleben reported that the Nunnery of St. George was inhabited by Greek Orthodox nuns. Muslim mobs plundered the church in the course of the anarchic year 1882. After the devastating fire of August 4, 1903, the church was rebuilt, and on November 1, 1909 consecrated by Photius, the Melkite Patriarch of Alexandria.

A flight of steps leads up to the church's entrance, which lies to the north. The present Church of St. George is a circular building or rotunda with a concentric inner colonnade, which supports an elevated cupola. The altar is located on its eastern side; icons of the Holy Virgin, Pentecost, and Christ adorn the iconostasis. It is not known how closely—or even if—the modern floor plan corresponds to the original design. It is traditionally believed that St. George was held prisoner next to the main church and martyred there. The little Sleeping Mary Greek Orthodox Church lies in the Greek Orthodox cemetery, which is to the north of the Church of St. George. Through the sanctuary to the left is a small cave and well where the Holy Family is believed to have stayed on their journey back to Jerusalem.

The Greek Orthodox Church of St. George: iconostasis with icons of Christ and the Holy Virgin.

Exterior view looking east to west of the Greek Orthodox Church of St. George, which was constructed on top of a Roman tower.

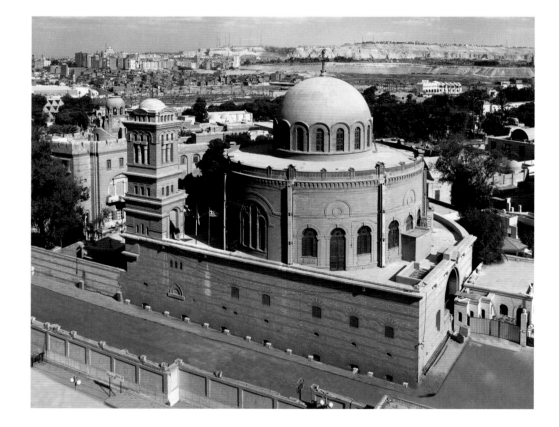

Sleeping Mary Greek Orthodox Church

THIS LITTLE CHURCH placed in the back northern area of the Greek Orthodox cemetery next to the Church of St. George in Old Cairo, is dedicated to The Virgin Mary. The formal name, the Church of the Dormition of the Virgin Mary, tells the story of the belief that the Virgin Mary simply went to sleep, her body never experienced decay in her tomb and was directly taken, assumed, into heaven. This was the belief of early Christian communities.

Four crosses adorn the front of the church. The church itself is surrounded by the cemetery.

Both Catholic and Orthodox Churches upheld this tradition even though it was not in the Gospels. During the sixth century the feast of the Dormition was begun by the Eastern Church. The Western churches taught the Assumption, the Orthodox that Mary went to sleep, her dormition.

Through the sanctuary to the left is a cave with a shrine to the Holy Family and a well that is said to have healing powers. It is also said the Holy Family stayed in this cave when on their return journey to Jerusalem.

Icon of the Dormition of Mary: Jesus flanked by two angels watches over His Mother

The shrine with an icon of the Holy Family in Egypt.

The Sleeping Mary Greek Orthodox Church: the well is believed to be a source of miraculous or healing water.

The Coptic Evangelical Church

THE COPTIC EVANGELICAL CHURCH is located on the square of Qasr al-Dubara facing the southern wall of the Mugamma' building on Midan al-Tahrir in Cairo.

In December 1941 Pastor Ibrahim Sa'id was able to raise funds to buy an old palace with a beautiful garden in the square known today as Midan al-Tahrir in order build a church in the place of that palace. He needed a royal decree that permitted the erection of the church. Ahmed Hussein Pasha, the tutor of King Farouk, had studied in England and lived in the house of Pastor Alexander White, a great preacher, in London. After the death of the latter his wife made a journey to Egypt. Hussein Pasha accompanied her to meet with Pastor Ibrahim Sa'id and asked the pastor if he could do anything for him. The pastor said to Hussein Pasha, "It would be great if Mrs. White would see the permission of building the church signed by his Majesty the King before she leaves Egypt." Thus the permission was secured and the church's foundation stone was laid in December 1947. The building was completed in 1950. When King Farouk saw the church in Cairo's most important square he was furious for he desired at that time to be regarded as the caliph of the Muslim world after the caliphate had been abolished in Turkey in 1923. Acting as a defender of the prominence of Islam, the king ordered the erection of a huge government building (al-Mugamma') in front of the church so that it could not be seen from Tahrir Square.

Following the 1952 Revolution and the exile of King Farouk to Italy, President Gamal 'Abd al-Nasser visited the church at Easter in 1955. Pastor Ibrahim Sa'id welcomed him, thanking him for his visit and saying to him, "King Farouk hated to see one cross of this church, and God sent him to a country where he will see many crosses."

Interior view of the Coptic Evangelical Church, Qasr al-Dubara, toward the pulpit.

Entrance court

Looking toward the gallery from the pulpit.

The Armenian Cathedral of St. Gregory the Illuminator

THE ARMENIAN ORTHODOX CATHEDRAL OF ST. GREGORY the Illuminator is situated at 179 Ramses Street, not far from the Cairo railway station. The site houses the Armenian Orthodox Patriarchate, the Torkomian Library, and the Apkarian Medical Center.

The building was constructed from August 1924 to May 1927 under the direction of architect Levon Nafilian and Des Pharos, Inc., together with the combined efforts of local and international artisans. It was financed by sums bequeathed by Gregory Eghiayan, Dikran Dabro Pasha, and Boghos Nubar Pasha. Archbishop Torkom Koushagian, the prelate of Egypt, consecrated the church in February 1928. The church is not parallel to the street but aligned so that the altar is on the east side and the vestibule (narthex) on the west.

There is a mosaic representing St. Gregory the Illuminator above the entrance. Upon entering the church one is surrounded by ornate designs, from the craftsmanship in the stone carvings and woodwork to the icons, of which the most significant is that of the Conversion of Armenia by St. Gregory the Illuminator. The southern end of the vestibule (narthex) was dedicated in 1965 to the victims of the 1915 massacres. The walls combine red Belgian marble and yellow Asian marble, while the tiles used on the walls were brought from Paris. The height of the church from the ground level to the dome is 35 meters high. The church's roof is supported by eighteen granite pillars with capitals decorated by leaves, birds, and animals. The wall paintings of the apse depict Christ in Majesty flanked by three kneeling angels on each side. Below him are the twelve apostles. The altar's dome is decorated with a dove, the symbol of the Holy Spirit. The church has nine bells, six of them named after Orthodox saints. The other three are used to ring in the Orthodox holy days.

Sanctuary interior and apse decoration.

Exterior of the Cathedral facing west.

Stone carving with a cross and vine-scrolls entwined with animal and human figures.

The Franciscan Church of the Assumption

Exterior view of the entrance to the Franciscan Church of the Assumption.

T HE CHURCH IS SITUATED at the end of Darb al-Barabra off Port Said Street in Muski. The history of this church begins in 1632 when Franciscan monks acquired a piece of land outside the 'Embassy of the Venetians.' This 'French Church,' as it came to be known, was enlarged in 1732. It is said that Napoleon Bonaparte prayed there during his 1798–1801 campaign. Around 1850, the church was demolished in order to build a new one, between 1852 and 1854. The church's designer was architect Fr. Serafino da Bacceno, who designed the Cathedral of St. Catherine in Alexandria.

The church's façade is adorned by two marble plaques that were executed in 1919. One of them commemorates the seventh centennial of the meeting of St. Francis of Assisi and the Ayyubid Sultan al-Kamil. The second plaque refers to the restoration of the church's façade on that occasion.

In 1860 Fr. Enrico Collado brought with him from Tripoli an icon of the Holy Virgin and a chapel was built specifically to house this famous icon. A large painting of the Assumption of the Holy Virgin Mary, which was donated by Emperor Franz Joseph, hangs in the apse. The Virgin is surrounded by three angels while the apostles are represented below her.

In 1952 Muhammad Naguib, president of Egypt, inaugurated the Franciscan Center for Eastern Christian Studies, which is attached to the church. Many scholars and students benefit from the treasures of its famous library.

Interior view looking toward the apse.

OPPOSITE:
Side altar of St. Therese.

Beam icon above the screen to the haykal *of the Archangel Gabriel, probably dating to ca. 1200. The seven major feasts of the Coptic Church are depicted: the Annunciation, the Nativity, the Baptism of Christ, the Entry into Jerusalem, the Resurrection, the Ascension, and Pentecost.*

The Church of the Holy Virgin

Harat Zuwayla.

THE CHURCH COMPLEX OF HARAT ZUWAYLA, situated in the center of the busy shopping district of Muski and Khan al-Khalili, consists of three churches. The main church is dedicated to the Virgin Mary, the northern church to St. Mercurius, and the upper church to St. George. The stairs descending to the entrance of the Church of the Virgin testify to its antiquity: since the building of the church, probably in the ninth century, the street level has risen about six meters. The church was repaired and renewed so many times that the original plan, a transept basilica, is barely recognizable, and there are hardly any parallel walls to be found. According to tradition, it was built on a spot where the Holy Family rested: it contains a well that was blessed by the Christ Child and whose water is believed to cure illness.

Patriarch John VII (1300–1320) moved the patriarchal seat to the Church of the Virgin, where it remained until Patriarch Matthew IV (1660–1675) took up residence at the Church of Harat al-Rum.

Through a doorway in the north wall of the church, one enters the Church of St. Mercurius, the equestrian saint with two swords. This church, also known as "the little church of St. Mercurius," was built in AM 1490/AD 1773–1774 by Mu'allim Ibrahim al-Guhari and was constructed on the foundations of an Armenian church dedicated to St. John the Baptist. In the nineteenth century, Alfred Butler reported that during Lent the Eucharistic wine "for all churches" was made in this church. Every year, a wine press belonging to the Church of St. Mercurius in Old Cairo was brought in for this purpose.[80] The Church of the Virgin and the Armenian Church are mentioned several times in *The History of the Churches and Monasteries of Egypt* (ca. twelfth century). One of the compilers, Abu al-Makarim, apparently lived in the vicinity of the church complex and reported on several festivities going on there.[81]

The upper church of St. George can be reached from the staircase outside. On account of multiple renovations, it is difficult to date. Annexed to these churches are two convents, the Convent of the Holy Virgin and the Convent of St. George.

OPPOSITE:
The interior of the ciborium crowning the main altar, showing Christ, surrounded by sun, moon, stars, and the Four Living Creatures of the Apocalypse, and carried by angels. Eighteenth centur; painted by the icon painter Yuhanna al-Armani.

Cherubs, painted on the interior of the ciborium of the main altar.

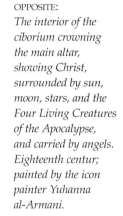

OPPOSITE:
View to the central haykal *with its magnificent screen, inlaid with ivory (fourteenth century).*

BELOW:
Dome over the shrine of the Virgin Mary.

Entrance to the shrine of the Virgin Mary in the southeastern corner of the church.

The Church of St. Menas

THE CHURCH OF ST. MENAS (MARI MINA) is significant in that it provides evidence for the expansion of churches north of Babylon and al-Fustat long before the foundation of Fatimid Cairo. It is located between Old Cairo and Historic or Fatimid Cairo, north of the medieval aqueduct, off al-Sadd al-Barrani. It bears the name of its patron, St. Menas, whose relics had been transferred from Mareotis to this church during the patriarchate of Benjamin II (1327–1339). In the early thirteenth century the church historian Abu al-Makarim/Abu Salih stated that the church was destroyed in 725 during the reign of Caliph Hisham ibn Abd al-Malik. According to the historian al-Maqrizi (1364–1442), the church was restored almost immediately, in 735. In medieval times, probably in the Fatimid period (eleventh and twelfth centuries), the northern part of the church was ceded to the Armenians, who returned it to the Copts in 1926 after accepting compensation. The church was partly destroyed again in 1164 and then restored during the pontificate of Patriarch John VI (1189–1216). It was pillaged in 1321 by a Muslim mob. In the twentieth century the Committee for the Preservation of Monuments of Arab Art has restored the church more than once.

Six pillars separate the nave from the northern and southern aisles. The principal sanctuary has an apse and two side chambers. Each chamber is connected with the sanctuary by a long passage through the partition wall. The wooden screen of the sanctuary is inlaid with ivory cross designs and surmounted by the icon of the Virgin and Child flanked by three icons on each side, each with a pair of apostles. Over the altar is a wooden ciborium (baldachin), supported by four graceful pillars. Its dome is ornamented with the usual scene of Christ Pantocrator. The paintings of the ciborium are stylistically assigned to the two artists Ibrahim al-Nasikh and Yuhanna al-Armani, who were active in the eighteenth century.

The apse features a depiction of Christ Pantocrator. The sanctuary's right wall shows the seraphim and cherubim (above); St. Basil, the prophet Isaiah, Simeon bearing a child (below). On the left wall are seraphim and cherubim (above); Aaron the priest, Samuel anointing David as king, St. Gregory (below). The shrine of St. Menas, which houses the relics of the saint, lies to the north of the sanctuary.

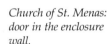

Church of St. Menas: door in the enclosure wall.

Exterior, modern Coptic art.

OPPOSITE:
Icon of the martyrs Behnam and his sister Sarah, painted by Yuhanna al-Armani in 1782.

ABOVE:
*Upper Church: Sanctuary of
St. George: Pantocrator. Note
the seraphim at each corner
of the ciborium.*

OPPOSITE:
*Upper Church: Sanctuary
of St. George*

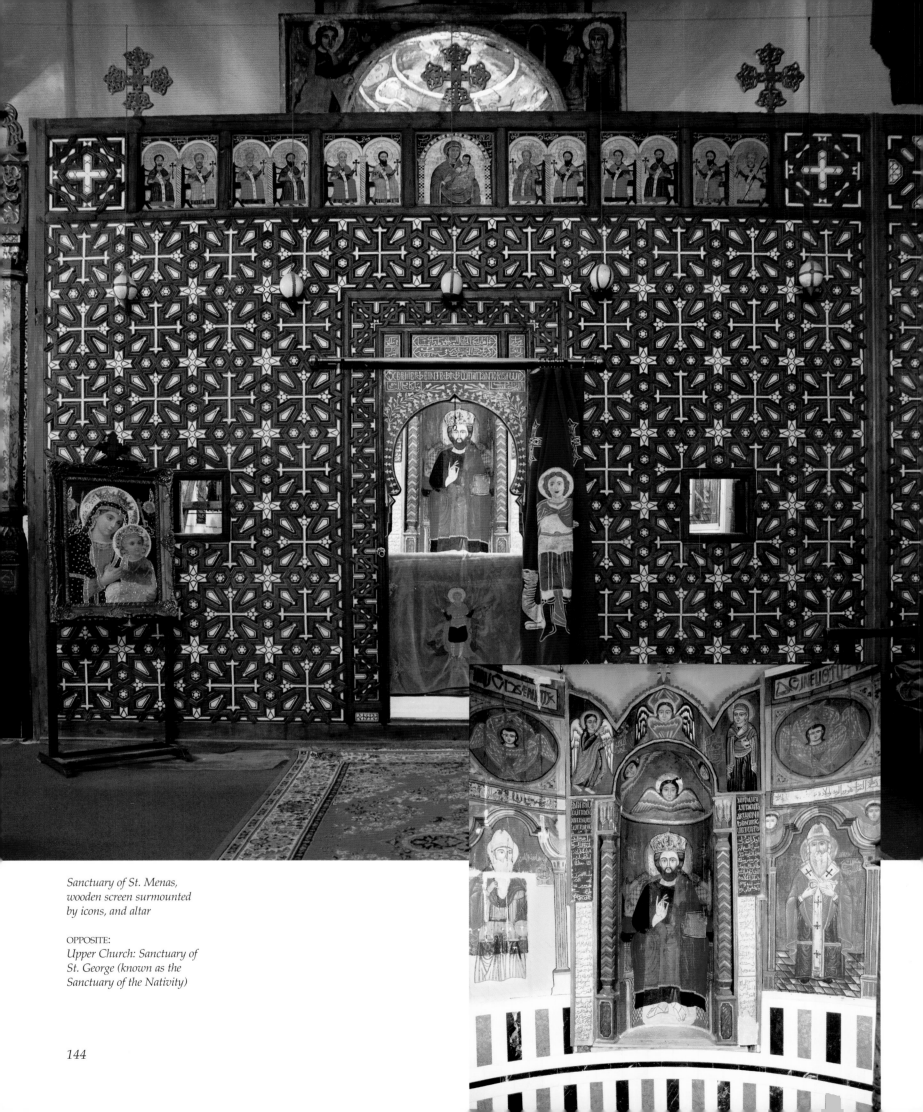

Sanctuary of St. Menas,
wooden screen surmounted
by icons, and altar

OPPOSITE:
Upper Church: Sanctuary of
St. George (known as the
Sanctuary of the Nativity)

144

The Catholic Cathedral of St. Mark

THE CATHEDRAL IS SITUATED ON AL-BI'THA (Mission) Street in Shubra. The street is named after the Society of African Missions, whose fathers served at the cathedral. The imposing cathedral was constructed in 1907. It is very rich in altars and sculptures but has no paintings. The cathedral's main high altar is dedicated to St. Mark the Evangelist, behind which is installed an altar to St. Joseph. The area of the high altar is decorated with the statues of St. Mark, St Augustine, St. Anne, St. Cyril, and St. Joan of Ark; all were executed by M. Marino. The northern side of the transept is occupied by the altar of the Sacred Heart of Jesus, the southern side by the altar of Our Lady of Lourdes. The three side altars on the northern wall of the nave are dedicated to St. Jean Baptiste de la Salle (1651–1719), the founder of the Order of the Christian Brothers, and St. Theresa of Lisieux; those on the southern wall are dedicated to St. Antony of Padua, Our Lady of Fatima, and Our Lady of Rosary. The baptistery, which stands at the nave's southwest corner, is ornamented with a statue of St. Peter Claver, patron of the Society of African Missions.

Interior view toward the entrance.

OPPOSITE:
Exterior view.

FOLLOWING PAGES:
Interior view toward the high altar.

The Jesuits' Holy Family Church

THE CHURCH IS SITUATED ON BUSTAN AL-MAQS STREET in Faggala near the Cairo railway station. In 1879 Pope Leo XIII ordered the Jesuit Fathers to establish a seminary to serve the Coptic Catholic community in Egypt. They founded it in Bughos Palace at Muski. In 1881 the French Jesuit missionary Michel Marie Jullien (1827–1911) became the director of the college. He quickly learned that the Palace of Boghus was not large enough, as many Egyptians desired to study with the Jesuit Fathers. In May 1882 he purchased a plot of land that measures 11,500 square meters in Faggala. The foundation stone was laid on April 22, 1888, and the college was transfered from Boghus Palace to Faggala. The work on the church of the college began April 2, 1889, under the supervision of the Jesuit architect François Mourier. Guido Corbelli, the apostolic delegate, consecrated the church on November 1, 1891.

The church entrance is decorated with a cross flanked by two angels. The nave measures 33 m in length and 15 m in width. The arches of the church's arcades are colored in black and red and are reminiscent of some Islamic monuments. The altar is dominated by a statue of the Sacred Heart of Jesus, to which the church is dedicated. The attractive colored glass of one of the windows shows the Annunciation to Joseph with the Holy Family and a pyramid in the background. In 1963 Father Henri Ayrout demolished the primitive altar and commissioned an Italian artist, Amedeo Trivisonno, to paint the wall behind the altar. The wonderful fresco features Christ Pantocrator flanked by the heads of the Four Living Creatures of the Apocalypse: eagle, ox, lion, and man. In the lower section, the Virgin Mary is surrounded by the twelve apostles in addition to two famous monks, St. Antony and St. Pachomius. His Beatitude Stephanous I Sidarouss inaugurated the fresco during Easter of 1965.

The Annunciation to Joseph.

Exterior view of the church.

*Stained glass window
(detail).*

*Interior view toward
the altar.*

The Coptic Evangelical Church

I N 1901 THE MEMBERS OF THE PRESBYTERIAN COMMUNITY of Faggala began their worship in a tent in the courtyard of the girls' school on Faggala Street. The tent burned down in 1912. By 1920 Pastor Ghubrial al-Dab' had been able to raise funds to acquire a plot of land, also in Faggala. The first donor was the famous Coptic gynecologist Naguib Mahfouz. The church was built in 1922 at a cost of LE9,000. The earthquake of October 1992 greatly affected the church, which was restored and renovated in 1994. When Nasser's nationalization policies compelled many of Egypt's long-standing communities and expatriates to leave Egypt in the early 1960s, the membership asked the Egyptian congregation to take on the responsibility of the orphanage that the congregation had been supporting. This was a very big challenge for all of them. The orphanage today is very successful. Girls of all ages live together, while going to school in the community.

OPPOSITE:
Exterior view of the Coptic Evangelical Church with the Jesuits' Holy Family Church in the background which is located directly across the street.

Interior view looking toward the pulpit.

Interior view of the sanctuary.

The Church of the Holy Virgin

Interior view looking toward the sanctuary.

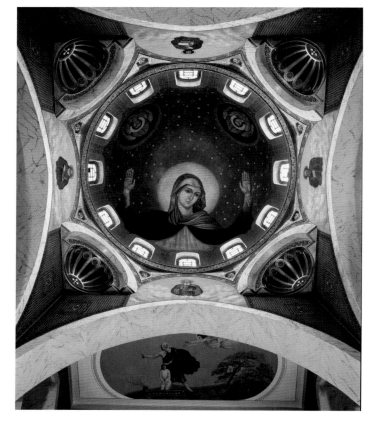

Large painting of the Holy Virgin on the dome.

OPPOSITE:
Exterior view of the church.

THE CHURCH STANDS ON TUMANBEY STREET IN ZAYTUN, CAIRO. In 1924 Tawfiq Bey Khalil entrusted the Italian architect Limongelli to erect a church there for the Holy Virgin Mary. We are told that Khalil Ibrahim Pasha had seen a vision of the Virgin, who ordered him to build a church in which she would appear fifty years later.

On the evening of April 2, 1968, the employees of the municipal garage in front of the church witnessed the first apparition of the Virgin. The apparitions in bright blue or orange light recurred several times until the beginning of September. The Virgin was often seen accompanied by doves on the dome or on one of the windows of the northeastern copula of the church. Thousands of pilgrims, both Christians and Muslims, flocked to witness the miraculous event.

In 1969 Patriarch Cyril VI (1959–1971) sanctioned a liturgical feast of the Transfiguration of the Holy Virgin Mary; it is celebrated on the fourth day of the Coptic month Baramhat.

The wooden screen of the sanctuary is decorated with two large depictions of Christ and the Virgin and Child. The dome features a large painting of the Virgin. In 2000 an Italian team of conservators cleaned and preserved the beautiful interior decoration of the church on the occasion of the two-thousand-year celebration of the Holy Family's Flight into Egypt.

Shrine to the Virgin
Mary with candles
of the faithful.

RIGHT:
Balcony overlooking
the sanctuary.

The Jesuits' Holy Family Church

Exterior view of the Jesuits' Holy Family Church, Matariya.

THE FRENCH JESUIT MISSIONARY MICHEL MARIE JULLIEN (1827–1911) is the initiator of the modern pilgrimage to the "Virgin of al-Matariya" in Cairo. The archives of the "Collège de la Sainte Famille" at Faggala, Cairo for the years 1883, 1885, 1890, 1910, and 1911 show that Father Jullien attempted, unsuccessfully, to purchase the garden and the land around the Tree of Mary. Instead, he purchased a plot of land very near to the Tree of Mary and enlarged it gradually. With the financial support of his family, in 1885 Father Jullien constructed a chapel surrounded by a fanciful garden. Processions were organized from Cairo to the chapel during the month of May. Many European pilgrims flocked to be blessed in that small chapel, and thus the need to build a church became imperative. The work began in 1902 under the supervision of Father Ponthier and the church was consecrated in December 8, 1904. Six large scenes were painted on canvas in Paris by Barbier, Schnorr, Overbeck, Zimmermann, and Esler. Each one is 1.5 meter high and 5 meters long. In August 1906 they were fixed to the church's walls. They represent the Massacre of the Innocents, the Order of Depart, the Flight into Egypt (north wall), Rest on the Bank of the River Nile, the Tree of the Virgin, and the Entrance into Heliopolis (south wall). The murals are in fragile condition but are still a moving sight.

The group of statues of the Holy Family that surmounts the altar is the work of the sculptor Millifaut. A copy of the statues stands in the garden in front of the church's entrance. The Coptic Catholic Church has been taking care of the church since 1997. The church commemorates the Flight into Egypt annually on February 17 by celebrating Mass.

The Jesuits' Holy Family Church, Matariya: interior view toward the altar.

ORDRE DU

*The Order of
Departure: angel
coming to Joseph.*

RIGHT:
Tree of the Virgin.

L'ARBRE DE LA VIERGE

Massacre of the Innocents.

The Holy Family Tree

ACCORDING TO MATTHEW 2:13, the angel of the Lord appeared to Joseph in a dream, saying, "Arise and take the young child and his mother and flee into Egypt, and be thou there until I bring thee word; for Herod will seek the young child to destroy him." The Holy Scripture does not tell us about the length of the sojourn of the Holy Family in Egypt and the sites they blessed during their journey. The details of the great Flight into Egypt and the itinerary of the journey were left to tradition.

One of the best-known sites visited by medieval pilgrims and modern tourists is al-Matariya, which is situated about five miles northeast of central Cairo. According to one tradition, the Holy Family found shade under a sycomore fig tree that is still standing there. It is said that Jesus created a well near the tree and blessed it. When Mary poured the water on the ground after the bath of Jesus, a balsam tree grew. It is believed that this plant was used for the preparation of the holy oil or *myron* that had been consecrated since the time of the apostles. Today the site of the "Tree of Mary" is visited by many Egyptians, both Christian and Muslim, and tourists from all over the world. As well as the Jesuits' Holy Family Church there is a 'Mosque of the Tree of Mary.' In 2000, the tree and the well beside it were protected by an attractive enclosure wall with beautiful interior decoration, and the site was renovated and landscaped on the occasion of the two-thousand-year celebration of the Holy Family's Flight into Egypt.

The Tree of Mary at al-Matariya. It is said that this is the fourth generation of the tree.

St. Cyril Melkite Catholic Church

THE CHURCH OF ST. CYRIL is located on al-Thawra Street, Corba, Heliopolis, Cairo. The church is dedicated to St. Cyril, Patriarch of Alexandria (412–444), who is considered one of the greatest figures of early Christianity because he defended the title of the Virgin Mary, "Mother of God," against Nestorius. The church was built in the early twentieth century to meet the needs of a growing suburban population of Greek Catholic elites. Originally from Syria and Lebanon, these Catholics moved to Heliopolis from the Cairo districts of Faggala and Shubra.

Habib Ayrouth drew the architectural plan of the church's Byzantine style in 1910. Baron Edouard Empain (1852–1919), who founded the Cairo Electric Railways and Heliopolis Oasis Company in 1904, donated six brown marble columns from Antwerp, Belgium, that still decorate the church's entrance. The church was consecrated by Patriarch Cyril VIII Moghabghab and the Latin Apostolic Nuncio Mgr. Deiry on June 8, 1912.

In 1945 the church erected a large wooden icon of Christ that was surrounded by icons of the apostles. At this time four chandeliers made of wrought iron were hung from the ceiling. In 1983 the church was restored and renovated.

The church also includes two modern icons that are modeled on two famous images from the Monastery of St. Catherine. The first icon imitates the famous twelfth-century icon of the 'Heavenly Ladder' of St. John Climacus from the Monastery of St. Catherine. It shows a ladder of thirty rungs symbolizing the thirty virtues that a monk should acquire. As the faithful seek to climb the ladder, devils pull them from their ascent. Saint John Climacus, the great abbot of the Monastery of St. Catherine, reaches heaven first, followed by Antuniyus, the first bishop of Sinai. Another modern icon depicts the Transfiguration, which is reminiscent of the magnificent sixth-century Transfiguration mosaic of Sinai. It shows Christ at the Transfiguration flanked by the prophets Moses and Elijah while the apostles Peter, John, and James prostrate themselves before him.

RIGHT:
Icon of the 'Heavenly Ladder' of St. John Climacus.

FAR RIGHT:
Icon of the Transfiguration.

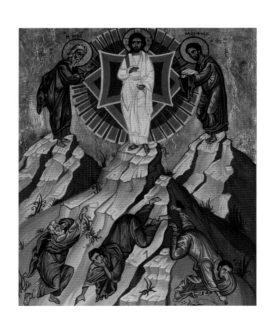

The Church of St. Cyril: interior looking toward the altar.

The Annunciation.

The Basilica of Our Lady

THE ROMAN CATHOLIC BASILICA OF OUR LADY in Heliopolis is situated on al-Ahram Street. It was donated by Baron Edouard Empain, who founded the beautiful quarter of Heliopolis northeast of Cairo in 1906. He entrusted the architect Alexandre Marcel, a member of the *Institut de France*, with its construction. The foundation stone of the basilica was laid in November 1910. The style of the basilica resembles that of the famous Hagia Sophia in Istanbul, although is much smaller. The wrought-iron gates were imported from Belgium and installed on July 10, 1929. At the entrance there is a porch with an arcade of four arches supported by eight columns of red granite. The baptistery stands at the southwest corner of the church. The west wall is decorated with modern paintings of two young saints of the nineteenth century: one depicts St. Maria Goretti (1890–1902), and the other St. Domenico Savio (1842–1857). The principal altar is dedicated to the Holy Virgin Mary, the northern altar to the Sacred Heart of Jesus, and the southern altar to St. Joseph. The interior of the church features twenty-two graceful columns of polished red granite, which support arches. Some of the column capitals are carved with acanthus leaves enclosing the monogram of Christ in the middle, which is surmounted by a Greek cross. Baron Empain is buried in the crypt, which was built of gray granite underneath the principal altar.

The baptismal font of carved marble is approximately four feet tall.

The Basilica of Our Lady, Heliopolis.

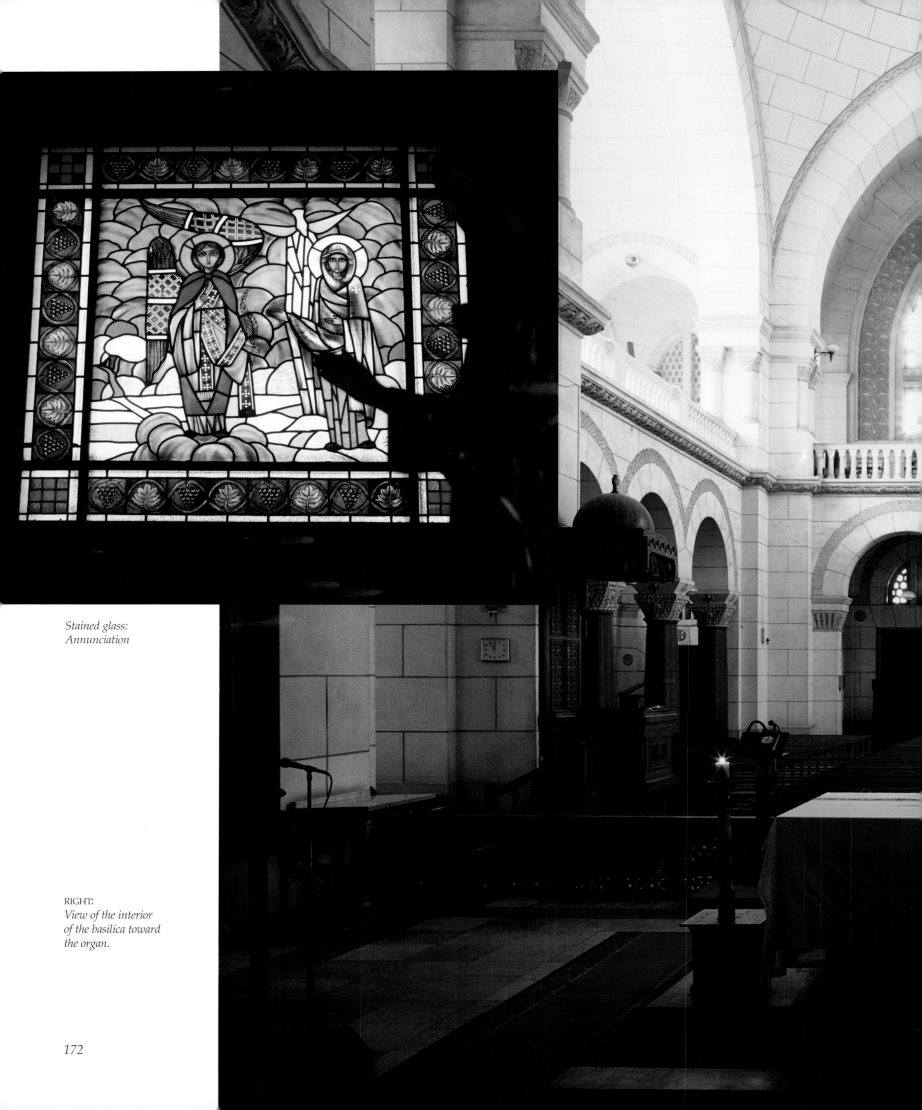

Stained glass:
Annunciation

RIGHT:
*View of the interior
of the basilica toward
the organ.*

172

The Old Cathedral of St. Mark

THE CATHEDRAL IS SITUATED on al-Murqusiya Street, Darb al-Wassa' (Clot Bey). Ibrahim al-Guhari, the famous Coptic official, was able to obtain permission from the Ottoman sultan to build a Coptic church in Azbakiya. Girgis al-Guhari, his brother, oversaw the completion of the church. In the late eighteenth century the church became the patriarchal residence of Patriarch Mark VIII (1796–1809). The church was later replaced by a cathedral. Patriarch Cyril IV (1854–1861) began the construction of the new cathedral, and it was finished during the patriarchate of Demetrius II (1862–1870). It housed the Coptic patriarchate from the 1850s until 1968, when the new cathedral was inaugurated at Anba Ruways, 'Abbasyia. The interior decoration was executed in the time of Patriarch Cyril V (1874–1927).

The cathedral was constructed in the style of nineteenth-century Greek Orthodox churches, with two rows of marble columns separating the nave from the northern and southern aisles. A wooden *ambon* is attached to one of the northern columns. It is reached by a spiral staircase. Three sanctuaries stand in the eastern part of the cathedral. They are separated from the nave by a continuous wooden screen. The central sanctuary, which is dedicated to St. Mark, features a marble *synthronon* that lies behind the altar. The northern sanctuary is dedicated to St. George and the southern to St. Mercurius. The paintings and the icons of the cathedral are executed in the Italo-Byzantine style of the nineteenth century. The semi-dome of the nave and the dome of the central altar are ornamented with Christ Pantocrator. The screen of the sanctuaries is decorated with icons representing Christ, the Virgin Mary, apostles, and saints.

Exterior view.

Nave, semi-dome of the nave, ornamented with Christ Pantocrator.

OPPOSITE:
Interior view toward the sanctuary.

Altar and dome with Christ Pantocrator.

OPPOSITE:
Altar, view looking toward the nave.

176

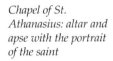

Anba Ruways

THE MOST IMPORTANT CONTEMPORARY COPTIC CENTER in Egypt, known as Anba Ruways, is located on Ramses street in Abbasiya. It is a compound of buildings with an enclosure wall comprising the Cathedral of St. Mark and his shrine, the Church of Anba Ruways, the Coptic papal residence, the Clerical College, the Higher Institute of Coptic Studies, the new cultural center with the library, and a number of episcopal and patriarchal offices.

In 970 a monastery (Dayr al-Khandaq) was founded there on an extensive area. It included a cemetery, which was mentioned by the historian al-Maqrizi (d. 1442). In the early thirteenth century the church historian Abu al-Makarim/Abu Salih stated that the monastery included eight churches. One of them, the Church of St. George, was later transformed into the Church of Anba Ruways.

The Chapel of St. Athanasius

ATHANASIUS (326–373) IS UNDOUBTEDLY the most important Coptic patriarch. He is considered an apostolic saint and played a crucial role in the theological controversies in the fourth century. He wrote a biography entitled the *Life of St. Antony* that significantly influenced monasticism in the West.

On May 6, 1973, Pope Shenouda III received the relics of St. Athanasius from Pope Paul VI in Rome. His relics repose in his chapel under the cathedral, which lies to the west of the two churches of the Holy Virgin and Anba Ruways and the Holy Virgin and St. Pshoi. There is an altar in the chapel with an apse decorated with the portrait of St. Athanasius. The ceiling is decorated with a scene of Christ and the Four Living Creatures.

Chapel of St. Athanasius: altar and apse with the portrait of the saint

The Cathedral of St. Mark

THE COPTIC CATHEDRAL OF ST. MARK in Cairo is the only Christian house of God to have been financed by the Egyptian government. President Gamal 'Abd al-Nasser laid its foundation stone on July 24, 1965. On July 26, 1968, Patriarch Cyril VI (1959–1971) and the Ethiopian emperor Haile Selassie I inaugurated the cathedral on the occasion of the translation of the relics of St. Mark the Evangelist from Venice to Cairo and the 1900th anniversary of his martyrdom. In 828 Venetian pirates stole the body of St. Mark from Alexandria and carried it to their city. The Venetians built the huge Cathedral of St. Mark and henceforth their commune was named the Republic of St. Mark.

The Cairo cathedral is an imposing structure 100 meters long, 36 meters wide, and 55 meters high. The belfry is 85 meters high. The huge vault is supported by two rows of six graceful pillars of Egyptian alabaster surmounted by two-zone basket-shaped capitals. The lower section of the capitals resembles a flat wicker basket executed in sharp relief. The corners of the capitals' upper sections are decorated with the heads of lions—the symbol of St. Mark—and the intervening spaces are filled with wreathed crosses. The huge vault of the cathedral features beautiful windows decorated with colored stained glass representing biblical scenes and saints. The southern windows represent from left to right: the Flight into Egypt, St. Mark the apostle, St. Antony, and St. Athanasius the Apostolic; northern side from right to left: the Good Shepherd, the Archangel Michael, St. George, and St. Dimyana surrounded by her forty virgins.

In the eastern part of the church stand three sanctuaries dedicated to St. Mark (center), St. Menas (north), and the Virgin Mary (south). The door of the central sanctuary is surmounted by an icon of the Last Supper, on which there is on which the crucifixion also appears, flanked by the Virgin Mary and St. John. On both sides there are six icons representing the twelve apostles. The door of the northern sanctuary is surmounted by two icons depicting the Flight into Egypt and the Magi. The two icons above the door of the southern sanctuary show the Nativity; one of them also depicts the shepherds. All the icons are painted by Budur Latif and Youssef Nassif. The Russian Orthodox Church presented the magnificent altar of the central sanctuary. It is of gilded metal with blue and white crosses, and features the Last Supper, the Passion of Christ, the Entombment, and Gethsemane.

Interior looking west.

OPPOSITE:
Interior looking east.

Part of the sanctuary's wooden screen decorated from left to right with the icons of Christ in Majesty, Baptism, St. George, and Sts. Paul and Antony.

The Church of the Holy Virgin Mary and St. Pshoi

THE CHURCH OF THE HOLY VIRGIN MARY AND ST. PSHOI lies to the west of the shrine of St. Mark in the ground floor beneath the Cathedral of St. Mark. Of special interest are two large modern mosaics on the two pillars in front of the sanctuary. They represent the Holy Virgin standing and holding the Christ Child, and St. Pshoi carrying Christ on his shoulder. The central sanctuary is dedicated to the Virgin and St. Pshoi; the northern sanctuary to St. Menas, and the southern to St. Michael. The wooden screen of the sanctuary shows nineteenth-century icons executed in Italo-Byzantine style. On the top there is an icon of the Last Supper. The central apse is decorated with the scene of Christ Pantocrator.

Church of the Holy Virgin Mary and St. Pshoi: interior view with the sanctuary and the two large mosaics.

Church of the Holy Virgin Mary and Anba Ruways: entrance, icons of the Flight into Egypt (above), Virgin and Child flanked by angels (left), and Anba Ruways (right).

The Church of the Holy Virgin Mary and Anba Ruways

THE CHURCH OF THE HOLY VIRGIN MARY AND ANBA RUWAYS lies to the west of the shrine of St. Mark on the ground floor beneath the Cathedral of St. Mark. Its wooden screen is decorated with modern icons representing the Last Supper, the apostles, a number of church fathers, and doctor-saints, as well as great figures of Coptic monasticism such as St. Moses the Black and St. Pachomius. Its apse features Christ Pantocrator and a beautiful stained glass icon representing the Virgin and Child and St. Pshoi carrying Christ on his shoulder. Above the church's entrance there is a large icon of the Flight into Egypt. All the icons are painted by Budur Latif and Youssef Nassif.

Three icons, from left to right: Moses and the Burning Bush, Elijah's Chariot, and the Sacrifice of Abraham.

183

The Church of Anba Ruways

THE CHURCH LIES BETWEEN THE PAPAL RESIDENCE and the cathedral. It is named after its patron Anba Ruways (ca.1334–1404). His original name was Ishaq Furayg. From his youth he devoted himself to a life of asceticism and prayer. He was called the man of miracles, and it is said that he had the power of healing the sick and predicting the future .

The church features three sanctuaries, which are covered by three beehive-shaped domes. A single wooden screen serves for the three sanctuaries. Above the door of the central sanctuary there is a large cross with the Crucifixion on its western face and the Resurrection on its eastern face. It is flanked by the icons of St. John and the women at Christ's tomb. The screen is surmounted by icons of the twelve apostles, the Archangel Michael, and St. Apoli. The southern sanctuary serves as a shrine. Eight steps lead down from the northern sanctuary to the crypt with the tomb of Anba Ruways and his companion St. Suleiman. In the crypt are also buried the patriarchs Matthew I (1378–1409), John XI (1427–1452), Matthew II (1452–1465), and Gabriel VI (1466–1475).

The Church of Anba Ruways. Interior view: entrance and wooden screen of the sanctuaries.

The Shrine of St. Mark. Top: Pantocrator; below: martyrdom of the saint and the translation of his relics.

The Shrine of St. Mark

WITH THE PROGRESS OF THE GROWING RELATIONSHIP between the churches of Rome and Alexandria in modern times, the Catholic papacy decided to return the relics of St. Mark in Venice to the Coptic Church in Egypt. The Shrine of St. Mark lies in the eastern part of the ground floor of the building of the Cathedral of St. Mark; the first floor of the building houses the cathedral, while there is a number of churches, including the shrine on the ground floor. The relics of the saint were transferred from Venice on July 26, 1968. In 1969 the famous Coptic artist Isaac Fanous, assisted by Mansur Farag, painted the walls of the shrine that houses the relics. St. Mark is depicted standing with the lion flanked by two scenes, which are very instructive. To his left is the martyrdom of the great saint. He is shown being dragged by the mobs over the cobbled roads of Alexandria. The angel of the Lord appears to him carrying the crown of martyrdom. The landscape shows Pharos or the lighthouse (right) and the temple of Serapis or the Serapeum (left). To the right of the saint is the other scene that depicts the translation of his relic. It shows three Coptic priests carrying the bier in which lies the wrapped body of the haloed saint. Behind his head are twenty-two representatives of the Church of Ethiopia, the Roman Catholic Church, the Coptic Catholic Church, the Syrian Orthodox Church, the Greek and Armenian churches, and the World Council of Churches. On the other side are Pope Cyril VI and Pope Paul VI followed by the clergy, the nuns, and the faithful communities. On the top appears the Holy Spirit flanked by the Cathedral of St. Mark in Cairo and his cathedral in Venice. The four angels Suryal, Gabriel, Raphael, and Michael are also represented. The stained glass of the shrine's windows is indeed attractive; of particular note are the three windows that depict Christ in Majesty flanked by the Flight into Egypt and St. Mark the Evangelist.

The Shrine of St. Mark: Stained-glass windows depicting Christ flanked by the Flight into Egypt and St. Mark the Evangelist.

The Church of St. Peter and St. Paul

THIS CHURCH IS POPULARLY KNOWN AS AL-BUTRUSIYA because it was built in 1911 over the tomb of Boutros Ghali, the first and last Coptic prime minister of Egypt, who was assassinated by Muslim fundamentalists in 1910. It is situated in Ramses Street near the new Cathedral of St. Mark at Abbasiya. Antoine Lasciac, the former chief architect of the khedivial mansions, was responsible for its construction. The church, built of dressed stone, measures 28 meters long and 17 meters wide. It was built in the traditional basilican style with a central nave and two aisles separated by a row of marble columns on each side. The Italian painter Primo Panciroli spent five years decorating the church with beautiful paintings representing episodes of Christ's cycle, and apostles and saints. The church boasts a remarkable mosaic of the Baptism, before which stands a graceful white marble baptismal font resting on four pillars.

Exterior view with the outer court, entrance, and belfries.

To the north of the sanctuary there is a flight of steps that leads down to the tomb of Boutros Ghali. The sarcophagus that contains his remains rests upon a black granite base. The last words of Boutros Ghali, "God knows that I have done no harm to my country," are inscribed in Arabic and French on its southern and northern sides.

LEFT:
The Church's paintings representing the life of Christ, the apostles, and saints by Primo Panciroli.

The Cathedral of the Holy Virgin Mary and St. Simeon the Tanner

The Cathedral of the Holy Virgin Mary and St. Simeon the Tanner: interior view toward the entrance.

RIGHT:
Entrance to the Cathedral of the Holy Virgin Mary and St. Simeon. Mosaic: moving the Muqattam Mountain, the Virgin Mary, Patriarch Abraham, and St. Simeon.

IN 1969 THE GOVERNOR OF CAIRO issued a decree that ordered all the trash collectors of Cairo to move to one of the Muqattam hills behind the Citadel. There they built themselves primitive houses, simple huts of tin that are called in their vernacular the *zabbalin* (garbage collectors). There are about twenty-five thousand, mostly Copts, who daily collect household trash from the huge city of Cairo, of more than fifteen million inhabitants, and haul it home in enormous green canvas bags, on truck beds, and in donkey carts. On the ground floors of their poor buildings, women and children recycle and sort out the plastics, paper, metal, glass, and textiles, then compress and clean the trash. They feed the organic trash to their pigs and goats.

In the early 1970s, one of the garbage collectors, Qiddis 'Agib 'Abd al-Masih, used to collect trash from the neighborhood of Shubra and regularly met a minister, who spoke with him about the life with Christ and his love and grace. Qiddis invited the minister to visit the Zabbalin area in the Muqattam, repeating his invitation for two years, from 1972 to 1974. Finally, on the morning of the first Friday in February 1974, the minister heard the voice of God confirming that this calling from Qiddis was from God. The minister stood amazed and overwhelmed and asked himself, "What God wanted to do in such an area that was crowded by men, boys, and girls sorting out heaps of trash?" Therefore, he asked the trash collector to take him to a quiet place to pray. He took the minister to the highest place of that cliff in the Muqattam hills, where the latter found a great gap under a huge rock. That huge cave became the nucleus of the monastery of St. Simeon the Tanner (St. Samaan).

A remarkable development took place in the garbage slums when a regular Sunday school started and youths from several churches began to serve the community. In June 18, 1977, Pope Shenouda III visited the church for the first time, and he celebrated the commemoration of St. Simeon the Tanner annually from 1978 till 1980 at his monastery in Muqattam. Many projects have been installed there during the last thirty years including a hospital, a kindergarten, a school for the deaf and mute, and a number of centers for training boys and girls in the crafts of tailoring, sewing, and carpentry.

The Monastery of St. Simeon is named after Simeon the Tanner, the medieval miracle worker who moved the Muqattam Mountain. The *History of the Patriarchs* tells us that the Fatimid Caliph al-Mu'izz wished Patriarch Abraham, known Ibn Zur'a (975–987), to prove the accuracy of the claim in the Gospel that faith the size of a mustard seed could move a mountain (Mt. 17:20). Failure to do so would mean the killing of all the Christians for this falsehood. We are told that the Virgin Mary appeared to the patriarch in a dream and directed him to Simeon, a poor tanner, who used to carry water for the poor and who was instrumental in the wonder of moving the mountain. The mountain moved after three days of fasting and prayer among Christians. When the caliph saw that miracle he said to the patriarch, "I have recognized the truth of your faith." He then granted the patriarch the restoration of many Coptic Churches. Pious Copts keep the three-day fast in remembrance of St. Simeon the Tanner and the miracle of moving the Muqattam Mountain.

The garbage slums have now been transformed into one of the most attractive places of worship in the world. The Monastery of St. Simeon the Tanner comprises the huge Cathedral of the Holy Virgin Mary and St. Simeon the Tanner, and a series of caves, including the two churches of St. Paul and Bishop Abraam. Work took place in the cathedral in the period from 1986 to 1994, during which about a million tons of limestone had to be removed from the Muqattam hills. The cathedral is a huge semi-natural amphitheater that has space for more than four thousand people. The cliffs of the site feature modern sculptures that represent episodes from the New Testament.

189

WILL SEE THE SON OF MAN COMING IN THE CLOUDS WITH GREAT POWER AND GLORY Mark 13:26

Sculpture of the Lord in his second coming from heaven flanked by four angels. Arabic and English texts: Mark 13:26.

RIGHT:
Cathedral of the Holy Virgin Mary and St. Simeon the Tanner: interior view toward the sanctuaries.

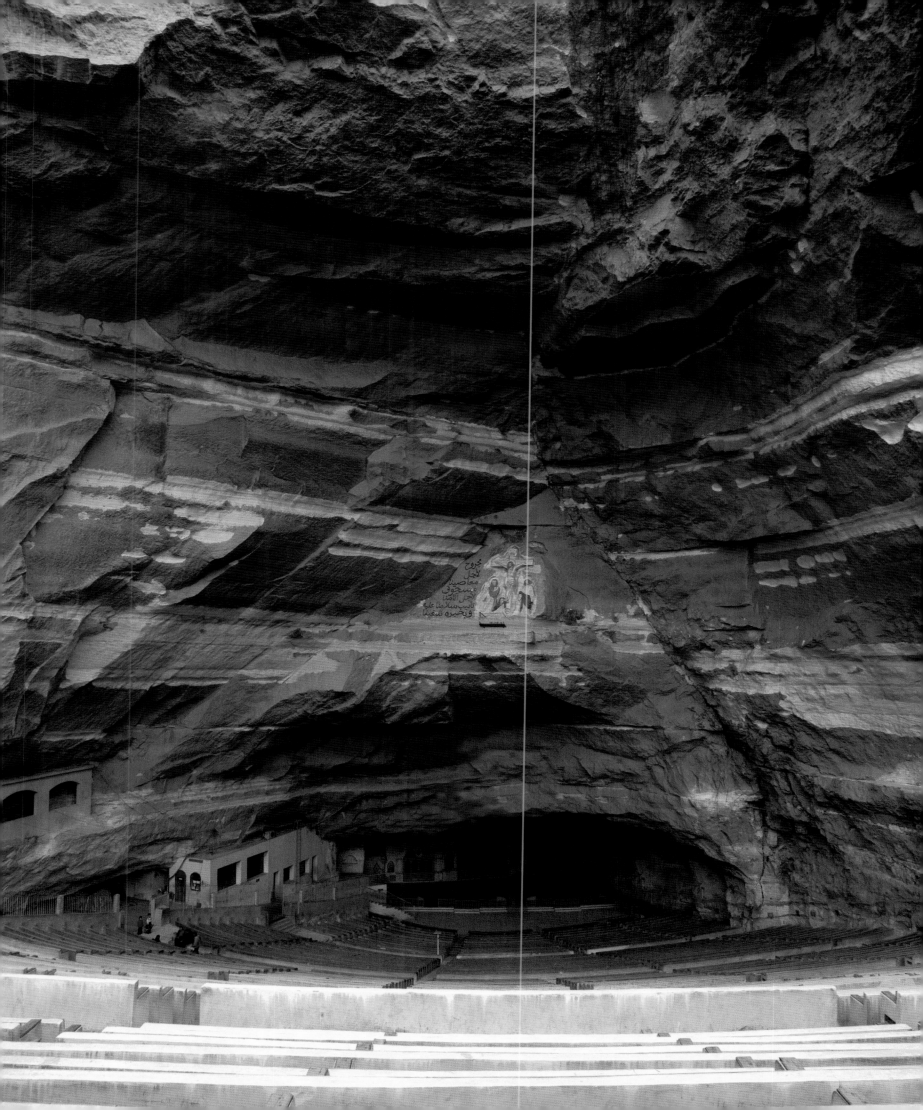

St. Mark's hall in one of the Muqattam caves.

The Church of the Holy Virgin

The Church of the Holy Virgin, Maadi: main entrance.

THIS CHURCH STANDS IN A BEAUTIFUL AREA on the Nile about ten kilometers south of Old Cairo. It is remarkable for its three beehive-shaped domes that cover the sanctuary. According to tradition, the Holy Family sailed from this site to Upper Egypt. Joseph was able to finance the travel by boat by using the gold, frankincense, and myrrh that the wise men had presented to the Christ Child in Bethlehem. On Friday, March 12, 1976 a deacon picked up a Holy Bible floating on the Nile. It was opened on the page of the prophecy of Isaiah (19:25): "Blessed be Egypt my people." Now the Arabic Bible, which was printed in Beirut in 1864, is on exhibit in the northern side chapel.

Abu al-Makarim/Abu Salih speaks of the church of the Lady Mary, known as al-Martuti, at al-'Adawiya, which was surmounted by a dome. Girgis al-Guhari (d. 1810) restored the church. Other restorations took place under the pontificate of Cyril V (1874–1927) and most recently in 1983. The sanctuaries stand at the eastern part of the church. They are dedicated to the Virgin Mary (center), Sts. Paul, Antony, and Shenute (north), and Sts. George, Menas, and Dimyana (south). Icons representing the twelve apostles surmount the wooden screen of the central sanctuary.

On the occasion of the two-thousand-year celebration of the Holy Family's Flight into Egypt in 2000, the three domes of the church and all of their icons were restored. Most of the icons in the church depict saints and were painted by the nineteenth-century icon painter Ibrahim al-Nasikh. One of the icons on the north chapel features the Virgin Mary surrounded by ten miniature scenes of her life. The flight of stairs with the tunnel leading from the church's yard to the Nile, which was used by the Holy Family, has been restored.

Icon of the Virgin Mary surrounded by ten miniatures of her life.

LEFT:
*Flight into Egypt
(Contemporary
Coptic art).*

RIGHT:
*Exterior view looking
onto the River Nile.
Note the three domes.*

BELOW:
*Modern icons
in the church.*

196

Modern mosaics of the
Purification of Isaiah
(left) and the Sacrifice
of Abraham.

Interior view toward
the central sanctuary.

Upper Egypt

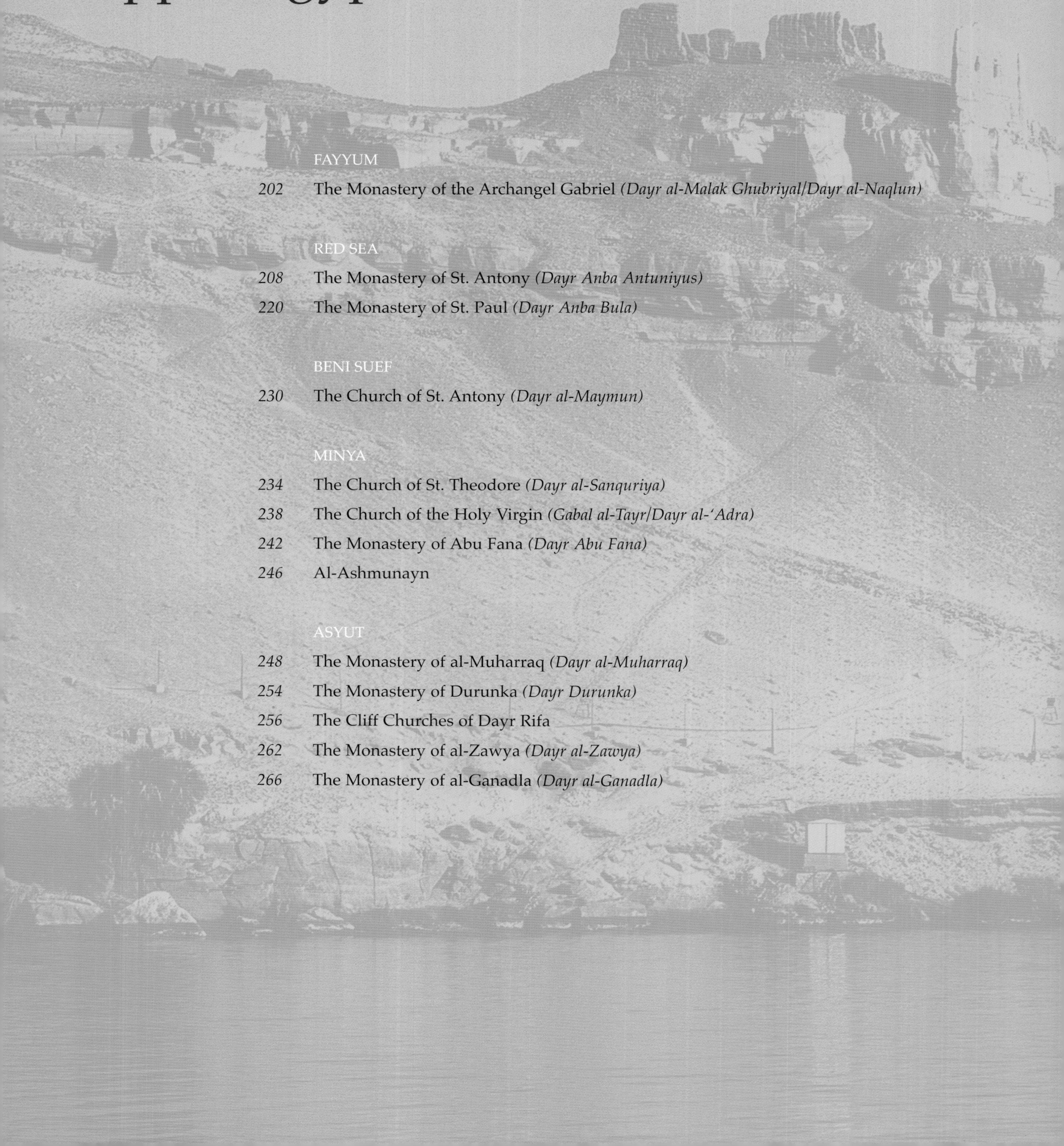

FAYYUM

202   The Monastery of the Archangel Gabriel *(Dayr al-Malak Ghubriyal/Dayr al-Naqlun)*

RED SEA

208   The Monastery of St. Antony *(Dayr Anba Antuniyus)*

220   The Monastery of St. Paul *(Dayr Anba Bula)*

BENI SUEF

230   The Church of St. Antony *(Dayr al-Maymun)*

MINYA

234   The Church of St. Theodore *(Dayr al-Sanquriya)*

238   The Church of the Holy Virgin *(Gabal al-Tayr/Dayr al-'Adra)*

242   The Monastery of Abu Fana *(Dayr Abu Fana)*

246   Al-Ashmunayn

ASYUT

248   The Monastery of al-Muharraq *(Dayr al-Muharraq)*

254   The Monastery of Durunka *(Dayr Durunka)*

256   The Cliff Churches of Dayr Rifa

262   The Monastery of al-Zawya *(Dayr al-Zawya)*

266   The Monastery of al-Ganadla *(Dayr al-Ganadla)*

AKHMIM

274   The Church of St. Mercurius *(Abu Sayfayn)*

SOHAG

278   The Red Monastery (of St. Pshai) *(al-Dayr al-Ahmar/Dayr Anba Bishai)*

284   The White Monastery (of St. Shenute) *(al-Dayr al-Abyad/Dayr Anba Shenute)*

NAQADA

290   The Monasteries of Naqada

290   The Monastery of the Cross *(Dayr al-Salib)*

292   The Monastery of St. Andrew *(Dayr Andra'us/Abu al-Lif)*

295   The Monastery of St. George *(Dayr Mari Girgis)*

296   The Monastery of St. Pisentius *(Dayr Anba Bisentiyus)*

297   The Monastery of St. Victor *(Dayr Mari Buqtur)*

299   The Monastery of the Archangel Michael *(Dayr al-Malak Mikha'il)*

LUXOR

300   Churches in Luxor Temple and Karnak Temple

ASWAN

304   The Monastery of St. Hatre *(Dayr Anba Hadra)*

308   The Monastery at Qubat al-Hawwa *(Dayr Qubbat al-Hawwa)*

The Monastery of the Archangel Gabriel

The equestrian saint Pichoshe on the west wall of the church. This is the only image preserved of this soldier and nothing is known about his life.

RIGHT:
The Church of the Archangel Gabriel, view from the south aisle to the sanctuary. The basin in the floor (laqqan) was used for the ceremony of foot washing on Maundy Thursday.

THE SAINTLY BISHOP AUR OF NAQLUN, the legendary founder of the monastery, was the secret son of a princess and a magician living somewhere in the East. His mother died when he was three years old. When he was eight years old, the king, the father of the princess, discovered his existence. Guided by the Archangel Gabriel, Aûr escaped with his father and two elder brothers to Fayyum. They settled in Naqlun, practicing magic. Shortly afterward, the father died. The Virgin Mary and the Archangel Gabriel appeared to the brothers and they were converted to Christianity. They promised to build a church in honor of the archangel, and Gabriel and the Virgin traced the ground plan. Legend has it that after much trouble caused by Satan, who wanted to stop the building, the church was completed. Saint Isaac, Bishop of Fayyum, consecrated the church and ordained Aûr priest. After St. Isaac's death, Aûr succeeded him as Bishop of Fayyum.

Although the origin of this story is uncertain, archaeological research in and around the monastery has been uncovering an extensive monastic community going back to at least the fifth century AD. Eighty-nine rock-cut hermitages in the hills and monastic buildings on the plateau at the foot of the hills were discovered. They testify to a way of life where monks lived on their own in hermitages, coming down for Mass and supplies. In around 900, the complex on the plateau completely burned down. A new monastic center was built and the current Church of the Archangel Gabriel presumably dates to this period. It has a basilican plan with a nave, side aisles and return aisle, an apse, and side chambers. Pieces of architectural sculpture (pilasters, columns, and capitals) dating to the fifth century and presumably originating from an older church on the plateau (not localized yet) were reused. From 1990–1996, wall paintings were discovered. On the walls of the nave, a series of equestrian saints (among others, Theodore and Mercurius), standing saints, Gabriel, Virgin and Child between archangels, and crosses were found. In the apse, the traditional pattern has been adapted to the architecture: Christ enthroned surrounded by the Four Living Creatures was depicted in the half-dome. Below, on either side of a window, the apostles were painted, accompanied by two monastic saints. The Virgin, who normally takes her place in the middle of the group of apostles, was painted on a lower level, in the central niche of the east wall. Inscriptions mentioning Patriarch Zacharias (1005–1030) point to a date of creation during his patriarchate. This makes the decorative program one of the few firmly dated assemblages in Christian wall painting in Egypt. In the apse, paintings of an earlier layer are still visible in the lateral niches: St. Mark and (presumably) St. Athanasius.

The hermitages seem to have been in use until the twelfth century, while the monastery was deserted in the fourteenth century. The Church of the Archangel Gabriel survived and has been the nucleus of a small complex. Renovations included a *khurus*, domes above the eastern end, and a wall closing the return-aisle, turning it into a narthex. Since the 1990s, the community has been revived and a new monastery is being developed.[82]

The apostles in the apse of the central haykal *on both sides of a window with stucco tracery.*

206

St. Mark (niche in the apse).

The Virgin enthroned with Child, accompanied by two archangels. The mural was painted on the west wall of the church, a most unusual place for this theme.

207

The Monastery of St. Antony

The Old Church of St. Antony, painting of St. Macarius the Great with the cherub showing him to the place where he should build his monastery. To the right an unidentified holy monk .

Saint Antony, the father of monks, found his final place of refuge in a cave in Mount Colzim (Qulzum) in the Wadi al-'Araba near the Red Sea. A spring at the foot of the mountain supplied water and he planted a small garden. After his death in 356, his disciples founded a monastic community that bears his name. The history of the Monastery of St. Antony repeats the ups and downs of many desert settlements: Bedouin attacks, renovation and rebuilding, fortification, and periods of abandonment and revival. The fame and stature of its patron saint has made it one of the most important monasteries of Egypt, both past and present.

The heart of the monastery is the Church of St. Antony, often simply called 'The Old Church' where St. Antony is believed to be buried. It is a small building with a nave divided into two domed bays, a *khurus*, and three altar rooms. To the south of the western bay of the nave is a small chapel, dedicated to the Four Living Creatures. This church not only houses one of the few rare, nearly complete decorative programs known but inscriptions also mention the painter, Theodore, and date this cycle of paintings to the years 1232–1233. Late thirteenth century paintings in the *khurus* and on the soffit of the arches to the *khurus* and the entrance to the Chapel of the Four Living Creatures complete the program as it is seen today.[83]

Theodore and his team were not only active in the church proper. In the Chapel of the Four Living Creatures, they painted an impressive Christ enthroned in *mandorla*, flanked by the Virgin Mary and St. John the Baptist, forming a deesis. The deesis was enlarged by the full-bodied images of the Four Living Creatures who, praying continuously, also mediate for mankind. In this case, angels carry the *mandorla* of Christ. The small niche below shows a draped cross with censing angels.

These paintings were not the first to be executed in the chapel or the church (although not in the altar rooms). During the recent restoration, conservators have found evidence of two earlier layers of painting. The fragments are small and badly preserved, with the exception of one example from the oldest layer, on the soffit of the sanctuary arch of the Chapel of the Four Living Creatures. The Christ enthroned and busts of his apostles in medallions may be dated to the sixth to seventh century. The absence of older fragments in the *haykals* may be an indication of the later addition of this section.

With the restoration of the church and the paintings, an important monument has been preserved. Moreover, it has greatly enriched and complemented the history of the Monastery of St. Antony. However, the monks and the numerous pilgrims traveling to the monastery, visiting his church and the cave in the mountains, do not need tangible evidence. St. Antony's presence and spirit are palpable everywhere.

One of the double towers of the new Church of St. Antony and St. Paul, through a window in the pulley room. For safety, desert monasteries had pulleys to hoist up goods and visitors.

OPPOSITE:
The Old Church of St. Antony, built in mud brick. View from the nave to the sanctuary. The paintings on the walls date to the years 1232–1233.

The Old Church of St. Antony. The two sections of the nave. The eastern part is decorated with monastic saints, the western part is painted with equestrian saints.

The dome of the central altar room with Christ and His heavenly hosts, the Twenty-Four Priests of the Apocalypse and two Old Testament scenes: Abraham's Sacrifice (Gen. 22:1–19) and Jephthah's Sacrifice (Judg. 11:30–40). In the niche, Christ enthroned surrounded by the Four Living Creatures. On the soffit of the arch to the khurus, six prophets. The beautifully decorated roof of the khurus is just visible.

213

OPPOSITE:
St. Mercurius (Abu Sayfayn) in the khurus
*is surrounded by elements from his life:
the angel bringing him a second sword, the killing of
the Emperor Julian after the prayers of St. Basil
(with St. Gregory depicted on the right), and the
killing of his grandfather by two dog-headed
creatures. The long inscription dates the paintings
to 1232–1233.*

From right to left in the khurus,
*the patriarchs Abraham, Isaac, and
Jacob in paradise. The small figures
represent the souls of the blessed.
On the far right, outside paradise,
the rich man in hell, indicating that
the poor Lazarus must have been
painted in Abraham's lap (Luke
16:19–31).*

215

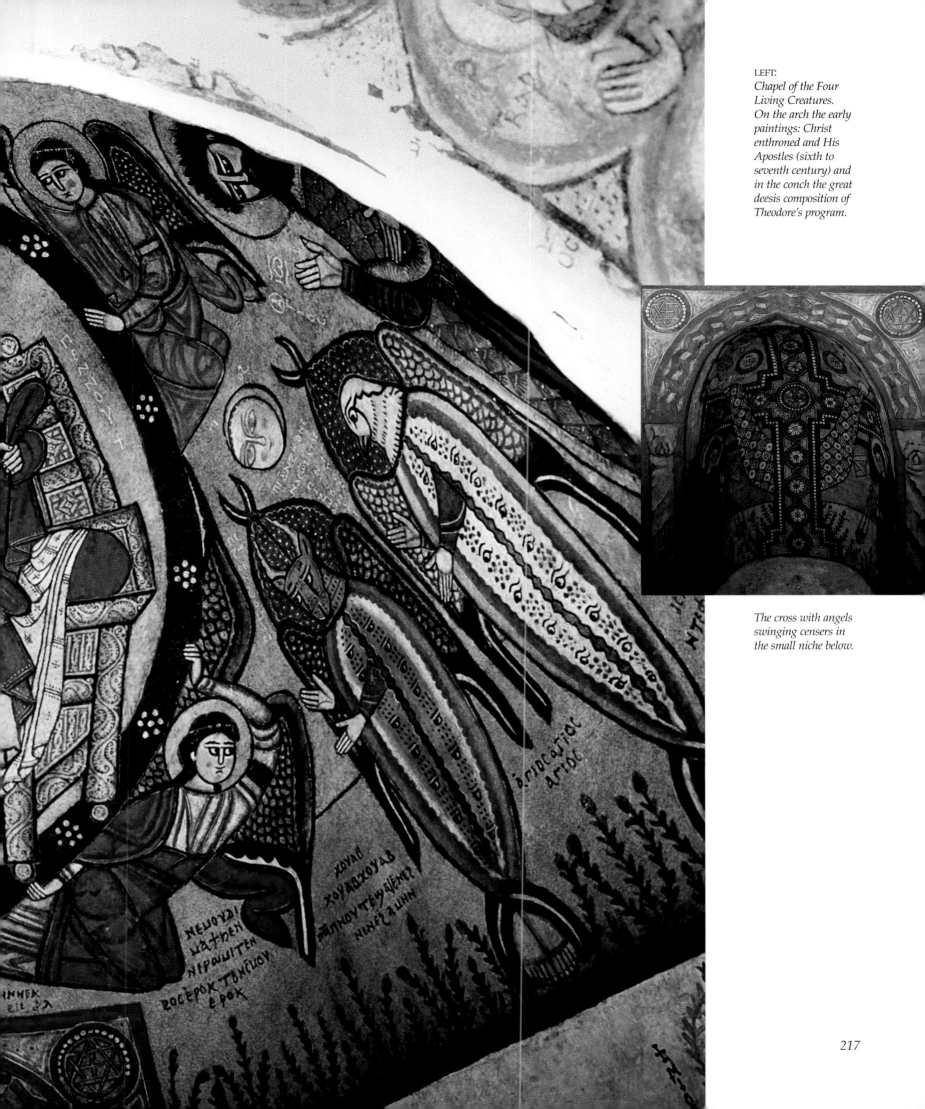

*The cross with angels
swinging censers in
the small niche below.*

217

Views of the Monastery of St. Antony. The double towers belong to the new Church of St. Antony and St. Paul (early twentieth century). The domed church outside the walls, built with stones from the mountain, is dedicated to St. Antony and the Virgin Mary. It was consecrated in 2004.

The Monastery of St. Paul

SAINT PAUL OF THEBES (Anba Bula, ca. 235–348?) is known as 'the first hermit.' For more than ninety years he lived in a cave near a natural spring and a palm tree. Daily, a raven brought him a piece of bread. The palm tree provided leaves for weaving his tunic and baskets, and some extra food. At the end of his life, St. Antony visited him and the raven brought a double portion. St. Paul died shortly afterward and, with the help of two lions who dug his grave, St. Antony buried him.

The cave where, according to tradition, St. Paul lived is the core of the monastery: the subterranean Church of St. Paul. Since it evolved around natural caves, the church has an irregular plan. There were two altar rooms (dedicated to St. Paul and St. Antony), a chamber with the tomb of St. Paul and a central room in front.

The Monastery of St. Paul is smaller and more remote than the nearby Monastery of St. Antony and lived most of its existence in its shadow. Vulnerable to Bedouin attacks, it was left uninhabited for long stretches of time. At the beginning of the eighteenth century, Patriarch John XVI renovated and repopulated the monastery. The subterranean church was enlarged with a third altar room, dedicated to the Twenty-Four Elders; the central room was extended and a staircase was constructed. The French Jesuit Claude Sicard visited the monastery in 1716 and he reported that the church was recently repaired and painted from wall to dome with "sacred histories," crudely executed. He met the painter, a monk from the monastery, who confessed that he had never learned to paint—a fact his work bears witness to, wrote Sicard.[84] In later times, the round faces of the saints depicted earned the monk the nickname of "the painter of the compass." Although this monk was certainly no master, he faithfully preserved the subjects of earlier murals. Fragments of these thirteenth- and fourteenth-century paintings are visible in the old parts of the church. The older monks' portraits bear a remarkable resemblance to the thirteenth-century paintings in the Old Church of the Monastery of St. Antony. At the end of the eighteenth century, Mu'allim Ibrahim al-Guhari built the Church of St. Mercurius partly on top of the old Church of St. Paul, with a connecting staircase. The most recent restoration of the church (completed in 2005) restored the paintings to their former colorful glory.[85]

Modern roads broke the silence and isolation of St. Paul's. Today, the monastery is enlarged with new buildings and guest houses outside the old walls. It is often bursting with pilgrims seeking spiritual guidance and visitors viewing the holy places.

Two layers of paintings: St. Shenute and St. John (with Coptic inscriptions) are just visible above a row of early eighteenth century saints (with Arabic inscriptions)

OPPOSITE:
Room of the Four Archangels, the eighteenth-century extension of the central room. To the right, the entrance of the altar room of the Twenty-Four Elders. The saints depicted are St. Sarapion, St. Antony, and St. Paul dressed in a palm-leaf tunic, with two lions at his feet and the raven bringing bread.

The Virgin Mary with Child accompanied by seraphim. The decorative motifs above belong to an earlier layer of paintings.

The dome of the eighteenth-century staircase, painted with an army of equestrian saints. The names of the saints are written in Arabic and Coptic. A Coptic inscription in the dome states the building date (1713) and names Patriarch John as "the one who took care of this church."

An angel carrying a child near the entrance of the tomb of St. Paul. It is believed to represent the Archangel Uriel bringing the baby St. John the Baptist into safety during the murder of the children of Bethlehem by the soldiers of King Herod.

RIGHT:
The dome of the altar room of the Twenty-Four Elders. Angels blowing trumpets surround Christ enthroned. Below, the Twenty-Four Priests of the Apocalypse. Their names are written in Coptic in the band above (eighteenth century).

In the garden is the cave of St. Mark, a fourteenth-century monk of St. Antony's. He lived for some years in this hermitage, which gives an impression of what a desert dwelling looked like.

Cave Church of St Paul: Holy monk (eighteenth century), probably one of the saintly brothers Domitius and Maximus in whose honor the Monastery of al-Baramus was founded. An earlier layer is visible to the left.

225

The old mill for grinding wheat. A donkey used to turn the large wheel. Grain was funneled through the wooden box on top of the millstones.

The old refectory of the monastery. At the end of the long stone table is a lectern for reading during the meal.

Cells in the Monastery of St. Paul.

The old entrance to the monastery with the pulley for hoisting up goods and visitors.

The churches of St. Mercurius and St. Paul with the keep of the monastery and the Church of St. Michael to the right.

The Church of St. Antony

IN AROUND THE YEAR 285, St. Antony set out for a mountain near the Nile called Pispir, where he lived twenty years before going into isolation near the Red Sea. The present-day Dayr al-Maymun, which is situated on the east bank of the Nile about thirteen miles north of Beni Suef and seven miles south of al-Kuaymat, is a modern village on the site of an early monastery that was used as a supply station of the Monastery of St. Antony at the Red Sea. Pispir, the site of the old monastery, has disappeared. Two churches at Dayr al-Maymun, which probably derive only from the Ottoman period, recall the old tradition about St. Antony and Pispir. Dayr al-Maymun was known to the church historian Abu al-Makarim/Abu Salih (early thirteenth century) and to the Arab historian al-Maqrizi (1364–1442) as 'Dayr al-Gumayza' (the Monastery of the Sycamore).

The two churches are situated beside each other. The smaller church, which is dedicated to St. Mercurius, is older and has an entrance along its southern wall. It features a domed nave with two columns, and a three-part sanctuary that is flanked by two side rooms. The larger church is dedicated to St. Antony. The many granite columns in its walls suggest that it was originally built in the basilican style. G.J. Chester and J.L. Petit visited the church in the middle of the nineteenth century and described its naos with a dome supported by four columns. The central and northern sanctuaries have been enlarged, while the southern sanctuary retained its original form of a small side room with an apse.

The Coptic inhabitants of the village in the site of Dayr al-Maymun take pride in the oral tradition that St. Antony lived in the cave which opens from the floor of the church's nave. The cave measures about 1.95 m in depth, 1.75 m in length, and 80 cm in width. The wooden screen of the sanctuary bears the date AM 1264 (AD 1529/1530).

OPPOSITE:
Entrance to the older Church of St. Mercurius.

The Church of St. Antony: exterior view (east/west).

The doors of the churches of St. Mercurius and St. Antony.

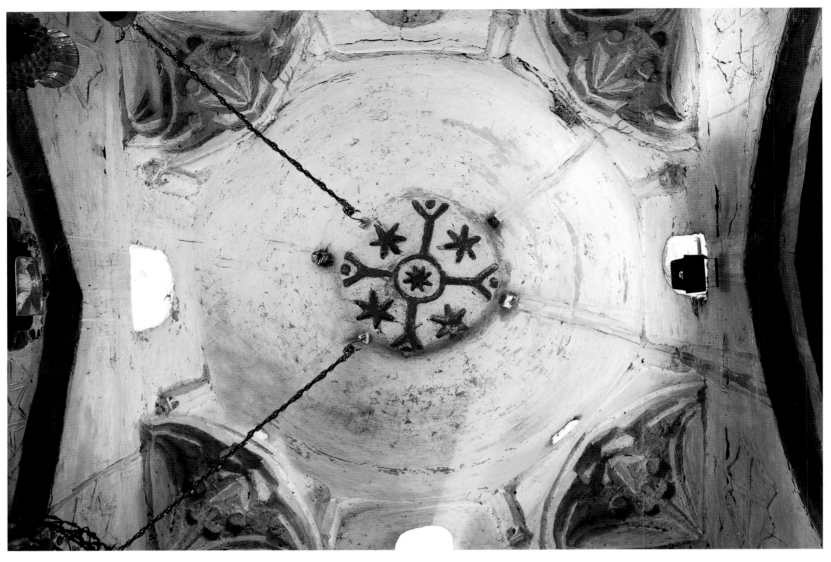

*The Church of
St. Antony: cross
decoration of
the dome.*

*The Church of
St. Antony: view
of the altar in
the sanctuary.*

LEFT:
*Interior view toward
the sanctuary.*

*Entrance to the
cave of St. Antony.*

The Church of St. Theodore

THE CHURCH OF ST. THEODORE is all that remains from the Monastery of al-Sanquriya. It is located on the east bank of Bahr Yusuf about thirteen miles west of the city of Beni Mazar in the Minya governorate. The church and a cemetery are surrounded by an enclosure wall. The church is situated in the southeast sector of the enclosure. It is a typical hall church with four columns and twelve domes. It dates from the eighteenth or nineteenth century. The church's northern and western sides open on a portico that is supported by fourteen red granite columns with old acanthus-leaf capitals. On the eastern part stand three sanctuaries dedicated to the St. Theodore (center), the Virgin Mary (north), and St. George (south). The wooden screens of the sanctuaries are decorated with geometric designs inlaid with ivory. The four marble columns, which are in the middle of the hall church, feature beautiful capitals decorated with acanthus leaves. They retain little of their natural appearance as their tips droop and might date to the sixth or the seventh century. These capitals must have been taken from an old building, perhaps from the ancient church of the old monastery that disappeared. The church's wooden *ambo*n (pulpit) has a spiral staircase winding around the northwestern column. It is adorned with the icons of the twelve apostles.

Interior of the ciborium over the altar.

Exterior view of the church within the enclosure wall.

234

The **ambon** *decorated with the icons of the twelve apostles.*

Interior view toward the **ambon** *and the sanctuaries.*

The Church of the Holy Virgin

VARIOUS MUSLIM AUTHORS mentioned Gabal al-Tayr ('the Mountain of the Birds'), south of Samalut on the east bank of the Nile, as one of the wonders of Egypt: migratory birds, a species called buqir (still not identified), would assemble in great numbers on this mountain that was also known as the Gabal Buqir.

According to tenth-century Coptic fragments of *The Homily of the Rock*, attributed to Timothy II, a fifth-century patriarch of Alexandria, the Holy Family spent some time on this mountain. The Virgin appeared to Timothy in a dream. She told him the story of their travels and ordered him to build a church on the rock. The origin of this homily might be sought in the sixth century and testifies to an ancient pilgrimage tradition.[86]

The History of the Churches and Monasteries of Egypt (ca. twelfth century) claims that the mountain is also called Gabal al-Khaff ('the Mountain of the Palm'), named after an imprint of the hand of Christ "which was made when he touched the mountain, when it worshipped before him, and restored it to its place with his hand; so that the mark of his palm remains impressed upon that mountain to the present day."[87] Where and how this mark appeared in the mountain, and how it disappeared, is surrounded by a number of legends.

Before the building of the Great Dam in Aswan, the Nile used to flow along the foot of the steep mountain plateau and the monastery could be reached by boat and a strenuous climb. Because of this picturesque location, it was from the seventeenth century onward often mentioned in accounts of European travelers sailing up the Nile. These travelers reported another name for the monastery: Dayr al-Bakara, or 'the Monastery of the Pulley.' To hoist goods (and sometimes also visitors), a pulley had been installed to the south of the complex. Traces of this lifting equipment are still visible.

In the eighteenth century, villagers had taken over most of the buildings around the Church of the Virgin, built in a late antique rock-cut tomb. The birds don't come any more, but pilgrims still flock in great numbers, although no longer by boat and prepared for a climb but in cars on comfortable roads. Their intentions to honor the Holy Family are most likely the same.

The west entrance of the church, hewn into the rock. The doorposts and lintel are original. The reliefs above the doorway are fragments of unknown provenance, showing human figures, plant motifs, and decorative borders. They were assembled in the late 1930s by the Supreme Council of Antiquities. The sign mentions the tradition of assigning the foundation of the church to Empress Helena (fourth century).

View of Gabal al-Tayr. The church is barely visible among the pilgrims' quarters, overcrowded in June (Feast of the Arrival of the Holy Family in Egypt) and August (Feast of the Assumption of the Virgin). At the far left is the residence of the Bishop of Samalut.

Cave of the Holy Family with an icon of the Virgin Mary and Child.

Interior of the church, with the massive rock-hewn pillars of the late antique tomb (probably fifth century).

241

The Monastery of Abu Fana

THE MONASTERY OF ABU FANA is situated eighteen kilometers south of al-Minya, at the edge of the Western Desert. It was named after the fourth-century hermit Apa Bane. According to the accounts of his life, Apa Bane, a gentle, wise, and humble man, lived in a pitch-dark cell for eighteen years. He was always on his feet, even sleeping in this position, leaning on a low wall built especially for this purpose. Bane means 'palm tree' in Coptic. It was not his name (his real name is not known) but it described his appearance: his body was stiff and stooped forward like a palm tree. After his death, miracles happened on his tomb in the church and the monastery became large and prosperous. The Arab historian al-Maqrizi (d. 1442) wrote that, formerly, a thousand monks lived there, although in his time no more than two survived.[88] It is not known when the decline set in.

At present, the 'Church on the Hill' is the only structure that survives from the old monastic complex. The sanctuary belongs to the original seventh-century structure. The eastern part looks like a triconch, as found in the churches of monasteries near Sohag, but was not built as such. The side rooms are narrower than the main apse and their half-domes are of later date. Originally, only the main apse had a half-dome (still in place) while the space in front was a khurus, most likely covered with a tunnel vault or a flat roof. The nave was remodeled several times and comprises now only part of the original space with a small courtyard at the western end. The Church is famous for its wall paintings: the huge, intricate patterned cross above the altar and the crosses in the southern and western half-dome (dating to the thirteenth century), that made the site also known as the 'Monastery of the Crosses.'

From 1987 to 1993, an Austrian team restored the church and excavated part of the monastic complex to the north. Below the pavement of a sixth-century church, they found the remains of a fourth-century church with the tomb of Apa Bane. The saint could be identified because his spine showed signs of the chronic illness ankylosing spondylitis, or Bechterew's Disease, a form of arthritis that primarily affects the spine and caused the stiffness of his body as described in his biographies.

The cult of Apa Bane, the oldest saint in Egypt whose remains have been identified, is still flourishing. Near the old church, a new monastery and church were built and solemnly inaugurated and consecrated in 2004.

The dome of the church from the desert.

The modern cemetery, surrounded by desert.

Crosses on the west wall of the courtyard. Originally, this space belonged to the nave of the church.

OPPOSITE:
View to the altar room with the large ornamental cross in the half dome. The altar screen with icons is modern. The Corinthian capitals of the columns flanking the entrance to the khurus *are reused building elements from the sixth century.*

Southern half-dome. The painting shows a large ornamental medallion with a cross under a canopy.

Al-Ashmunayn

Late antique Hermopolis Magna (modern al-Ashmunayn) was an important administrative center in Middle Egypt, with a long history. In pharaonic times, one of the largest temples in honor of Thot, the ibis-headed god, scribe, and vizier of the gods, was built here. The Arabic *al-Ashmunayn* derives from the Egyptian name of the city. In the middle of the third century, Christianity established itself and Hermopolis became a bishop's see. At present, the ancient city is in ruins. Archaeological research has revealed numerous churches in the region. Among these is a great basilica (mid-fifth century) that was one of the most impressive houses of worship in Egypt.[89] The remains of the basilica, with columns of the nave still standing, testify to a prosperous past.

A pilgrim's account from the late fourth century connects Hermopolis with the Holy Family. The unknown author relates that when Christ first entered the city, all idols fell to the ground, fulfilling the prophesy in Isaiah 19:1 "the idols of Egypt shall be moved at his presence" Already at that time extensive ruins of Egyptian temples were visible everywhere and must have seemed convincing proof to visitors.[90]

Later traditions and sources supported the view that the Holy Family traveled through the area and stories and legends were woven around their sojourn. Hermopolis became an important pilgrimage site and it became the first city that was explicitly related to the Holy Family's travels in Egypt.

The basilica of al-Ashmunayn.

The Monastery of al-Muharraq

This altar stone of the main altar was previously used as a tombstone for a man named Colluthos in the year 746.

THE MONASTERY OF AL-MUHARRAQ (Dayr al-Muharraq) near the mountains of Qusqam is considered the most sacred of the Holy Family pilgrimage centers in Egypt. According to tradition, the Holy Family stayed here for more than six months in an old abandoned house on the edge of the desert at the end of their journey through Egypt. *The History of the Churches and Monasteries of Egypt* (ca. twelfth century) tells this story and adds that after his resurrection, Christ traveled back to Qusqam on a cloud, in the company of his mother and the apostles. He consecrated their former home as a church, the first church in Egypt. Near the church was a well, blessed by Christ, whose water cured diseases and to which pilgrims came in multitudes.[91] The author has based his account on The Vision of Theophilus, which is attributed to Patriarch Theophilus (d. 412?), but the text is most likely the work of a later writer. This source records the journey of the Holy Family, the miraculous events during their sojourn in Egypt, and the foundation of the first church at the place that was to become the Church of the Virgin in the Monastery of the Holy Virgin. The consecration of the church, fulfilling Isaiah's prophesy, "On that day there will be a church in the center of the land of Egypt" (Is. 19:19), is still commemorated each year on November 15.

Historical facts on the monastery are scarce. Originally, it belonged to the Upper Egyptian monasteries that followed the Pachomian Rule and has undoubtedly been rebuilt and renovated several times. *The History of the Churches and Monasteries of Egypt* mentions the restoration of a keep. Four monks from the Monastery of the Holy Virgin became patriarchs in the fourteenth and fifteenth centuries. In the thirteenth to eighteenth century, groups of Ethiopian monks lived in the monastery, which was one of their stops on their way from Ethiopia to Jerusalem.

Today, the Monastery of the Holy Virgin is situated in a sea of fertile fields. The crenelated enclosure walls with gates (1910–1928) give the impression of a medieval castle. The ancient Church of the Virgin and the keep belong to the oldest part of the monastery. Like the keep, the present church building was most probably part of a twelfth-century renovation. However, the extensive renovations and reconstructions at the end of the nineteenth and early twentieth century dominate the current appearance of the monastery.

The veneration of the Holy Family and the reputation of the first church make the Monastery of the Holy Virgin one of the oldest and most beloved pilgrimage goals in Egypt. Every June, thousands of people gather at the monastery to celebrate the feast of the Virgin Mary.

OPPOSITE:
The ancient Church of the Virgin Mary, the central altar room.

The ancient Church of the Virgin Mary, view from the nave to the sanctuary. According to tradition, Christ consecrated the house where the family lived during their stay in Egypt as a church, the first church in Egypt. The present building most probably dates to the twelfth century.

The Ark or Throne of the Chalice (Kursi al-kas). During liturgy, the prepared chalice is put in the Ark until Holy Communion. The icon painter A[na]stasi al-Qudsi al-Rumi decorated the Ark with The Last Supper (photograph), the Virgin and Child and the archangels Michael and Gabriel (dated AM 1581/AD 1864–1865).

OPPOSITE:
The main gate of the monastery.

250

*The interior of the keep with the Chapel of the Archangel Michael (*LEFT *and* ABOVE LEFT*) with a wooden lectern. The reused columns were placed upside down.* RIGHT: *the well on the ground floor of the keep.*

The Monastery of Durunka

OPPOSITE:

*The Quarry Church
of the Virgin.*

AFTER THEY HAD LIVED SIX MONTHS in the place that was to become Dayr al-Muharraq, an angel brought the Holy Family the message that Herod had died and that it was safe to return to Palestine. According to tradition, attested to by medieval manuscripts, they traveled by boat. The manuscript traditions also agree that they did not go farther south than the Monastery of al-Muharraq.

Recent oral tradition, however, maintains that in order to go home, the Holy Family had to journey some fifty kilometers farther south to Lycopolis (present-day Asyut), the closest main Nile port. They found a cave to the southwest of the city where they lodged before finding a boat to take them north. This cave, originally a pharaonic quarry, became the Church of the Holy Virgin in the Monastery of the Holy Virgin at Durunka.

In the 1950s, Bishop Mikha'il of Asyut began to renovate the existing Monastery of the Holy Virgin around the cave and to build accommodations for pilgrims. The annual Feast of the Holy Virgin in the Monastery of Durunka has rapidly become the largest pilgrimage site in Egypt. Since 1968, visitors have been reporting appearances of the Virgin or the miraculous appearance of lights. These lights are interpreted as signs that the Holy Family blessed this spot. Hundreds of thousands of people visit Durunka during two weeks of August, culminating in the Procession for the Virgin Mary on August 21, the eve of the Feast of the Assumption. From afar, the monastery resembles a gigantic beehive glued to the hills: in order to house the huge number of pilgrims, hundreds of apartment buildings and hotel rooms have been built on the slope of the mountain.

*A miracle of light
inspired the belief that
the Holy Family
stayed in this chapel.*

The Cliff Churches of Dayr Rifa

THE HISTORY OF THE MONASTERIES AND CHURCHES IN EGYPT (ca. twelfth century) and the historian al-Maqrizi (d. 1442) both mention monasteries in the region of Dayr Rifa. However, none of these can be identified with certainty as the monastic settlement in the northern part of the Middle and New Kingdom tomb complex in the hills. In the seventeenth century, the Dominican monk Vansleb mentioned a Monastery of the Blessed Virgin in the mountain behind the village of Rifa. In 1901, the Jesuit priest Jullien and the architect Somers Clarke both visited the site. They found a village community occupying the monastery and described both churches. A plan of the Church of the Virgin supplements Somers Clarke's description.

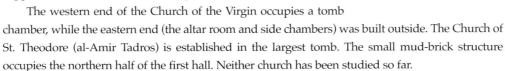

Western part of the Church of the Virgin Mary.

The western end of the Church of the Virgin occupies a tomb chamber, while the eastern end (the altar room and side chambers) was built outside. The Church of St. Theodore (al-Amir Tadros) is established in the largest tomb. The small mud-brick structure occupies the northern half of the first hall. Neither church has been studied so far.

When the villagers left the monastery to settle in the village of Rifa at the foot of the mountains is not known. Dayr Rifa is now designated a military area and is difficult to visit. Twenty years ago the churches were dilapidated and empty. At present, they have been carefully renovated and are in use again.

Somers Clarke already noted the love and pride shown by the villagers for the Church of the Virgin. Prince Johann Georg, Duke of Saxony, who visited Dayr Rifa in 1930, confirms this affection. He recounts that at that time the authorities wanted to place the sculptured lintel from the entrance to the church in the Coptic Museum. The villagers declared that, if necessary, they were willing to defend their church by force of arms. Fortunately, it was unnecessary and the lintel is still in place. This example of protection of monuments deserves to be mentioned, wrote Prince Johann Georg.[92]

The tombs of Rifa. The Church of St. Theodore is built in the large tomb with two columns. The Church of the Virgin Mary is installed in a tomb to the left.

OPPOSITE:
The Church of the Virgin Mary. The screen with inlay veils the haykal. *The lattice screens divide the space into a* khurus, *a men's section, and a women's section.*

ABOVE AND OPPOSITE:
The baptismal font.

*The Church of the
Virgin Mary.
Engraving of the
Virgin in a mother-
of-pearl inlay in the
altar screen.*

LEFT AND ABOVE:
The Church of
St. Theodore.

The Monastery of al-Zawya

THE MONASTERY OF AL-ZAWYA, near the village of al-Zawya, resembles a fortress. High walls topped with ornamental brickwork surround houses and a church in an area of about 80x100 meters. The gate is situated in the west wall and narrow streets lead to a church in the center, dedicated to St. Athanasius, the twentieth patriarch (d. 373) and author of the *Life of Antony*. Fragments of stone sculpture, decorative motifs, funerary stelae, and inscriptions are built into the mud-brick walls of the houses and the enclosure walls. The monastery has become a small village, preserving its original outline completely.

The Monastery of al-Zawya.

OPPOSITE:
One of the narrow streets through the ancient village.

Nothing is known about the history of the site or the church. Medieval sources are silent. Father Vansleb visited the Monastery of St. Athanasius in Zawya (Sauvie) in 1673. He had hoped to see some antiquities but was bitterly disappointed, and he does not mention anything about walls, a church, or the presence of monks.[93] In 1901, Father Jullien admired the church (at that time severely damaged) and complained that no one could tell him the real name of the monastery or to whom the church was dedicated. He described the church and draws a parallel with the famous churches near Sohag, dedicated to St. Shenute and St. Pshai.[94]

In contrast to these churches, the Church of St. Athanasius has no trilobed sanctuary but an apse with two side chambers, a *khurus*, a nave, and side aisles, and a narthex. The narthex and *khurus* are both barrel vaulted. The heavy brick columns in the nave most probably conceal more elegant columns: The upper part of capitals is still visible. When a dome replaced the wooden roof, stronger supports were required and the original columns were encased. The resemblance to the monasteries near Sohag lies in the system of decorative niches in the apse. Three round-headed niches flanked by pilasters were built in the lower wall and two doorways give access to the side chambers. Above, five smaller niches with broken pediments on half-columns are set on a continuous band of sculpture. Finely sculptured bands accentuate all architectural features.

The high, fortress-like walls of the village with the main gate.

The architecture and sculpture have never been studied. Undoubtedly, the church has undergone several building phases. The reuse of older building elements in enclosure walls, houses, and the façade of the church point to an ancient past. Sir Flinders Petrie concluded, "This great Deir or Coptic village must be early, as it is surrounded by a wide stretch of rubbish mounds which go back to Roman times."[95] Only thorough research will cast light on the history of the Monastery of al-Zawya.

The Church of St. Athanasius.

OPPOSITE:
The central altar room with the two stories of niches. In the upper niches, the sculpted shells in the niche heads are just visible above the modern icons.

The Monastery of al-Ganadla

The Monastery of al-Ganadla.

THE MONASTERY OF AL-GANADLA, also called the Monastery of the Virgin (Dayr al-'Adra), was established in pharaonic quarries to the west of the village of al-Ganadla, about 25 kilometers south of Asyut. It is often confused with the Monastery of St. Macrobius (Dayr Abu Maqrufa), a nearby laura dedicated to the sixth-century hermit St. Macrobius (Abu Maqrufa).

The Monastery of al-Ganadla has two churches, one from the nineteenth century, and an older church dedicated to the Virgin Mary. A narrow corridor, through which the visitor enters a doorway to the southern part of the old church, separates the houses of worship. The naos is formed by the irregular shape of a quarry with the ceiling highest in the central part. At the wide former entrance to the quarry, an apse was constructed with a small room to the north. The brickwork of the sanctuary dates from the nineteenth century, but the quarry was used as a church during earlier times. The altar screen was built of masonry and reused pieces of sculpture, decorative borders, and stelae. Their provenance is unknown, but they probably date to the time of the original church.

Niches were cut in all walls of the quarry. They have beautiful conches and a gable-shaped upper part, reminiscent of the niches in the churches of the monasteries in Sohag (see pages 278–89). As in the church of the Monastery of St. Pshai (Red Monastery), all architectural elements of the niches, the walls, and the ceiling were painted, probably in the sixth century. The interiors of the niches were decorated with crosses set with gemstones (not one is alike) and inscriptions of the names of Christ as Savior through the cross. Ornamental borders, gemstone crosses, branches, and leaves in various patterns decorate the walls. The ceiling was painted with a cassette pattern filled with decorative motifs and a series of similar crosses in medallions. The upper part of the walls, along the high ceiling, presents a series of unique paintings: canopies (a domed roof resting on columns) with plant motifs in between. Curtains, drawn back, hang between the columns, revealing a vase or a cross. The architecture of the niches with painted crosses inside them seems to be repeated in paint on the walls.

The early murals were plastered over in the eleventh or twelfth century and repainted, this time with a series of saints, angels, and, on the north wall, *The Communion of the Apostles*: Christ, standing behind the altar as a priest, is distributing bread and wine to his disciples. These paintings were, unfortunately, inexpertly restored, suffering great loss of detail. Although damaged, the extraordinary quality of the murals of the earlier layer is still discernible.

The altar screen of the main haykal, *constructed of reused sculpture.*

*The upper part of the
east wall: fragments of
a series of canopies of
the first layer and two
saints of the second
layer of paintings.*

OPPOSITE:
*The ceiling with the
cassette pattern.*

268

*The west wall.
Fragments of saints
of the second layer
show in the upper
part. All other
decoration belongs
to the older layer.*

The north wall. In the upper part is the mural of The Communion of the Apostles.

273

The Church of St. Mercurius

THE CHURCH OF ST. MERCURIUS *(Abu Sayfayn)* stands at the center of the city of Akhmim near the police station. Its floor is about three meters below the level of the street. The design of the church follows the domed-hall type that began to appear in the fourteenth century. Thus, it belongs typologically to the last phase of development in Egyptian church building.

The current church dates to the sixteenth or seventeenth century. It was originally five bays wide and three rooms deep: the eastern part comprises three semi-circular sanctuaries flanked by two rectangular rooms with two bays in front of each sanctuary and room. The northern corner room and the northern two bays do not exist because an adjoining church was built in their place. The two bays in front of the central sanctuary are covered by domes on squinches surmounted by windows. The church's columns, arches and domes are built of baked bricks, which are painted dark red in cross patterns. The wooden screens of the sanctuaries are decorated with crosses and geometrical designs. Nineteenth-century wooden ciboria (baldachins) supported by four pillars are erected above the altar in each of the three sanctuaries. The ciboria are ornamented with scenes of Christ, the Virgin Mary, and angels.

Icon of the Resurrection, nineteenth century.

Icon of the Entombment painted by A[na]stasi al-Qudsi al-Rumi, nineteenth century.

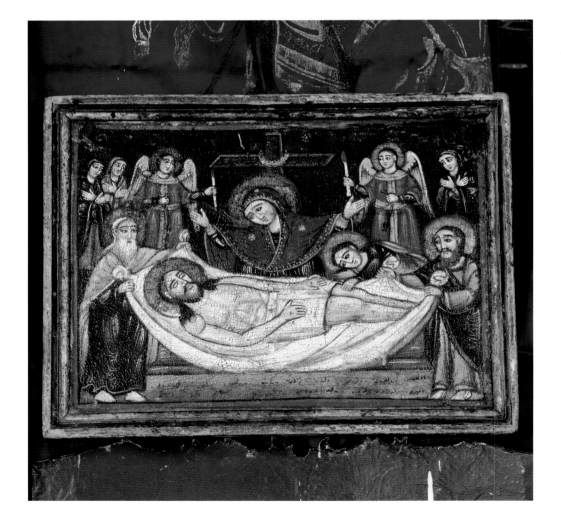

LEFT:
*Wooden screen of
the central altar.*

OPPOSITE:
*Interior of new
church adjoining
the old church of
Abu Sayfayn.*

*Ciborium (baldachin)
of the southern altar.*

The Red Monastery

THE MONASTERY OF ST. PSHAI is more commonly known as the Red Monastery (*al-Dayr al-Ahmar*). The historian al-Maqrizi (d. 1442) used this name, explaining that it was built of red bricks.[96] Saint Pshai was a hermit and companion of St. Bigul, St. Shenute's uncle. As a young boy, Shenute (d. ca. 465), abbot of the neighboring monastery that later carried his name (also called the White Monastery), was initiated to monastic life by his uncle and St. Pshai. Although it is not known whether St. Pshai founded the monastery or whether it was dedicated to his memory, it is most likely situated on the place where he lived. When Shenute became head of the White Monastery, he also assumed authority of the Monastery of St. Pshai as it became a component of his monastic federation.

Historical documentation is scarce. In 1301 the painter Mercurius left a dated inscription in the sanctuary of the church. Father Vansleb visited the site in 1673, to find only the church with its high enclosure walls. He wrote that the sanctuary, where Mass was celebrated, was preserved but the nave had been ruined. The columns were still standing and he admired the beauty of the capitals.[97] The evening before Vivant Denon visited Sohag in 1798, Mamluks had sacked the church complex and it was still burning.[98]

On the north wall of the nave of the Church of St. Pshai faint remains of a pattern of crosses in medallions survive.

Scholars have mainly been interested in the larger, mid-fifth-century church of Shenute's monastery. The Church of St. Pshai (early sixth century) was similar in outline but smaller and built with cheaper materials: brick instead of limestone blocks. High brick walls enclose a basilican type church with a trilobed sanctuary and a long narrow hall along the south wall. Reused sculptured friezes surmount the northern and southern entrances. At present, the sanctuary (the only part of a building preserved inside the walls) functions as a church.

The architectural system of the trilobed sanctuary consists of richly decorated niches in two superimposed registers. Columns between the niches are carrying architraves for the upper register and the semi-dome. Two features make this sanctuary unique: first, most of the decorative sculpture is original to the construction of the church and, second, the walls are painted throughout. Color enlivens the sculpture pieces and imitation stone patterns or decorative designs cover all architectural elements. The semi-domes were painted with Christ enthroned with the Four Living Creatures, flanked by archangels (east); the nursing Virgin enthroned, accompanied by prophets, saints, and angels in a richly decorated framework (north), and a similar architectural framework with Christ enthroned, surrounded by St. John the Baptist and his father Zacharias, angels, evangelists, and patriarchs (south).

Through the centuries, soot and grime had been blackening the paintings, and a process of restoration began in 2002.[99] The northern lobe has been finished and shows its former splendor. New research dates the semi-dome murals (the fourth layer of wall painting) to around 800, while the architectural paintings belong to the second layer. The wealth of details coming to light will considerably enrich our knowledge of painting in late antique Christian Egypt, as well as of the history of the monastery.

The entrance in the north wall, embellished with reused architectural sculpture.

Triptych showing the
holy monks Bigul,
Pshai, and Shenute.

Church of St. Pshai,
north lobe of the
trilobed sanctuary. St.
Shenute is represented
in the niche.

Fragment of a face from an earlier layer coming through.

RIGHT:
The northern semi-dome: the Virgin Mary enthroned, nursing her son and surrounded by angels and prophets. From left to right: Ezekiel, Jeremiah, Isaiah, and Daniel. On the columns, an unidentified saint and St. Paul are depicted.

The White Monastery

The Archangel Michael.

OPPOSITE:
The Church of St. Shenute, the north lobe of the trilobed sanctuary.

SAINT SHENUTE OF ATRIPE (d. ca. 465) was five or seven years old when his father entrusted him to his maternal uncle, the monk St. Bigul. After a vision that the boy would be a great leader of men, St. Bigul made him a monk and kept him with him. Shenute became head of a monastic federation comprising several monasteries for men and women, where the Pachomian Rule of shared work and prayer was strictly interpreted. He was the first prolific writer in Coptic, the language of the common people. Much of his work survives and is an endless source of information on various aspects of fifth- and sixth-century monastic life in the region.[100]

In the twelfth century, the Monastery of St. Shenute was still functioning, but al-Maqrizi (d. 1442) reported that it was in ruins.[101] The church, built in the middle of the fifth century, survives. It was constructed of large limestone blocks (hence its name) on a basilican plan with a trilobed sanctuary, a baptistery, and a narthex. Along the south wall of the church runs a long narrow hall with a square room at the east end, probably a library. The high outer walls of the complex include a cornice such as was often used in the construction of pharaonic temples.

An unidentified patriarch.

In the sanctuary, two registers of elaborately decorated niches are built in the walls. Columns set between the niches carry the architraves for the upper register and the semi-dome. Undoubtedly, the architectural system was once completely painted, as still evident in the church of the Monastery of St. Pshai. Similar niches were set in the walls of the side aisles. The sculpture consisted of reused elements from older buildings and sculpture that was made to order.

Fire heavily damaged the church in the seventh century. It was renovated faithfully to the old plan and columns and capitals were reused. A *khurus* was inserted in front of the trilobed sanctuary, although the existing *khurus* was most likely built in the eleventh or twelfth century. Father Vansleb's description of the church in 1673 is still accurate: the sanctuary is functioning as a church while the nave and side aisles are unroofed and ruined.[102]

Paintings survive in the central and southern semi-domes, and on the ground floor. The eastern semi-dome shows Christ enthroned with the Four Living Creatures surrounded by four medallions with the Evangelists working on their Gospels. Bilingual inscriptions (Coptic and Armenian) date the painting to the twelfth century and are witness to the presence of Armenians in the monastery at that time. In the southern semi-dome, angels are carrying a triumphal cross in *mandorla*, flanked by the Virgin Mary and St. John the Baptist. Together, they form a deesis. The Virgin and Child and St. Michael flank the central semi-dome, while an unidentified patriarch was painted on a pillar. Further study will have to prove whether all paintings belong to the same phase of decoration.

Excavations of the monastic settlement surrounding the church are in progress. In conjunction with the results of an extensive study of Shenute's writings, a new history of the monastery will be written.

The enthroned Christ in the eastern semi-dome. The four Evangelists working on their Gospels are depicted in four roundels (twelfth century).

The Virgin Mary and Child.

OPPOSITE:
The south lobe of the trilobed sanctuary. In the semi-dome, angels are carrying a triumphal cross in mandorla, flanked by the Virgin Mary and St. John the Baptist.

The steps of the old
throne-like ambon
in the nave.

OPPOSITE:
The nave of the
church. View to
the southwest.

The Monasteries of Naqada

S IX MONASTIC SETTLEMENTS SURVIVE TO THE SOUTHWEST OF NAQADA at the edge of the cultivated land and the desert. They trace their roots to the sixth century, when the area, known as the Mountain of Benhadab or Tsenti, was populated with hermits and small monasteries. Traditionally, St. Pisentius (569–632) is associated with this region. This popular bishop of Qift (Coptos, about 15 kilometers north of Naqada, on the east bank of the Nile) was famous as a preacher and wonder-worker, but was also a good organizer. Many of his writings and correspondence are preserved. St. Pisentius's influence on monastic life in the region is widely attested to.

Unfortunately, the ancient structures of existing monasteries have rarely survived. The majority of the churches date to the eighteenth and nineteenth centuries or even later. For most of the twentieth century, travelers and scholars visiting the deserted monasteries in the Naqada region found nearly all churches, old and new, neglected or in ruins. However, during the past twenty-five years, the monasteries have been extensively rebuilt, restored, and reoccupied by monks or nuns.

The Church of the Cross. The haykal *with two altars. Because of an oil-miracle (oil appeared on the altar top and found its way down) witnessed regularly, the oldest altar could no longer be used for masses. A new altar was built in the 1960s, leaving the older altar in place.*

The Monastery of the Cross.

The Monastery of the Cross

The Monastery of the Cross *(Dayr al-Salib)* has an uncommon dedication. Churches and monasteries in Egypt were (and are) usually dedicated to the Virgin Mary or saints. The provenance of the name is not clear and the history of the monastery is virtually unknown. In the seventh century, Apa Andreas, a friend of Bishop Pisentius, was most probably one of the abbots. By 1668 the Capuchin fathers Protais and François reported that this was the only inhabited monastery in the region.[103]

The architect Somers Clarke described and measured the Church of the Cross in 1901. At that time, it had already fallen into ruin. He noted hieroglyphs on the columns, which were

taken from a pharaonic building. The two churches of the monastery were completely pulled down in 1917 and new churches were built shortly afterward. A thorough renovation of the Church of St. Shenute and the Church of the Cross has just been completed. In the latter church, remains of late antique building elements and pharaonic columns were found. These photographs were taken during the restoration.

The Monastery of St. Andrew

The Monastery of St. Andrew (Dayr Andra'us) is also called Dayr Abu al-Lif, the Monastery of the Father of the Beard. Whether Andrew was the abbot of the Monastery of the Cross and a friend of St. Pisentius is not certain. The old churches of the monastery have not survived. A modern, almost square church building with sixteen domes contains the three-aisled Church of St. Andrew and, in the southern bay, a small Church of the Virgin, separated from the main church by a wooden screen.

LEFT AND OPPOSITE: *The Church of St. Andrew.*

The ruins of the Church of St. John.

OPPOSITE:
The Church of St. George.

The Church of St. George. The architect designed the church building as an altar. The horns on the corners of the roof refer to a so-called horned altar, used for burning incense or for burnt offerings in various pagan cults in late-antique Egypt.

The Monastery of St. George

The Monastery of St. George *(Dayr Mar Girgis)* is also known as Dayr al-Magma'. The name al-Magma' might be interpreted as 'of the assembly.' In local tradition however, it means 'place of provisioning,' the place where supplies for monasteries in the neighborhood were kept. Little is known about the history of the monastery that was once the largest and most important of the Christian settlements in the Naqada area.

The History of the Churches and Monasteries of Egypt (ca. twelfth century) appears to refer to this monastery as the Monastery of St. Pisentius and says that the tomb of the bishop was "outside the monastery." However, the author also claims that St. Pisentius's tomb was near the Monastery of the Archangel Michael.[104] The Capuchin fathers Protais and François (1668) reported that St. Pisentius was buried near the Monastery of St. George.[105]

The western part of the Church of St. George. The large stone might originally have been placed as a screen, partitioning off the entrance. Locally, it is called "the priest's step."

The History of the Churches and Monasteries of Egypt continues, "and to the west of it, there is a well of water which was visited by our Lady and the Lord Christ with the righteous old man Joseph."[104] A Holy Family tradition this far south of the Monastery of al-Muharraq, customarily their most southern resting place, has not been attested elsewhere. There is a well to the west of the monastery. In local tradition, it is called "the well of the mud." The mud is believed have miraculous powers and villagers mark their houses with crosses of mud to assure divine protection.

Originally, the monastery possessed four churches. One of these was rebuilt in the 1920s: the Church of St. George. Part of the ruined Church of St. John is still visible. It has undergone several building phases. The original building date is hard to ascertain but a rebuilding with domes probably took place in the twelfth century.

The Monastery of St. Pisentius

The monastery dedicated to the famous St. Pisentius, Bishop of Qift, is situated about 400 meters to the south of the Monastery of St. George. It seems that originally, only the tomb of St. Pisentius existed at this site. At the beginning of the twentieth century, a church and enclosing walls were built around the burial place of the bishop.

The Monastery of St. Pisentius, domes of the church.

The Monastery of St. Victor. In the foreground are the remains of a deserted extension of the monastery. It might date to medieval times.

The Monastery of St. Victor

The Church of St. Victor (Mar Buqtur) is the only early building that is still in use in the Naqada monasteries. The outer walls of the church most likely belong to an eighth-century basilica, while the interior and sanctuary area were renovated and restored several times.

St. Victor was (and still is) a popular equestrian saint, martyred under the Emperor Diocletian (late third to early fourth century). It is said that Bishop Pisentius revived his cult in this monastery.

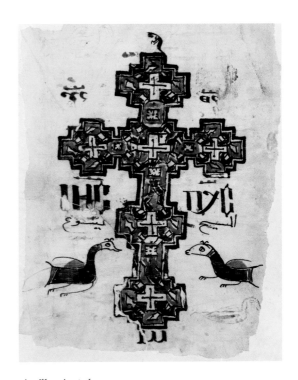

An illuminated liturgical manuscript.

LEFT:
The Church of Saint Victor. The screens of the altar rooms consist of a brick wall with a central window and two doorways.

The Church of the Virgin Mary.

OPPOSITE:
The Church of the Archangel Michael.

The Monastery of the Archangel Michael

The Monastery of the Archangel Michael *(Dayr al-Malak Mikha'il)* was in former times also called Dayr al-'Ayn, the Monastery of the Well. It was known for its fresh water, as *The History of the Churches and Monasteries of Egypt* (ca. twelfth century) reported "from which travelers drink when they pass through the district. The monastery contains a keep, and is surrounded by an enclosing wall. It is said to possess the body of St. Pisentius."[107]

For a long time, it was the church and the cemetery of the Christians of nearby Qamula. Recently, the monastery has been rebuilt and extended. The two churches of the monastery are dedicated to the Virgin Mary and the Archangel Michael. The latter church may date from the fourteenth century.

Churches in Luxor Temple and Karnak Temple

At THE END OF THE THIRD CENTURY AD, the great temple of Amun in Luxor was no longer in use. Under the Emperor Diocletian (284–305), it was enclosed by defensive walls and became the center of a Roman military camp. The Persian army used it as administrative headquarters during their occupation of Egypt (619–629). After they left, the complex seems to have fallen into ruin.

A treasure of silver liturgical objects and coins dates the earliest Christian church in the former temple and camp to the first half of the seventh century. Two other churches were discovered that are dated to a slightly later period. One of these churches is situated under the mosque of Abu al-Haggag that was built in the court of Ramesses II. The west wall with a row of windows is well preserved. A fourth church was excavated in front of the pylon of Ramesses II, the gateway of the temple, while a fifth was built along the avenue of sphinxes that connected Luxor with Karnak. Built with dressed stone, partly using blocks from the temple, they all show a basilican plan with a return aisle and an apse with side chambers. Little is left of the churches and even the plans cannot be reconstructed with certainty. During the restoration of the temple, a number of later structures were demolished in order to replace the reused temple blocks.

OPPOSITE:
Column of the southwest church in Luxor Temple. In the background is the Forecourt of Amenhotep III.

Sculptured block of one of the churches in the temple complex.

Fragments of sculptured friezes.

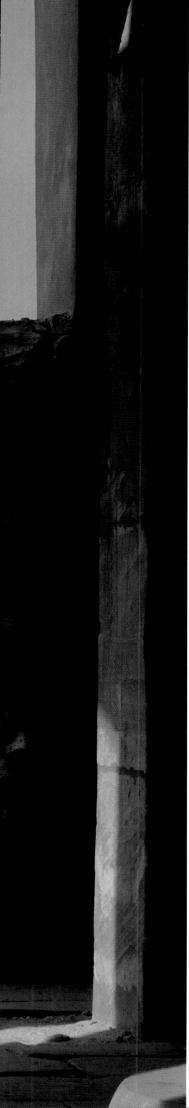

The Festival Hall of Thutmosis
III in Karnak Temple. View to
the north. The Festival Hall
was converted in the late
antique period to a church.

Painting of a saint
on one of the
monumental columns
of the Festival Hall
of Thutmosis III.

The Monastery of St. Hatre

SAINT HATRE (ANBA HADRA) WAS THE SON of Christian parents who lived as a hermit in a cave near the city. His reputation as a healer of mental and physical illness grew quickly and he was ordained bishop of Aswan under Patriarch Theophilus (385–412).

Where St. Hatre's cave was situated is not clear. The monastery that bears his name (called St. Simeon by later travelers) was built on the west bank of the Nile at Aswan. It might already have existed in the fifth century, and it was deserted in the thirteenth century. The layout of the monastery consists of two levels connected by a staircase. The two areas follow the natural terraces of the site, dividing the monastery in to a public part and a private part. An enclosure wall with towers once surrounded the whole complex and each section had its own entrance. The lower terrace includes the church with a baptistery and guest houses while the upper terrace was reserved for the monks. A huge keep (eleventh to twelfth century), which contained permanent living quarters, a refectory, and a kitchen, dominates this area, supplemented by utility and workrooms, a bakery, an oil press, and pottery kilns.

A doorway on the upper terrace.

The church was built in the eleventh century, following a domed oblong plan: the nave consists of two domed sections. Side aisles were elongated to flank the sanctuary where a *khurus* and a rectangular altar room make up a trefoil. In the altar room, the semi-dome contains remains of paintings showing an enthroned Christ in mandorla, carried by two angels. To the right is a standing person with a rectangular nimbus, a type seldom used in Christian art in Egypt. As a rule, saints and biblical persons have a round nimbus. A rectangular nimbus might have been used when the person depicted was still alive when the painting was made. Below, on the upper part of the walls, fragments of a frieze of the Twenty-Four Priests are still visible. The Virgin Mary and Child are painted between angels in the niche in the west wall. Traditionally, the murals are dated to the eleventh to twelfth century. However, at the beginning of the twentieth century, the painted program was better preserved and scholars visiting the monastery observed two layers of painting in the church. The murals have not been studied properly so far.

At the western end of the church is an entrance to a cave in the rock (most probably created by quarry activities) that served as an anchorite's cell. It belongs to an earlier period and still has paintings dating to the sixth to eighth century. The walls were decorated with a row of saints while the ceiling has a geometrical pattern, filled with busts of saints. It is possible that this cave is the former cell of St. Hatre.

An oil press.

The ceiling paintings of the cave at the western end of the church.

307

The Monastery at Qubbat al-Hawwa

SOME SIX KILOMETERS NORTH of the Monastery of St. Hatre, pharaonic tombs for the governors of Aswan were cut into the cliff. Around these tombs, the monastic settlement of Qubbat al-Hawwa developed. It is named after the tomb of a shaykh who was buried nearby. The original name of the monastery is unknown.

In the early Christian period, hermits used these tombs for dwellings and they installed a church in the Tomb of Khune, probably in the sixth or seventh century. During the eleventh to twelfth centuries, the settlement expanded in the same way as St. Hatre. A staircase connected two natural terraces. Residential buildings, a refectory and utility rooms were constructed on the upper terrace and a new church was built on the lower terrace, outside the Tomb of Khune. It was enlarged at a later stage. The layout of the church is still traceable and is similar in plan to the Church of St. Hatre. Only the western part of the second building stage has been preserved. It contains a large niche with a semi-dome (a peculiarity of the Aswan churches) that is decorated with a bust of Christ in a mandorla carried by angels. In the lower zone, the twelve apostles surround the Virgin Mary. A graffito in the niche contains the date 1125 and makes clear that these murals were painted before that date. On the wall to the right, the west wall of a rectangular room or corridor, six standing figures were painted; five of these have rectangular nimbi. Their identity is unknown.

The choice of themes, the use of a rectangular nimbus, and other aspects of the paintings, as well as the architecture, inscriptions and graffiti (in Coptic and Arabic) still await an extensive study.

OPPOSITE:
View of the Monastery at Qubbat al-Hawwa from the Nile.

The niche in the west wall with the painting of Christ in mandorla, carried by angels in the semi-dome, and the Virgin Mary and the apostles below. To the right, the row of figures with rectangular nimbi.

Glossary

Abuna: Father

ambon: Pulpit

ciborium: canopy. A freestanding domed structure covering the altar. The surviving ciboria in Egyptian churches consist of a wooden dome resting on four stone, marble or wooden columns. The interior of the dome and the spandrels of the exterior are painted with figural scenes.

deesis: (Gr. 'entreaty') a representation of Christ accompanied by his mother Mary and St. John the Baptist, who intercede for mankind.

haykal: altar room.

iconostasis: a wooden screen that partitions off the sanctuary of a church. It is decorated with icons.

khurus: a transverse space reserved for the clergy between the altar room(s) and the nave of the church.

laqqan: basin in the floor of a church, used for the ceremony of foot washing on Maundy Thursday.

laura: A semi-organized monastic community. The monks lived on their own or in small groups, assembling once a week for Mass and a common meal.

mandorla: an almond-shaped halo enlosing a whole person.

martyrion: early Christian shrine, built in commemoration or as the burial place of a martyr.

mashrabiya: projecting oriel window that features wooden latticework made up of intricately carved segments connected without nails.

Melkite: Christians accepting the decrees of the Council of Chalcedon of 451. They support Christ's two separate human and divine natures after the Incarnation.

monophysite: adherent to the belief of the union of Christ's human and divine natures after the Incarnation.

naos: the area of a church in which the laity assembles, the nave, and, when provided, the side aisles and return aisle.

narthex: tranverse vestibule of a church.

Nilometer: A small building with gauges for measuring the Nile river's water levels.

orans: figure depicted frontally with arms raised in an attitude of prayer.

reredos: the ornamental screen at the back of an altar.

soffit: the underside of an architectural structure, such as an arch.

synaxarion: a liturgical book containing texts about saints and feasts, arranged according to the calendar.

synthronon: a bench or raised platform for the clergy set against the east wall of the apse in a church, usually incorporating a bishop's throne.

The Four Living Creatures, cherubim and seraphim: these were angelic beings. Their body was covered with four or six eye-studded wings and they had the head, hands, and feet of a man, except for The Four Living Creatures, who had the faces of a man, lion, ox, and eagle. They were part of the heavenly court, standing around the throne of God and praising Him continuously. The characteristics of these heavenly beings, described in Is. 6:2–7, Ez. 1, and Rev. 4:6–9 are often mixed up in visual art.

The Twenty-Four Priests (or Elders): appear as seated around the throne of God, praying and praising Him continuously (Rev. 4–5). From an early date, they were held in high regard in the Coptic Church. They are seen as intercessors for mankind (the incense in their censers symbolizes the prayers of saints). In magical texts, the reciting of their names protected against evil.

vita: life, biography.

Notes

1   Den Heijer 1996, 69–77, with earlier literature.
     Translations: Evetts 1907, Evetts 1910, Evetts 1915, 'Abd
     el-Masih and Burmester 1943, Atiya, 'Abd el-Masih, and
     Burmester 1948, Atiya, A.S., 'Abd el-Masih, and
     Burmester 1949, Khater and Burmester 1968, Khater and
     Burmester 1970 and Khater and Burmester 1974.

2   Den Heijer 1993, 1994, and 1996, 77–80; Zanetti 1995.
     Translations: Evetts and Butler 1895; al-Suryani 1992.

3   Wüstenfeld 1845; Evetts and Butler 1895, 305–46.

4   Vansleb 1677; on his life and travels see Delahaye 2003.

5   Martin 1982.

6   Denon 1802. Reprint 1989–1990, with a historical
     introduction by J.C. Vautin.

7   Mayeur-Jaouen 1992.

8   Bradshaw 2004.

9   Frend 1996, 199.

10   P. Grossmann, "Early Christian Architecture in the Nile
     Valley," in *Coptic Art and Culture*, ed. H. Hondelink
     (Cairo: Shouhdy Publishing House, 1990), 3.

11   Grossmann 1979, 232–36.

12   Similar to a church at Arcadius in Maryut.

13   Emmel 2004.

14   Grossmann 1998b, 281–302.

15   Capuani 1999, 51.

16   Kleinbauer 1987, 277–93.

17   Grossmann 1982, 7–13.

18   Bolman (ed.) 2002, xvi.

19   Jones 2002, 30.

20   Grossmann 2002, 542.

21   Famous hermits, monks, and founders of monasteries:
     St. Antony the Great (d. 356), St. Pachomius (d. 346), St.
     Paul the Hermit (d. 348?), and St. Macarius the Great (d.
     390).

22   Coptic Orthodox patriarchs of the See of St. Mark: St.
     Mark the Evangelist, the first patriarch (d. 68). There
     were four patriarchs called Peter before Benjamin. The
     most famous was Peter I, the last martyr (d. 311);
     Athanasius I (d. 373); Liberius, Pope of Rome (352–366),
     supporter of Athanasius's theological views; Kyrillos
     (Cyril) I (d. 444), and Dioscoros I (d. 458).

23   Paris, BnF, 12914, fol. 125r-v (Sahidic), ninth–tenth
     century, provenance: Sohag, White Monastery ? (Müller
     1959, 341–42 [text] and 345–46 [trans.]; cf. Coquin 1975,

34–35). J. van der Vliet (Leiden University) made a new
     English translation from the original text.

24   Dayr Abu Maqar, Ms. 207*Taa* (Bohairic), AD 1348, fol. 23
     v–24v; ed. and trans. Coquin 1975, 130–33.

25   'Paradise' could mean first, the Garden of Eden of the
     Book of Genesis. Second, it was used for the Kingdom of
     God, Heaven, or the Heavenly Jerusalem. Third, it could
     also point to an intermediate place, the abode of the
     souls of the righteous where they await the Resurrection
     of the Dead and the Last Judgment. The latter two
     definitions were sometimes mixed up or used
     indiscriminately (Daniélou 1954, 433–72; Dumuleau
     1992, 37–51.

26   Horner 1902, 394–95 and 13.

27   For example in *The Book of the Investiture of the Archangel
     Gabriel* attributed to Stephen Protomartyr (New York,
     Pierpont Morgan Library M 593, 892–93, fol. 45v°
     (Depuydt 1993 I, 214–16: no. 111-2; ed. and trans. Müller
     1962, I:77 (text), II: 95 [trans.]). Cf. Meinardus 1986–1987.

28   Ibn Sabba, *The Book of the Precious Pearl of Ecclesiastical
     Sciences*, after the first quarter of the fourteenth century
     (ed. and trans. Périer 1922, 738 and 753).

29   Van Loon 1999, 109–24.

30   Fifth–seventh century Syriac dedication hymns for
     churches, partly based on Alexandrian theological ideas,
     underline this theory (McVey 1983 and 1993).

31   Saqqara: for bibliography see Wietheger 1992; Bawit: for
     bibliography see note 35.

32   All wall painting conservation work at the Red
     Monastery has been funded by the United States
     Agency for International Development (USAID) and
     administered by the American Research Center in Egypt
     (ARCE), with the collaboration of the Coptic Church
     and the Egyptian Supreme Council of Antiquities (SCA).
     The project director is E. Bolman, and the head of
     conservation is L. De Cesaris, assisted by A. Sucato
     (Bolman 2004a and 2006b).

33   The restoration was a similar ARCE–USAID funded
     Egyptian Antiquities Project in cooperation with the
     SCA and the Coptic Church, 1996–1999. The results are
     presented and studied in Bolman (ed.) 2002.

34 Reports on the ongoing restoration of the Church of the Virgin (a joint Dutch–Polish project under direction of K.C. Innemée (Leiden University) and a bibliography can be found in various issues of *Hugoye*: http://syrcom.cua.edu/Hugoye. L. Van Rompay (Duke University, Durham, NC) studies the inscriptions in the church.

35 The excavations in Bawit are a joint project of the Louvre (D. Bénazeth and M.-H. Rutschowscaya) and the Institut français d'archéologie orientale in Cairo. News of the excavations and a bibliography can be found at www.louvre.fr/media/repository/ressources/ sources/pdf/src_document_51210_v2_m5657756983066 9676.pdf: *Nouvelles fouilles sur le site copte de Baouit.*

36 For example the Imperial Cult Room in Luxor Temple (mainly known from nineteenth-century watercolors by J.G. Wilkinson, see Kalavrezou-Maxeiner 1975, figs. 6–14 and pls. I–IV; at present the paintings are being restored (an ARCE–Egyptian Antiquities Conservation project in collaboration with the University of Chicago Epigraphic Survey in Luxor [Chicago House – dir. R. Johnson]); in tombs in Alexandria (Venit 2002) and in a villa in Amheida (Dakhla Oasis in the Western Desert, see www.mcah.columbia.edu/amheida, dir. R.S. Bagnall. Field reports 2005: H. Whitehouse).

37 Van Loon 2004.

38 Bolman 2004a and 2006b (see also note 32).

39 As described by the prophets Isaiah and Ezekiel and in John's Revelation. The Four Living Creatures, cherubim, and seraphim were angelic beings. Their bodies were covered with four or six eye-studded wings and they had the head, hands, and feet of a man, except for the Four Living Creatures who had the faces of a man, lion, ox, and eagle. They were part of the heavenly court, standing around the throne of God and praising Him continuously. The characteristics of these heavenly beings, described in Is. 6:2–7, Ez. 1, and Rev. 4:6–9, are often mixed up in visual art.

40 According to apocryphal stories, a midwife called Salomé was one of the first persons to adore the Christ child. She might have been a relative of the Virgin Mary, and she accompanied the Holy Family on their flight into Egypt (Van Loon 2006).

41 Van Moorsel and De Grooth 2000.

42 Van Moorsel 2000b–d.

43 Van Moorsel 2000d, 188–89.

44 Hymns on Mary, no. 7. Trans. Brock 1984, 60.

45 Innemée in Innemée and Van Rompay 2002, [1]–[11].

46 For the thirteenth-century paintings, see Leroy 1982, 61–74 and pls. 107–46; Hunt 1985.

47 Innemée in Innemée, Van Rompay, and Sobczynski 1999, [7].

48 Young 1981, 349–50 (text) and 353–54 (trans.).

49 Inv. no. 1172, from the Church of Sts. Sergius and Bacchus, Old Cairo (Gabra and Alcock 1999, 93; Gabra and Eaton-Krauss 2007, 194–95).

50 Van Moorsel 1995a; Bolman (ed.) 2002. See also note 33.

51 The Twenty-Four Priests or Elders are seated around the throne of God, praying and praising Him continuously (Rev. 4–5). From an early date, they have been held in high regard in the Coptic Church. They are seen as intercessors for mankind (the incense in their censers symbolizes the prayers of saints). In magical texts, the reciting of their names protected against evil (Van Loon 1999, 153n with literature).

52 Van Moorsel 1995a; Van Loon 1999, 81–106, 126–41, 154–58, 163–67; Bolman in Bolman (ed.) 2002, 91–125; Van Loon 2003 and 2004. The resurrected Christ meeting the women in the garden and the women at the empty tomb (Matt. 28:1–9) above the entrance to the central *haykal*, and the two archangels on the soffit of the arch between *khurus* and nave, and nave and southern side chapel, are later additions, probably from the second half of the thirteenth century (Bolman in Bolman (ed.) 2002, 127–40).

53 Recently, fragments of this theme were discovered in the apse of the southern altar room in the Church of Sts. Sergius and Bacchus in Old Cairo. It turned out to be the second layer of painting, repeating the same subject. On the basis of stylistic parallels, it might be dated to around 1200. (Milward Jones 2006; Bolman 2006a, who assigns a somewhat later date to this painting. The restoration was an ARCE-funded project.)

54 A team from the Polish Center of Mediterranean Archaeology of the University of Warsaw under direction of W. Godlewski discovered and restored the wall paintings during the years 1991–1999 (Godlewski 2000; Godlewski 2005a).

55 Jeudy in Snelders and Jeudy 2006, 114–22; Jeudy in Immerzeel and Jeudy, in press.

56 Coptic Museum, Cairo, inv. no. 7118 (Gabra and Alcock 1999, 58–59).

57 'Crusader art' consists of works of art produced in the Middle East (for example icons, miniatures, wall paintings) characterized by a choice of themes, composition, and styles from Europe and lands where crusaders created a stronghold, the Crusader kingdoms. There was a mutual influence. Through contact with artists working in a Christian environment in the Middle East, themes, iconography, and compositions were introduced into European art.

58   Bolman and Lyster in Bolman (ed.) 2002, 77–154.

59   Leroy 1982, pls. 29–30; Van Loon 1999, 45–47, 141–45.

60   Van Loon 1999, 50–51, 158–63 and figs. 54–57.

61   Leroy 1982, pls. 85–90.

62   Van Moorsel 1992, 177.

63   Hunt 1985.

64   Lyster in Bolman (ed.) 2002, 140–54; Jeudy in Snelders and Jeudy 2006, 114–22; Jeudy in Immerzeel and Jeudy, in press.

65   The restoration of the paintings was an ARCE–USAID funded Egyptian Antiquities Project in cooperation with the SCA and the Coptic Church, 2001–2005. The results will be presented and studied in Lyster (ed.), in press.

66   Van Moorsel 2000a; Lyster 1999; Van Moorsel 2002; Lyster (ed.), in press.

67   For the history of icon painting in Egypt and a catalog with examples from all periods, see Skálová in Skálová and Gabra 2006. The following paragraphs are largely based on this book.

68   Zanetti 1991.

69   Rutschowscaya 1998; Skálová in Skálová and Gabra 2006, 168–69.

70   Z. Skálová directed these restoration projects.

71   Jeudy 2004.

72   Van Moorsel 1991.

73   At present, this monastic complex is being excavated by the University of Leiden, under direction of K.C. Innemée (Innemée 2005).

74   See "The Art of Coptic Churches," in this volume, note 34 and page 32.

75   The chrism is the holy oil for sacramental use. With the assistance of bishops from all over Egypt, the patriarch himself consecrates the chrism. The ceremony takes place on Maundy Thursday, although not every year, only whenever a new supply of the chrism is necessary. From the twelfth to the fourteenth century, the ceremony often took place in the Monastery of St. Macarius.

76   This miracle is, with various details, among others, described in the *History of the Patriarchs, The Churches and Monasteries of Egypt* (see following note) and the Coptic *Synaxarion* (the Calendar of Saints; cf. den Heijer 2004, 49–57).

77   Evetts and Butler 1895, 116–22.

78   A *katib* (scribe or secretary) was a high official, to be compared with the modern function of minister, secretary of state, or deputy secretary (Sellheim and Soudel 1978).

79   Inv. no. 738 (Gabra and Alcock 1999, 102–103; Gabra and Eaton-Krauss 2007, 215–17); Inv. no. 778 (Jeudy in Snelders and Jeudy 2006, 114–22).

80   Butler 1884, vol. I: 115–16, 277; vol. II: 281–82. Eucharistic wine is made from raisins that are soaked in water and crushed in a wine press or squeezed by hand. After forty days, the juice is fit for sacramental use.

81   Evetts and Butler 1895, 3, 6, and 10–11. Abuna Samuel al-Suryani 1992, 1–9.

82   Since 1986, The Polish Center of Mediterranean Archaeology of the University of Warsaw, under direction of W. Godlewski, has been conducting research and excavations in and around the monastery. From 1991–1999, they also uncovered and restored the wall paintings in the Church of the Archangel Gabriel (for literature see Bibliographic References, page 317. C.E. ten Hacken (Leiden University) researches the manuscript tradition of the story of Aûr (ten Hacken 2004).

83   See chapter "The Art of Coptic Churches," in this volume, pages 33–34.

84   Martin 1982 vol. I, 41.

85   See "The Art of Coptic Churches," page 35 and note 65.

86   The complete story is known from Arabic and Ethiopian manuscripts (Boud'hors, Boutros, and Colin 2001). This homily was part of a group of texts promoting pilgrimage sites of the Holy Family.

87   Evetts and Butler 1895, 218.

88   Evetts and Butler 1895, 314.

89   For an architectural discussion, see "The Architecture of Coptic Churches" in this volume, pages 24–25.

90   *Historia Monachorum* VIII–1 (Russell and Ward 1980, 70). Cf. Davis 2001, 138–40.

91   Evetts and Butler 1895, 225–27.

92   Johann Georg, Duke of Saxony, 1931, 11.

93   Vansleb 1677, 364 and 377–78.

94   Munier 1940, 154–55.

95   Petrie 1907, 2.

96   Evetts and Butler 1895, 317–18.

97   Vansleb 1677, 376–77.

98   Denon 1802, 99.

99   See pages 31–32 and note 32.

100   Shenute's literary corpus is being edited and studied by an international group of scholars under the direction of Prof. Stephen Emmel (University of Münster, Germany). This project is part of the Consortium for Research and Conservation in the Monasteries of the Sohag Region (dir. E.S. Bolman), including work in the Monastery of St. Pshai, and survey and excavations around the Church of St. Shenute.

101   Evetts and Butler 1895, 235–40 and 317.

102   Vansleb 1677, 372–76.

103   Sauneron 1969, 137.

104   Evetts and Butler 1895, 233–34 (with corrections by
       Coquin, Martin, and Grossmann 1991b, 819–20) and 284.

105   Sauneron 1969, p. 137.

106   Evetts and Butler 1895, 233–34.

107   Evetts and Butler 1895, 283–84.

Bibliographic References

History of Christianity in Egypt (general)
Atiya (ed.) 1991; idem 1968; Badawy 1978; Bagnall 1993; Basset 1907–1929; Davis 2004; Gabra and Alcock 1993; Gabra and Alcock 1999; idem 2001; idem 2002; Gabra 2003 111–19; Guirguis 2000, 23–44; Hardy 1952; Haas 1997; Krause 1981; idem 1998; Meinardus 1977; idem 2006; Partrick 1996; Pearson 1986; Porkurat et al. 1996; Tagher 1998; Wilfong 1998; Wipszycka 1988.

The Cathedral of the Holy Virgin, Port Said
Meinardus 1977, 267 f.

The Pilgrimage Center of St. Dimyana Monastery
Grossmann 1982, 51–54; Samuel and Habib 1996, 100–102.

Churches of Alexandria (introduction)
Atiya 1991; Meinardus 1977, 170 ff.

The Coptic Patriarchal Church of St. Mark, Alexandria
Meinardus 1977, 170; Father Yuhanna of the Coptic Cathedral of St. Mark at Alexandria: personal communication of October 25, 2006.

The Church of St. Catherine, Alexandria
Meinardus 1977, 179 f; "Cronica" 1996.

The Anglican Church of St. Mark, Alexandria
Meinardus 1977, 184.

The Greek Orthodox Cathedral of St. Saba, Alexandria
Meinardus 1977, 172 f.

Monasteries in Wadi al-Natrun (general)
Evelyn White 1932; Evelyn White 1933; Grossmann 1997; Burmester 1954; Coptica 2 (2003) and Coptica 3 (2004): Proceedings of the Wadi al-Natrun Symposium, Wadi al-Natrun, Egypt, February 1–4, 2002; Grossmann 2004b.

The Monastery of al-Baramus, Wadi al-Natrun
Butler 1884, vol 1, 326–40; Johann Georg, Duke of Saxony 1914, 29–31; Johann Georg, Duke of Saxony 1930, 44; Meinardus 1977, 206–209; Meinardus 1989, 52–71; Cody, Grossmann, and Van Moorsel 1991; Van Moorsel 1992; Grossmann and Severin 1997; Van Loon 1999, 61–74; Gabra 2002, 38–42; Grossmann 2002, 499–501; Zibawi 2003, 136–45 and figs. 173–85; Van Loon 2004; el-Baramusi 2004.

The Monastery of the Syrians, Wadi al-Natrun
Butler 1884, vol 1, 306–26; Johann Georg, Duke of Saxony 1914, 31–36; Johann Georg, Duke of Saxony 1930, 44–45; Meinardus 1977, 217–24; Leroy 1982, 51–74; Hunt 1985; Meinardus 1989, 121–43; Cody and Grossmann 1991b; Van Moorsel 1995b; Innemée/Van Rompay 1998; Gabra 2002, 47–56; Grossmann 2002, 501–503; Hunt 2003; Van Loon 2003; Zibawi 2003, 128–33 and figs. 132, 161–67; den Heijer 2004; Immerzeel 2004a and 2004b; Parandowska 2004. Innemée, Van Rompay, and others in various issues of *Hugoye*: http://syrcom.cua.edu/Hugoye.

The Monastery of St. Pshoi, Wadi al-Natrun
Butler 1884, vol 1, 308–16; Johann Georg, Duke of Saxony 1914, 36–37; Johann Georg, Duke of Saxony 1930, 45; Meinardus 1977, 214–17; Meinardus 1989, 105–20; Cody and Grossmann 1991a; Van Loon 1999, 75–82; Gabra 2002, 43–46; Meinardus 2002, 74; Zibawi 2003, 134–35 and figs. 168–72.

The Monastery of St. Macarius, Wadi al-Natrun
Butler 1884, vol 1, 294–307; Johann Georg, Duke of Saxony 1914, 37–41; Johann Georg, Duke of Saxony 1930, 46; Leroy 1982, 3–49; Meinardus 1977, 214–17; Meinardus 1989, 72–104; Abuna Matta al-Miskin 1991; Van Loon 1999, 31–60; Gabra 2002, 56–63; Hunt 2004; Zibawi 2003, 134–35 and figs. 168–72.

The Church of the Holy Virgin Mary, Sakha
Gabra (ed.) 2001, 30, 50–52, 150 f; Samuel and Habib 1996, 103 f.

The Churches of Old Cairo (General)
Burmester 1955; Habib 1967; Coquin, Ch. 1974; Meinardus 1994.

The Church of St. Mercurius, Old Cairo
Butler 1884, vol 1, 75–135; Johann Georg, Duke of Saxony 1914, 9–13; Johann Georg, Duke of Saxony 1930, 12–13; Meinardus 1977, 228–92; Coquin, Ch. 1991a; Grossmann 1991a, 320–21; Van Loon 1999, 17–30; Middeldorf Kosegarten 2000, 36–44; Grossmann 2002, 505–507; Zibawi 2003, 164–75 and figs. 133–36, 214–29, 281, and 285; Jeudy in Snelders and Jeudy 2006, 114–22; Skálová in Skálová and Gabra 2006, 180–95, 198–99; Gabra and Eaton-Krauss 2007, 242–54.

The Tomb of Ibrahim and Girgis al-Guhari.
Atiya 1968, 100.

The Church of Sts. Sergius and Bacchus, Old Cairo
Butler 1884, vol 1, 181–205; Johann Georg, Duke of Saxony 1914, 5–6; Johann Georg, Duke of Saxony 1930, 15; Meinardus 1977, 275–79; Grossmann 1991a, 318; Meinardus 2002, 60–61; Grossmann 2002, 414–16; Zibawi 2003, figs. 137–40; Bolman 2006a; Grossmann 2006b; Milward Jones 2006; Gabra/Eaton-Krauss 2007, 231–39.

The Hanging Church, Old Cairo
Butler 1884, vol 1, 206–35; Johann Georg, Duke of Saxony 1914, 6–9; Johann Georg, Duke of Saxony 1930, 15; Meinardus 1977, 273–75; Hunt 1989; Coquin, Ch. 1991b; Grossmann 1991a, 319–20; Middeldorf Kosegarten 2000, 44–56; Zibawi 2003, 162–63 and figs. 43–45, 208–13, 283, and 286; Gabra and Eaton-Krauss 2007, 221–31.

The Church of St. Barbara, Old Cairo
Butler 1884, vol 1, 235–47; Johann Georg, Duke of Saxony 1914, 9; Patricolo and Monneret de Villard and Munier 1922; Johann Georg, Duke of Saxony 1930, 14; Meinardus 1972–1973; Meinardus 1977, 279–80; Grossmann 1991a, 318–19; Middeldorf Kosegarten 2000, 29–36; Grossmann 2002, 417; Zibawi 2003, figs. 41–42, 130, 282; Skálová in Skálová and Gabra 2006, 176–79; Jeudy in Snelders and Jeudy 2006, 114–22; Gabra and Eaton-Krauss 2007, 240–42.

The Greek Orthodox Church of St. George and the Sleeping Mary Greek Orthodox Church, Old Cairo
Coquin, Ch. 1974, 152–69; Meinardus 1977, 283–86; Grossmann 1991a, 320.

The Coptic Evangelical Church, Qasr al-Dubara
Rev. Dr. Abdel-Masih Estafanous: e-mail of October 18, 2006.

The Armenian Cathedral of St. Gregory the Illuminator, Ramses
Meinardus 1977, 321 f.

The Franciscan Church of the Assumption, Muski
Le Messager 1987

The Church of the Virgin, Harat Zuwayla
Butler 1884, vol 1, 271–78; Meinardus 1977, 301–304; Grossmann 1991a, 322–23; Wissa 1991; Meinardus 1994, 63–68; Zanetti 1995, 95–98; Middeldorf Kosegarten 2000, 56–58; Skálová in Skálová/Gabra 2006, 200–207; Jeudy in Immerzeel and Jeudy, in press.

The Church of St. Menas, Fumm al-Khalig
Habib 1967, 82–87; Coquin, Ch. 1974, 1–5; Burmester 1955, 56–59; Meinardus 1994, 48–51; Jeudy 2004, 67–87.

The Catholic Cathedral of St. Mark, Shubra
Meinardus 1977, 329.

The Jesuits' Holy Family Church, Faggala
Father Jacques Masson: e-mail of February 9, 2007.

The Coptic Evangelical Church, Faggala
Rev. Dr. Abdel-Masih Estafanous, e-mail message to the author, October 18, 2006.

The Church of the Holy Virgin, Zaytun
Meinardus 1977, 313 f; idem 1994, 80 f; Viaud 1979, 35.

The Jesuits' Holy Family Church, Matariya
Meinardus 1977, 333–35; Father Jacques Masson: e-mail of February 9, 2007.

The Holy Family Tree, Matariya
Meinardus 1987; Zanetti 1993; Gabra 1999; idem 2001

St. Cyril Melkite Catholic Church, Heliopolis
"Iconostase: St. Cyril." http://www.saintcyrille.com/icon.htm

The Basilica of Our Lady, Heliopolis
Meinardus 1977, 328 f.

The Old Cathedral of St. Mark, Azbakiya
Burmester 1955, 80 f; Habib 1967, 101; Meinardus 1994, 68–70.

The Cathedral of St. Mark, Abbasiya
Meinardus 1994, 72 f.

The Church of the Holy Virgin Mary and St. Pshoi, Abbasiya
Meinardus 1994, 73 f.

The Church of the Holy Virgin Mary and Anba Ruways, Abbasiya
Meinardus 1994, 73 f.

The Church of Anba Ruways, Abbasiya
Burmester 1955, 87–89; Habib 1967, 105 f; Meinardus 1994, 71 f.

The Chapel of St. Athanasius, Abbasiya
Meinardus 1994, 73–75.

The Shrine of St. Mark, Abbasiya
Meinardus 1994, 73 f.

The Church of St. Peter and St. Paul
Habib 1967, 102–104.

The Cathedral of the Holy Virgin Mary and St. Simeon the Tanner
Labib 1991, 10 f; Anonym. 1998.

The Church of the Holy Virgin, Maadi
Gabra 2001, 65, 73; Meinardus 1994, 82–84

The Monastery of the Archangel Gabriel, Fayyum
Johann Georg, Duke of Saxony 1930, 19; Meinardus 1977, 447–57; Timm 1984–92, vol. 2, 762–66; Meinardus and Grossmann 1991; Godlewski 2000; Gabra 2002, 64–71; Grossmann 2002, 513; Meinardus 2002, 53–56 and 77; Ten Hacken 2004; Godlewski 2005a and 2005b (with earlier literature); Czaja-Szewczak 2005; Łyżwa-Piber 2005; Parandowska 2005.

The Monastery of St. Antony, Red Sea
Johann Georg, Duke of Saxony 1930, 32–43; Meinardus 1977, 491–501; Timm 1984–92, vol. 2, 1287–330; Meinardus 1989, 1–32; Meinardus, Coquin, Martin, and Van Moorsel 1991; Van Moorsel 1995a; Van Loon 1999, 83–108; Bolman (ed.) 2002; Gabra 2002, 73–86; Zibawi 2003, 176–89 and figs. 129, and 230–49; Bolman 2004b; Van Loon 2004.

The Monastery of St. Paul, Red Sea
Johann Georg, Duke of Saxony 1931, 15–25; Meinardus 1977, 502–507; Meinardus 1989, 33–47; Timm 1984–92, vol. 2, 1359–1373; Meinardus, Coquin, Martin, and Van Moorsel 1991; Van Moorsel 2000a; Lyster 1999; Meinardus 2000; Gabra 2002, 87–93; Zibawi 2003, 190–91, 203–209 and figs. 250–52 and 270–80; Jones 2004; Lyster (ed.), in press.

The Church of St. Theodore, Minya
Meinardus 1977, 361f; al-Suryani 1990, 135 f.

The Church of the Holy Virgin, Minya
Johann Georg, Duke of Saxony 1930, 21–22; Meinardus 1977, 362–64; Timm 1984–92, vol. 2, 817–23; Grossmann, Coquin, Martin 1991; Ovadiah 1995; Boud'hors/Boutros 2000; Boutros 2000; Grossmann 2002, 343, n. 639; Meinardus 2002, 78–79; Boutros 2004.

The Monastery of Abu Fana, Minya
Munier 1940, 147–51; Martin 1972, 120–24; Meinardus 1977, 364–66; Timm 1984–92, vol. 2, 573–74; Coquin, Martin, and Grossmann 1991a; Meinardus 2002, 57–58; Grossmann 2002, 516–20; Buschhausen 2003.

Al-Ashmunayn, Minya
Timm 1984–92, vol. 1, 198; Grossmann and Severin 1991; Davis 2001, 137–43; Grossmann 2002, 441–43; Bagnall and Rathbone 2004, 162–67.

The Monastery of al-Muharraq, Asyut
Johann Georg, Duke of Saxony 1930, 23–25; Meinardus 1977, 379–84; Timm 1984–92, vol. 2, 750–56; Meinardus 1989, 155–67; Coquin and Martin 1991d; Davis 2001, 144–47; Hulsman 2001, 106–14; Meinardus 2002, 79, 83–84.

The Monastery of Durunka, Asyut
Meinardus 1977, 394–95; Timm 1984–92, vol. 2, 892–99, Coquin and Martin 1991c; Hulsman 2001, 115–20; Meinardus 2002, 80, 84.

The Cliff Churches of Dayr Rifa, Asyut
Johann Georg, Duke of Saxony 1931, 10–11; Pillet 1935–1938; Meinardus 1977, 395–96; Timm 1984–92, vol. 2, 1009–12; Coquin/Martin 1991e.

The Monastery of al-Zawya, Asyut
Petrie 1907, 2, 31; Munier 1940, 154–55; Meinardus 1977, 397; Timm 1984–92, vol. 4, 1648–49; Abuna Samuel al-Suryani 1990, 89; Coquin and Martin 1991f.

The Monastery of al-Ganadla, Asyut
Johann Georg, Duke of Saxony 1931, 8–10; Meinardus 1977, 397–98; Timm 1984–92, vol. 2, 634–36; Coquin and Grossmann 1991; Buschhausen and Korshid 1998; Meinardus 2002, 81; van Loon 2004.

The Church of St. Mercurius, Akhmim
Grossmann 1982, 196 f; al-Suryani 1990, 74 f; Moorsel 1994, 60; Jeudy 2004, 67–87.

The Red Monastery, Sohag
Johann Georg, Duke of Saxony 1914, 47; Monneret de Villard 1925–1926; Meinardus 1977, 404-406; Timm 1984–92, vol. 2, 639–42; Coquin, Martin, Severin, and Grossmann 1991; Laferrière 1993; Gabra 2002, 101–104; Grossmann 2002, 536–39; Meinardus 2002, 81; Zibawi 2003, 96–101 and figs. 113–25; Bolman 2004a; Bolman 2006b; Grossmann 2006a.

The White Monastery, Sohag
Johann Georg, Duke of Saxony 1914, 45–46; Monneret de Villard 1925–1926; Meinardus 1977, 401–404; Timm 1984–92, vol. 2, 601–34; Coquin, Martin, Grossmann, and Severin 1991; Gabra 2002, 94–100; Grossmann 2002, 528-536; Zibawi 2003, 192–96 and figs. 153–263; Brooks Hedstrom 2005. State of research on Shenute's life and writings: *Coptica* 4 (2005): The Life and Times of St. Shenouda the Archimandrite. A Conference held in Los Angeles, August 13–14, 2004.

Churches of Naqada
Somers Clarke 1912, 121–40; Johann Georg, Duke of Saxony 1914, 56–58; Johann Georg, Duke of Saxony 1930, 47–48; Sauneron 1969, 137; Meinardus 1977, 421–26; Timm 1984–92, vol. 1, 797–99; Timm 1984–92, vol. 5, 1727–34; al-Suryani and Habib 1990, 50–56; Coquin and Martin 1991a and 1991b; Coquin, Martin, and Grossmann 1991b, c, d, and f; Gabra and Müller 1991; Timm 1984–92, vol. 5, 2100–2105; Boutros and Décobert 2000; Grossmann 2002, 553–54; Van der Vliet 2002; Grossmann 2004a.

Churches in Luxor Temple and Karnak Temple
Grossmann 1991b; Grossmann 2002, 448–54; Bagnall and
Rathbone 2004, 188–92.

The Monastery of St. Hatre, Aswan
Johann Georg, Duke of Saxony 1914, 60–62; Monneret de
Villard 1927; Johann Georg, Duke of Saxony 1930, 48–49;
Meinardus 1977, 444–45; Timm 1984–92, vol. 2, 664–67;

Coquin, Martin, Grossmann, and Du Bourguet 1991; Gabra
2002, 108–14; Grossmann 2002, 562–65, Meurice 2006.

The Monastery at Qubbat al-Hawwa
Meinardus 1977, 443–44; Coquin, Martin, and Grossmann
1991e; Timm 1984–92, vol. 6, 2160–61; Gabra 2002, 105–107;
Dekker 2006.

Bibliography

Abd el-Masih, Y. and O.H.E.-Khs Burmester, eds. 1943. *History of the Patriarchs of the Egyptian Church known as the History of the Holy Church*, vol. II–i. Publications de la Société d'Archéologie Copte, Textes et Documents III. Cairo.

Anon. 1998. *The Biography of Saint Samaan the Shoemaker "the Tanner,"* 2nd ed. Cairo.

Atiya, A.S. 1952. "The Monastery of St. Catherine and the Mount Sinai Expedition." *Proceedings of the American Philosophical Society* 96, no. 5, 578–86.

———. 1968. *A History of Eastern Christianity*. London.

———. 1991. "Alexandria, Historic Churches," in *The Coptic Encyclopedia*, vol. 1, 92–95.

———., ed. 1991. *The Coptic Encyclopedia*, 8 vols. New York.

Atiya, A.S., Y. 'Abd el-Masih, and O.H.E.-Khs Burmester, eds. 1948. *History of the Patriarchs of the Egyptian Church known as the History of the Holy Church*, vol. II–ii. Publications de la Société d'Archéologie Copte, Textes et Documents IV. Cairo.

———. 1959. *History of the Patriarchs of the Egyptian Church known as the History of the Holy Church*, vol. II–iii. Publications de la Société d'Archéologie Copte, Textes et Documents V. Cairo.

Badawy A. 1978. *Coptic Art and Archaeology. The Arts of the Christian Egyptians from the Late Antique to the Middle Ages*. Cambridge, MA.

Bagnall, R.S. 1993. *Egypt in Late Antiquity*. Princeton, NJ.

Bagnall, R.S. and D.W. Rathbone, eds. 2004. *Egypt. From Alexander to the Copts*. London.

el-Baramusi, Zakaria (Abuna). "The Kasr of Saint Mary Baramus Monastery after the last restoration from AD 1994 to 1995," in *Coptic Studies on the Threshold of a New Millennium. Proceedings of the Seventh International Congress of Coptic Studies. Leiden, August 27–September 2, 2000*, eds. M. Immerzeel and J. van der Vliet, 1105–18. Louvain.

Basset, R. 1907–1929. "Le Synaxaire arabe-jacobite (rédaction copte). Texte arabe publié, traduit et annoté." *Patrologia Orientalis* 1 (1907) 215–379; 3 (1909) 243–545; 11 (1915) 505–859; 16 (1922) 185–424; 17 (1923) 525–782; 20 (1929) 741–90.

Bolman, E.S. 2004a. "Chromatic Brilliance at the Red Monastery Church." *Bulletin of the American Research Center in Egypt* 186, 1–9.

———. 2004b. "Scetis at the Red Sea: Depictions of Monastic Genealogy in the Monastery of Saint Antony." *Coptica* 3 (Proceedings of the Wadi al-Natrun Symposium, Wadi al-Natrun, Egypt, February 1–4, 2002), 1–16.

———. 2006a. "The Newly Discovered Paintings in Abu Serga, Babylon, Old Cairo: the Logos Made Visible." *Bulletin of the American Research Center in Egypt* 190, 14–17.

———. 2006b. "Late Antique Aesthetics, Chromophobia, and the Red Monastery, Sohag, Egypt." *Eastern Christian Art* 3, 1–24.

———., ed. 2002. *Monastic Visions: Wall Paintings in the Monastery of Saint Antony at the Red Sea*. New Haven and London.

Boud'hors, A. and R.W. Boutros. 2000. "La Sainte Famille à Gabal al-Tayr et l'Homélie du Rocher," in *Études Coptes* 7, 59–76. Cahiers de la bibliothèque copte 12. Leuven.

Boud'hors, A., R. Boutros, and G. Colin. 2001. "L'homélie sur l'église du Rocher attribuée à Timothée Ælure (textes copte, arabe, ethiopien et traductions)." *Patrologia Orientalis* 49–1/2.

Boutros, R.W. 2000. "Dayr al-'Adra – Gabal al-Tayr (Moyenne Égypte) d'après les polygraphs arabes et les voyageurs européens," in *Études Coptes* 6, 107–119. Cahiers de la bibliothèque copte 11. Leuven.

———. 2004. "Dayr Gabal al-Tayr: Monastère ou église d'un village?" in *Coptic Studies on the Threshold of a New Millennium. Proceedings of the Seventh International Congress of Coptic Studies, Leiden, August 27–September 2, 2000*, eds. M. Immerzeel and J. van der Vliet, 1053–68. Louvain.

Boutros, R.W. and C. Décobert 2000. "Les installations chrétiennes entre Ballâs et Armant: implantation et survivance" in *Études Coptes* 7, 78–108. Cahiers de la bibliothèque copte 12. Leuven.

Bradshaw, Paul. 2004. *Eucharist Origins*. Oxford.

Brock, S. 1984. *The Harp of the Spirit. Eighteen Poems of Saint Ephrem*, 2nd enlarged ed. San Bernardino.

Brooks Hedstrom, D.L. 2004. "An Archaeological Mission for the White Monastery." *Coptica* 4 (The Life and Times of St. Shenouda the Archimandrite. A Conference Held in Los Angeles, August 13–14, 2004), 1–26.

Burmester, O.H.E. 1954. *A Guide to the monasteries of the Wadi 'n-Natrun*. Cairo.

———. 1955. *A Guide to the Ancient Churches of Cairo*. Cairo.

Buschhausen, H. and F.M. Khorshid. 1998. Die Malerei zu Deir al-Genadla, in ΘΕΜΕΛΙΑ – *Spätantike und koptologische Studien Peter Grossmann zum 65. Geburtstag*, eds. Krause, M. and S. Schaten, 55–67. Wiesbaden (Sprachen und Kulturen des christlichen Orients 3).

Buschhausen, H. 2003. "Die Obere Kirche in Dayr Abu Fano in Mittelägypten. Probleme der Restaurierung und Wiederherstellung." *Steine Sprechen* 126.

Butler, A.J. 1884. *The Ancient Coptic Churches of Egypt*, vols. 1–2. London.

Capuani, M. 1999. *Christian Egypt: Coptic Art and Monuments through Two Millennia*. Collegeville, MN.

Cody, A. and P. Grossmann. 1991a. "Dayr Anba Bishoi." *Coptic Encyclopedia*, vol. 3, 734–36.

———. 1991b. "Dayr al-Suryan." *Coptic Encyclopedia*, vol. 3, 876–81.

Cody, A., P. Grossmann, and P.P.V. van Moorsel. 1991. "Dayr al-Baramus." *Coptic Encyclopedia*, vol. 3, 789–94.

Coquin, Ch. 1974. *Les édifices chrétiens du Vieux-Caire.* Bibliothèque d'études coptes 11. Cairo.

———. 1991a. "Church of Abu Sayfayn," in *The Coptic Encyclopedia*, vol. 2, 549–52.

———. 1991b. "Church of al-Mu'allaqah," in *The Coptic Encyclopedia*, vol. 2, 557–60.

Coquin, R.-G. 1975. *Livre de la consécration du sanctuaire de Benjamin.* Bibliothèque d'études coptes XIII. Cairo.

Coquin, R.-G. and P. Grossmann. 1991. "Dayr Abu Maqrufah and Dayr al-Janadlah," in *The Coptic Encyclopedia*, vol. 3, 704–706.

Coquin, R.-G. and M. Martin. 1991a. "Dayr Abu al-Lif," in *The Coptic Encyclopedia*, vol. 3, 703–704.

———. 1991b. "Dayr Anba Pisentius," in *The Coptic Encyclopedia*, vol. 3, 757.

———. 1991c. "Dayr Durunkah," in *The Coptic Encyclopedia*, vol. 3, 799–800.

———. 1991d. "Dayr al-Muharraq," in *The Coptic Encyclopedia*, vol. 3, 840–41.

———. 1991e. "Dayr Rifah," in *The Coptic Encyclopedia*, vol. 3, 855–56.

———. 1991f. "Dayr al-Zawiyah," in *The Coptic Encyclopedia*, vol. 3, 884.

Coquin, R.-G., M. Martin, and P. Grossmann. 1991a. "Dayr Abu Fanah," in *The Coptic Encyclopedia*, vol. 3, 698–700.

———. 1991b. "Dayr al-Majma," in *The Coptic Encyclopedia*, vol. 3, 819–22.

———. 1991c. "Dayr al-Malak Mikha'il," in *The Coptic Encyclopedia*, vol. 3, 827–28.

———. 1991d. "Dayr Mar Buqtur," in *The Coptic Encyclopedia*, vol. 3, 829–30.

———. 1991e. "Dayr Qubbat al-Hawwa" in *The Coptic Encyclopedia*, vol. 3, 850–52.

———. 1991f. "Dayr al-Salib" in *The Coptic Encyclopedia*, vol. 3, 858–60.

Coquin, R.-G, M. Martin, P. Grossmann, and P. Du Bourguet. 1991. "Dayr Anba Hadra," in *The Coptic Encyclopedia*, vol. 3, 744–45.

Coquin, R.-G., M. Martin, P. Grossmann, and H.G. Severin. 1991. "Dayr Anba Shinudah," in *The Coptic Encyclopedia*, vol. 3, 761–70.

Coquin, R.-G., M. Martin, H.G. Severin, and P. Grossmann. 1991. "Dayr Anba Bishoi," in *The Coptic Encyclopedia*, vol. 3, 736–40.

"Cronica." *1996: Studia Orientalia Christiana. Collectanea* 26–27: Studia-Documenta, 75 ff.

Czaja-Szewczak, B. 2005. "Tunics from Naqlun," in *Christianity and Monasticism in the Fayoum Oasis*, ed. G. Gabra, 133–42. Cairo.

Daniélou, J. 1954. "Terre et Paradis chez les Pères de l'Église." *Eranos-Jahrbuch* 22, 433–72.

Davis, S.J. 2001. "Ancient Sources for the Coptic Tradition," in *Be Thou There. The Holy Family's Journey in Egypt*, ed. G. Gabra, 133–62. Cairo.

———. 2004. *The Early Coptic Papacy. The Egyptian Church and Its Leadership in Late Antiquity.* Cairo.

Dekker, R. 2006. "Dayr Anba Hadra, Dayr Qubbat al-Hawwa and

Dayr al-Kubaniyyah and their relations with the world outside the walls." M.A. Thesis, Leiden University.

Delahaye, G.-R. 2003. "Johann Michael Vansleb (1635–1679). Voyageur en Égypte et en Orient pour le compte de la Bibliothèque royale." *Le Monde Copte* 33, 113–22.

Denon, V. 1802. *Voyage dans la basse et la haute Égypte, pendant les campagnes du Général Bonaparte.* Paris (reprint Institut Français d'Archéologie Orientale 1989–1990).

Depuydt, L. 1993. *Catalogue of Coptic Manuscripts in the Pierpont Morgan Library*, vols. 1–2. Corpus of Illuminated Manuscripts, 4–5/Oriental Series, 1–2. Louvain.

Dumuleau, J. 1992. *Une histoire du Paradis I : Le Jardin des délices.* Paris.

Emmel, S. 2004. *Shenoute's Literary Corpus.* Louvaii.

Encyclopædia Britannica. 2007. "Catherine of Alexandria, Saint." Encyclopædia Britannica Online (http://search.eb.com/eb/article-9021811).

Evans, H. and W.D. Wixom, eds. 1997. *The Glory of Byzantium.* New York.

Evelyn White, H.G. 1926. *The Monasteries of the Wâdi'n Natrûn I: New Coptic Texts from the Monastery of Saint Macarius.* New York.

———. 1932. *The Monasteries of the Wâdi'n Natrûn II: The History of the Monasteries of Nitria and of Scetis.* New York.

———. 1933. *The Monasteries of the Wâdi'n Natrûn III: The Architecture and Archaeology.* New York.

Evetts, B.T.A., ed. 1907. History of the Patriarchs of the Coptic Church of Alexandria, vol. I and II, *Patrologia Orientalis* I, 99–214 and 381–518.

———. 1910. History of the Patriarchs of the Coptic Church of Alexandria, vol. III, *Patrologia Orientalis* V, 1–215.

———. 1915. History of the Patriarchs of the Coptic Church of Alexandria, vol. IV, *Patrologia Orientalis* X, 357–551.

Evetts, B.T.A. and A. J. Butler, eds. 1895. *The Churches and Monasteries of Egypt and some neighbouring countries attributed to Abu Salih, the Armenian.* Oxford (reprint 2001).

Frend, W.H.C. 1996. The Archaeology of Early Christianity. Minneapolis.

Gabra, G. 1999. "Über die Flucht der Heiligen Familie nach koptischen Traditionen." *Bulletin de la Societé d'Archéologie Copte* 38, 29–50.

———. 2002. *Coptic Monasteries: Egypt's Monastic Art and Architecture.* Cairo.

———. 2003. "The Revolts of the Bashmuric Copts in the Eights and the Ninth Centuries," in *Die Koptische Kirche in den ersten drei islamischen Jahrhunderten, Leucorea Kolloquium* 2002, ed. W. Beltz (= Hallesche Beiträge zur Orientwissenschaft 36/2003), Halle (Saale) 2003, 111–19.

Gabra, G., ed. 2001. *Be Thou there. The Holy Family's Journey in Egypt.* Cairo.

———. 2005. *Christianity and Monasticism in the Fayoum Oasis.* Cairo.

Gabra, G. and A. Alcock. 1993. *Cairo, the Coptic Museum and Old Churches.* Cairo. (reprint 1999).

Gabra, G. and M. Eaton-Krauss. 2007. *The Treasures of Coptic Art in the Coptic Museum and Churches of Old Cairo.* Cairo.

Gabra, G. and C.D.G. Müller. 1991. "Saint Pisentius," in *The Coptic Encyclopedia*, vol. 6, 1978–80.

Godlewski, W. 2000. "Les peintures de l'église de l'Archange Gabriel à Naqlun." *Bulletin de la Societé d'Archéologie Copte* 39, 89–101.

Godlewski, W. 2005a. "Excavating the Ancient Monastery at Naqlun," in *Christianity and Monsasticism in the Faymoum Oasis*, ed. G. Gabra, 155–71.

———. 2005b. The Medieval Coptic Cemetery at Naqlun, in *Christianity and Monsasticism in the Faymoum Oasis*, ed. G. Gabra, 173–83.

Grossmann, P. 1979. "The Basilica of St. Pachomius." *Biblical Archaeologist* 42, no. 4, 232–36.

———. 1982. *Mittelalterliche Langhauskuppelkirchen und Verwandte Typen in Oberägypten*. Abhandlungen des deutschen archäologischen Instituts Kairo, Koptische Reihe, 3. Glückstadt.

———. 1989. "Early Christian Architecture in the Nile Valley," in *Beyond the Pharaohs*, ed. F.D. Friedman, 81–88. Providence, RI.

———. 1990. "Early Christian Architecture in the Nile Valley," in *Coptic Art and Culture*, ed. H. Hondelink, 3. Cairo.

———. 1991a. "Babylon," in *The Coptic Encyclopedia*, vol. 2, 317–23.

———. 1991b. "Luxor Temples, Churches in and outside," in *The Coptic Encyclopedia*, vol. 5, 1484–86.

———. 1997. "Zur datierung der ersten Kirchenbauten in der Sketis." *Byzantinische Zeitschrift* 90, 367–95.

———. 1998a. "Koptische Architektur," in *Ägypten in spätantik-christlicher Zeit*, ed. M. Krause, 209–67. Wiesbaden.

———. 1998b. "The Pilgrimage Center of Abu Mina," in *Pilgrimage and Holy Space in Late Antique Egypt*, ed. David Frankfurter, 281–302. Leiden.

———. 2002. *Christliche Architektur in Ägypten*. Handbook of Oriental Studies, section 1: The Near and Middle East 62. Leiden.

———. 2004a. "A Journey to Several Monasteries Between Naqada and Qamula in Upper Egypt." *Bulletin de la Societé d'Archéologie Copte* 43, 25–32.

———. 2004b. "On the Architecture in the Wadi al-Natrun." *Coptica* 3 (Proceedings of the Wadi al-Natrun Symposium, Wadi al-Natrun, Egypt, February 1–4, 2002), 17–42.

———. 2006a. "Zum Dach über dem Ostumgang der Kirche des Bishuyklosters bei Suhag." *Eastern Christian Art* 3, 37–46.

———. 2006b. "Neue Beobachtungen zur Sergioskirche von Alt-Kairo." *Bulletin de la Societé d'Archéologie Copte* 45, 9–24.

Grossmann, P. and H.-G. Severin. 1991. "al-Ashmunayn," in *The Coptic Encyclopedia*, vol. 1, 285–88.

———. 1997. "Zum antiken Bestand der al-Adra kirche des Dair al-Baramûs im Wâdî Natrûn." *Mitteilungen der Christlichen Archaeologie* 3, 30–52.

Grossmann, P., R.-G. Coquin, and M. Martin. 1991. "Dayr al-Ahdra," in *The Coptic Encyclopedia*, vol. 3, 715–16.

Guirguis, M. 2000. "Athar al-Arakhinah 'ala awda' al-Qabat fi-l-qarn al-thamin 'ashr." *Annales Islamologiques* 34, 23–44.

Haas, Chr. 1997. *Alexandria in Late Antiquity: Topography and Social Conflict*, Baltimore and London.

Habib, R. 1967. *The Ancient Churches of Cairo: A Short Account*. Cairo.

Hacken, C.E. ten. 2004. "The Legend of Aûr: Arabic Texts concerning the foundation of the Monastery of Naqlun," in *Coptic Studies on the Threshold of a New Millennium. Proceedings of the Seventh International Congress of Coptic Studies. Leiden, August 2–September 2, 2000*, eds., M. Immerzeel and J. van der Vliet, 337–48. Louvain.

Hardy, E.R. 1952. *Christian Egypt, Church and People: Christianity and Nationalism in the Patriarchate of Alexandria*. New York.

Heide, B. and A. Thiel, eds. 2004. Sammler, Pilger, Wegbereiter. *Die Sammlung des Prinzen Johann Georg von Sachsen. Mainz, Landesmuseum 5.12.2004–10.4.2005*. Mainz.

den Heijer, J. 1993. "The Composition of the 'History of the Churches and Monasteries of Egypt': some Preliminary Remarks," in *Acts of the Fifth International Congress of Coptic Studies, Washington D.C. 12–15 August 1992.*, eds., T. Orlandi and D.W. Johnson, vols. 1–2, 209–19. Rome.

——— 1994. "The Influence of the 'History of the Patriarchs of Alexandria' on the 'History of the Churches and Monasteries of Egypt' by Abu-l-Makarim." *Parole de l' Orient* 19, 415–39 (ed. S.K. Samir, Actes du 4eme Congrès International d'Études Arabes Chrétiennes, Cambridge September 1992, vol. 2).

———. 1996. "Coptic Historiography in the Fatimid, Ayyubid and Early Mamluk Periods." *Medieval Encounters* 2, 67–98 (ed. D. Thomas, Papers from the Second Woodbrooke-Mingana Symposium on Arab Christianity and Islam, Woodbrooke College, Selly Oak Colleges, Birmingham, 19–22 September 1994).

———. 2004. "Relations between Copts and Syrians in the Light of Recent Discoveries at Dayr al-Suryan," in *Coptic Studies on the Threshold of a New Millennium. Proceedings of the Seventh International Congress of Coptic Studies. Leiden, August, 27–September 2, 2000*, eds., M. Immerzeel and J. van der Vliet, 923–38. Louvain.

Hobbs, J.J. 1996. *Mount Sinai*. Cairo: The American University in Cairo Press.

Horner, G., ed. and trans. 1902. *The Service for the Consecration of a Church and Altar According to the Coptic Rite*. London.

Hulsman, C. 2001. "Tracing the Route of the Holy Family Today," in *Be Thou There. The Holy Family's Journey in Egypt*, ed. Gabra, G., 31–131. Cairo.

Hunt, L.A. 1985. "Christian-Muslim Relations in Painting in Egypt of the Twelfth to mid-Thirteenth Centuries: Sources of Wallpainting at Deir es-Suriani and the Illustration of the New Testament MS Paris, Copte-Arabe 1/Cairo, Bibl. 94." *Cahiers Archéologique* 33, 111–55.

———. 1989. "The al-Mu'allaqa Doors Reconstructed: An Early Fourteenth-Century Sanctuary Screen from Old Cairo." *Gesta* 28, 61–77.

———. 2003. "Stuccowork at the Monastery of the Syrians in the Wadi Natrun: Iraqi-Egyptian artistic contact in the 'Abbasid period," in *Christians at the Heart of Islamic Rule. Church Life and Scholarship in 'Abbasid Iraq*, ed., D. Thomas, 93–127. Leiden.

———. 2004. "Art in the Wadi al-Natrun: An Assessment of the Earliest Wallpaintings in the Church of Abu Makar, Dayr Abu Maqar." *Coptica* 3 (Proceedings of the Wadi al-Natrun Symposium, Wadi al-Natrun, Egypt, February 1–4, 2002), 69–103.

Immerzeel, M. 2004a. "The Stuccoes of Deir al-Surian: A Waqf of the Takritans in Fustat?" in *Coptic Studies on the Threshold of a New Millennium. Proceedings of the Seventh International Congress of Coptic Studies. Leiden, August 27–September 2, 2000*, eds. M. Immerzeel and J. van der Vliet, 1303–20. Louvain.

———. 2004b. "A Play of Light and Shadow: The Stuccoes of Dayr al-Suryan and Their Historical Context." *Coptica* 3 (Proceedings of the Wadi al-Natrun Symposium, Wadi al-Natrun, Egypt, February 1–4, 2002), 104–29.

Immerzeel, M. and A. Jeudy, in press. "Christian Art in the Mamluk Period," in *Proceedings of the Symposium 'Towards a Cultural History of Bilad-al-Sham in the Mamluk Era. Prosperity or Decline, Tolerance or Persecution?' Balamant 3rd to 7th May 2005*.

Innemée, K.C. 2001. "Deir al-Surian (Egypt): Conservation work of Autumn 2000." *Hugoye: Journal of Syriac Studies* 4–2 (http://syrcom.cua.edu/hugoye).

———. 2005. "Excavation at the site of Deir el-Baramus 2002–2005." *Bulletin de la Société d'Archéologie Copte* 44, 55–68.

Innemée, K.C. and L. Van Rompay. 1998. "La presence des Syriens dans le Wadi al-Natrun (Egypte)." *Parole de l'Orient* 23, 167–202.

———. 2002. "Deir al-Surian (Egypt): New Discoveries of 2001–2002." *Hugoye: Journal of Syriac Studies* 5–2 (http://syrcom.cua.edu/hugoye).

Innemée, K.C., L. Van Rompay, and E. Sobczynski. 1999. "Deir al-Surian (Egypt): Its Wall-paintings, Wall-texts and Manuscripts." *Hugoye: Journal of Syriac Studies* 2–2 (http://syrcom.cua.edu/hugoye).

Jeudy, A. 2004. "Icones et ciboria: relation entre les ateliers coptes de peinture d'icônes et l'iconographie du mobilier liturgique en bois." *Eastern Christian Art* 1, 67–87.

Johann Georg, Duke of Saxony. 1914. *Streifzüge durch die Kirchen und Klöster Ägyptens*. Leipzig/Berlin.

———. 1930. *Neue Streifzüge durch die Kirchen und Klöster Ägyptens*. Leipzig/Berlin.

———. 1931. *Neueste Streifzüge durch die Kirchen und Klöster Ägyptens*. Leipzig/Berlin.

Jones, M. 2002. "The Church of St. Antony: The Architecture," in *Monastic Visions: Wall Paintings in the Monastery of Saint Antony at the Red Sea*, ed. Bolman, 30. New Haven and London.

———. 2004. "Conservation Continues at St. Paul's Monastery." *Bulletin of the American Research Center in Egypt* 186, 10–12.

Kalavrezou-Maxeiner, I. 1975. "The Imperial Chamber at Luxor." Dumbarton Oaks Papers 29, 225–51.

Khater, A. and O.H.E. Burmester, eds. 1968. *History of the Patriarchs of the Egyptian Church known as the History of the Holy Church*, vol. III–i. Publications de la Société d'Archéologie Copte, Textes et Documents XI. Cairo.

———. 1970. *History of the Patriarchs of the Egyptian Church known as the History of the Holy Church*, vol. III–ii and iii. Publications de la Société d'Archéologie Copte, Textes et Documents XII–XIII. Cairo.

———. 1974. *History of the Patriarchs of the Egyptian Church known as the History of the Holy Church*, vol. IV–i and ii. Publications de la Société d'Archéologie Copte, Textes et Documents XIV–XV. Cairo.

Kleinbauer, W.K. 1987. "The Double-Shell Tetraconch Building at Perge in Pamphylia and the Origin of the Architectural Genus." *Dumbarton Oaks Papers* 41, 277–93.

Krause, M. 1998. "Heidentum, Gnosis und Manichäsmus, ägyptische Survivals," in *Ägypten in spätantik-christlicher Zeit. Einführung in die koptische Kultur*, ed., M. Krause, 1–116. Sprachen und Kulturen des christlichen Orients 4. Wiesbaden.

———. 1981. "Das christliche Alexandrien und seine Beziehungen zum koptischen Ägypten," in eds. G. Grimm, H. Heinen, and E. Winter, *Alexandrien: Kulturbegegnungen dreier Jahrtausende im Schmelztiegel einer mediterranen Großstadt*, Aegyptiaca Treverensia. Trierer Studien zum griechisch-römischen Ägypten, vol. 1, 53–62. Mainz.

Labib, S.Y. 1991. "Abraham, Saint." *The Coptic Encyclopedia* 1, 10 f.

Laferrière, P.-H. 1993. "Les croix murales du monastère Rouge à Sohag." *Bulletin de l'Institut Français d'Archéologie Orientale du Caire* 91, 299–311.

Le Messager 1987. *Journal of the Franciscans in Egypt*. "L'église de L'Assomption du Mousky," August 30, 1987, September 6, 1987, September 20, 1987.

Leroy, J. 1982. *Les peintures des couvents du Ouadi Natroun*, Cairo (La peinture murale chez les Coptes II—Mémoires Publiés par les Membres de l'Institut Français d'Archéologie Orientale 101).

van Loon, G.J.M. 1999. *The Gate of Heaven–Wall Paintings with Old Testament Scenes in the Altar Room and the Hurus of Coptic Churches*. Uitgaven van het Nederlands Historisch-Archeologisch Instituut te Istanbul/Publications de l'Institut historique-archéologique néerlandais de Stamboul 85. Leiden.

———. 2003. "Abraham, Isaac and Jacob in Paradise in Coptic Wall Painting." *Visual Resources. An International Journal of Documentation* XIX–1, 67–79.

———. 2004. "The Meeting of Abraham and Melchizedek" and "The Communion of the Apostles" in *Coptic Studies on the Threshold of a New Millennium. Proceedings of the Seventh International Congress of Coptic Studies. Leiden, August 27–September 2, 2000*, eds., M. Immerzeel and J. van der Vliet, 1381–1400. Louvain.

———. 2006. "The Virgin Mary and the Midwife Salomé. The So-called Nativity Scene in 'Chapel' LI in the Monastery of Apollo in Bawit." *Eastern Christian Art* 3, 81–104.

Lyster, W. 1999. *The Monastery of Saint Paul*. Cairo.

———., ed. In press. *The Cave Church of Saint Paul the Hermit*.

Łyżwa-Piper, A. 2005. "The Basketry from Excavations at Naqlun," in *Christianity and Monsasticism in the Faymoum Oasis*, ed. G. Gabra, 231–45.

Martin, M., ed. 1972. "Notes inédites du P. Jullien sur trois monastères chrétiens d'Égypte: Dêr Abou Fâna—Le couvent des 'Sept-Montagnes'—Dêr Ambâ Bisâda." *Bulletin de l'Institut Français d'Archéologie Orientale du Caire* 71, 119–28.

———. 1982. Sicard, Cl., Oeuvres I–III. Bibliothèque d'études LXXXIII–LXXXV. Cairo.

Matta al-Miskin (Abuna). 1991. "Dayr Anba Maqar." *Coptic Encyclopedia*, vol. 3, 748–56.

Mayeur-Jaouen, C. 1992. "Un jésuite français en Égypte, le père Jullien," in *Itinéraires d'Égypte. Mélanges offerts au Père Maurice Martin S.J.*, ed. C. Décobert, 213–47. Bibliothèque d'études 107. Cairo.

McVey, K.E. 1983. "The Domed Church as Microcosm: Literary Roots of an Architectural Symbol." *Dumbarton Oaks Papers* 37, 91–121.

———. 1993. "The Soghitha on the Church of Edessa in the Context of Other Early Greek and Syriac Hymns for the Consecration of Church Buildings." *ARAM* 5, 329–70 (A Festschrift for Dr. Sebastian P. Brock).

Meinardus, O.F.A. 1972–1973. "St. Barbara in the Coptic Cult." *SOC-Collectanea* 15, 123–32.

———. 1977. *Christian Egypt, Ancient and Modern*, 2nd (revised) ed. Cairo.

———. 1986–1987. *The Eucharist in the historical experience of the Copts*, Texts and Studies 5–6, 155–70.

———. 1987. *The Holy Family in Egypt*, 2nd ed. Cairo.

———. 1989. *Monks and Monasteries of the Egyptian Deserts*, revised ed. Cairo.

———. 1994. *The Historic Coptic Churches of Cairo*. Cairo.

———. 2000. "Im Schatten des heiligen Antonius: das St. Paulus-kloster." Kemet 3/2000.

———. 2002. *Coptic Saints and Pilgrimages*. Cairo.

———. 2006. *Christians in Egypt: Orthodox, Catholic, and Protestant Communities Past and Present*. Cairo.

Meinardus, O.F.A. and P. Grossmann. 1991. "Dayr al-Naqlun," in *The Coptic Encyclopedia*, vol. 3, 845–47.

Meinardus, O.F.A., R.-G. Coquin, M. Martin, and P.P.V. van Moorsel. 1991. "Dayr Anba Bula," in *The Coptic Encyclopedia*, vol. 3, 741–44.

Meinardus, O.F.A., R.-G. Coquin, M. Martin, P. Grossmann, and P.P.V. van Moorsel. 1991. "Dayr Anba Antuniyus," in *The Coptic Encyclopedia*, vol. 3, 719–28.

Meurice, C. 2006. "Découverte et premières études des peintures du monastère de Saint-Siméon à Assouan" in *Études Coptes* 9, 291–303. Cahiers de la bibliothèque copte 14. Paris.

Middeldorf Kosegarten, A. 2000. "Die mittelalterlichen Ambonen aus Marmor in den koptischen Kirchen Alt-Kairos." *Marburger Jahrbuch für Kunstwissenschaft* 27, 29–81.

Milward Jones, A. 2006. "Conservation of the Mediaeval Wall Painting in the Church of Sts. Sergius and Bacchus (Abu Serga)." *Bulletin of the American Research Center in Egypt* 190, 9–13.

Monneret de Villard, U. 1925–1926. *Les Couvents près de Sohâg*, vols. 1–2. Milan.

———. 1927. *Il monastero di S. Simeone presso Aswân*, vols. 1–2. Milan.

van Moorsel, P.P.V. 1991. "Ein Thron für den Kelch" in Tesserae. *Festschrift für Josef Engemann*, 299–303. Jahrbuch für Antike und Christentum—Ergänzungsband 18.

———. 1992. "Treasures from Baramous, with some Remarks on a Melchizedek Scene," in *Actes du IVe Congrès Copte. Louvain-la-Neuve, 5–10 septembre 1988*, vol. 1, eds. M. Rassart-Debergh and J. Ries, 171–77. Publications de l'Institut Orientaliste de Louvain 40. Louvain-la-Neuve.

———. 1995a. *Les peintures du Monastère de Saint-Antoine près de la Mer Rouge*, vols. 1–2, Cairo (La peinture murale chez les Coptes III—Mémoires Publiés par les *Membres de l'Institut Français d'Archéologie Orientale* 112).

———. 1995b. "La grande annonciation de Deir es-Sourian." *Bulletin de l'Institut Français d'Archéologie Orientale du Caire* 95, 517–37.

———. 2000a. "The Medieval Iconography of the Monastery of St. Paul as Compared with the Iconography of St. Antony's Monastery," in *Called to Egypt. Collected Studies on Painting in Christian Egypt*, 41–62. Leiden.

———. 2000b. "Analepsis? Some Patristic Remarks on a Coptic Double-Composition," in *Called to Egypt. Collected Studies on Painting in Christian Egypt*, 97–106. Leiden,

———. 2000c. "The Vision of Philotheus (On Apse-Decorations)," in *Called to Egypt. Collected Studies on Painting in Christian Egypt*, 107–114. Leiden.

———. 2000d. "Forerunners of the Lord. Saints of the Old Testament in Medieval Coptic Church Decoration," in *Called to Egypt. Collected Studies on Painting in Christian Egypt*, 179–202. Leiden.

———. 2002. *Les peintures du Monastère de Saint-Paul près de la Mer Rouge*. Cairo (La peinture murale chez les Coptes IV—*Mémoires Publiés par les Membres de l'Institut Français d'Archéologie Orientale* 120).

van Moorsel, P.P.V. and M. De Grooth. 2000. "The Lion, the Calf, the Man and the Eagle in Early Christian and Coptic Art," in *Called to Egypt. Collected Studies on Painting in Christian Egypt*, 115–38. Leiden.

van Moorsel, P.P.V., M. Immerzeel, and L. Langen. 1994. *Catalogue général du Musée copte: The Icons*. Cairo.

Müller, C.D.G. 1959. "Neues über Benjamin I, 38. und Agathon, 39. Patriarchen von Alexandrien." *Le Muséon* 72, 323–47.

———. 1962. "Die Bücher der Einsetzung der Erzengel Michael und Gabriel." Corpus Scriptorum Christianorum Orientalium 225–26. Louvain.

Munier, H. 1940. "Les monuments coptes d'après les explorations du père Michel Jullien." *Bulletin de la Societé d'Archéologie Copte* 6, 141–68.

Ovadiah, A. 1995. "Deir el-'Adra: The Resting Place of the Holy Family on the Flight to Egypt," in *Akten des XII. Internationalen Kongresses für Christliche Archäologie, Bonn 22.–28. September 1991*, 1065–68. Münster.

Parandowska, E. 2004. "Results of the Recent Restoration Campaigns (1995–2000) at Dayr al-Suryan." *Coptica* 3, 130–40 (Proceedings of the Wadi al-Natrun Symposium, Wadi al-Natrun, Egypt, February 1–4, 2002).

———. 2005. "Preservation of the Wall Paintings in the Church of the Archangel Gabriel at Naqlun," in *Christianity and Monsasticism in the Faymoum Oasis*, ed. G. Gabra, 2005, 279–89. Cairo.

Partrick, Th. H. 1996. *Traditional Egyptian Christianity*. Greensboro, NC.

Patricolo, A., U. Monneret de Villard and H. Munier. 1922. *La chiesa di Santa Barbara al vecchio Cairo*. Florence.

Pearson, B.A. 1986. "Earliest Christianity in Egypt: Some Observations," in *The Roots of Egyptian Christianity*, eds., B.A. Pearson and J.E. Goehring. Philadelphia.

Périer, J., ed. 1922. "La perle précieuse traitant des sciences ecclésiastiques (chapitres I-LVI) par Jean, fils d'Abou-Zakariya, surnommé Ibn Sabâ`." *Patrologia Orientalis* 16, 592–760.

Petrie, W.M. Flinders. 1907. *Gizeh and Rifeh*. London.

Pillet, M. 1935–1938. "Structure et décoration architectonique de la nécropole antique de Deïr-Rifeh." *Mélanges Maspero I : Orient Ancien*, 61–75. Cairo (*Mémoires Publiés par les Membres de l'Institut Français d'Archéologie Orientale 66*).

Porkurat, M, A. Golitzin, and M.D. Peterson. 1996. *Historical Dictionary of the Orthodox Church*. Lanham, MD and London.

Rossi, Corinna and A. de Luca. 2006. *The Treasures of the Monastery of Saint Catherine*. Cairo: The American University in Cairo Press.

Russell, N., trans. 1981. *The Lives of the Desert Fathers*, with introduction by B. Ward SLG. Cistercian Studies series 34. Oxford/Kalamazoo.

Rutschowscaya, M.-H. 1998. *Le Christ et l'abbé Ména*. Louvre, Collection Solo 11 – Département des Antiquités égyptiennes. Paris.

Samuel (Bishop) and Badie Habib. 1996. *Ancient Coptic Churches & Monasteries in Delta, Sinai, and Cairo*. Cairo.

Sauneron, S. 1969. "Villes et légendes de l'Égypte (§ XXV–XXIX)." *Bulletin de l'Institut Français d'Archéologie Orientale du Caire 67*, 117–145.

Sellheim, R. and D. Sourdel. 1978. "Katib," in *The Encyclopedia of Islam*, vol. 4, 754–57.

Skálová, Z. and G. Gabra. 2006. *Icons of the Nile Valley*, 2nd ed. Cairo.

Snelders, B. and A. Jeudy. 2006. "Guarding the Entrances: Equestrian Saints in Egypt and North Mesopotamia." *Eastern Christian Art* 3, 103–40.

Somers Clarke. 1912. *Christian Antiquities in the Nile Valley*. Oxford.

al-Suryani, S. 1990. *Guide to the Ancient Coptic Churches and Monasteries in Upper Egypt*. Cairo.

———. 1992. *Abu al-Makarem*, Cairo.

al-Syriany, S. and B. Habib. 1990. *Guide to Ancient Coptic Churches and Monasteries in Upper Egypt*. Cairo.

Tagher, J. 1998. *Christians in Muslim Egypt: An Historical Study of the Relations Between Copts and Muslims from 640 to 1922*. Arbeiten zum spätantiken und koptischen Ägypten 10. Altenberge.

Timm, S. 1984–1992. *Das christlich-koptische Ägypten in arabischer Zeit*. 6 vols. Beihefte zum Tübinger Atlas des vorderen Orients, Reihe B (Geisteswissenschaften) Nr. 41/1–6. Wiesbaden.

UNESCO. 2002. World Heritage Committee, Twenty-sixth Session, Budapest, Hungary, 24–29 June 2002, *Information on Tentative Lists and Examination of nominations of cultural and natural properties of the List of World Heritage in Danger and the World Heritage List*, (WHC-02/CONF.202/20), http://whc.unesco.org/p_dynamic/document/document_download.cfm?id_document=1353.

Vansleb (Wansleben), J.M. 1677. *Nouvelle Relation en forme de Journal d'un Voyage fait en Egypte en 1672 & 1673*. Paris.

Venit, M.J. 2002. *Monumental Tombs of Ancient Alexandria. The Theater of the Dead*. Cambridge.

Viaud, G. 1979. *Les pèlerinages coptes en Égypte*. Bibliothèque d'Études Coptes XV. Cairo.

van der Vliet, J. 2002. Pisenthios de Coptos (569–632): moine, évêque et saint. Autour d'une nouvelle édition de ses archives, in *Autour de Coptos: actes du colloque organisé au Musée des Beaux-Arts de Lyon (17–18 mars 2000). (=TOPOI.Supplément 3)*, ed., M.-F. Boussac, 61–72.

Walters, C.C. 1974. *Monastic Archaeology in Egypt*. Warminster, UK.

White, L. Michael. 1996. *The Social Origins of Christian Architecture*. Valley Forge, PA.

Wietheger, C. 1992. *Das Jeremias-Kloster zu Saqqara unter besonderer Berücksichtigung der Inschriften*. Arbeiten zum spätantiken und koptischen Ägypten 1. Altenberge.

Wilfong, T. G. 1998. "The Non-Muslim Communities: Christian cCmmunities," in *The Cambridge History of Egypt I: Islamic Egypt, 640–1517*, ed., C.F. Petry, 175–97. Cambridge.

Wipszycka, E. 1988. "La christianisation de l'Égypte aux IVe–VIe siècles. Aspects sociaux et ethniques." *Aegyptus 68*, 117–65.

Wissa, M. 1991. "Harit Zuwaylah," in *The Coptic Encyclopedia*, vol. 4, 1207–1209.

Wüstenfeld, F., trans. 1845, *Macrizi's Geschichte der Copten*. Göttingen (reprint 1979).

Young, D.W. 1981. "A Monastic Invective against Egyptian Hieroglyphs" in *Studies Presented to Hans Jacob Polotsky*, ed., D.W. Young, 348–60. Beacon Hill, MA.

Zanetti, U. 1991. "Les icônes chez les théologiens de l'église copte." *Le monde Copte* 19, 77–98.

———. 1993. "Matarieh, La Sainte Famille et les Baumiers." *Analecta Bollandiana* 111, 21–68

———. 1995. "Abu'l-Makarim et Abu Salih." *Bulletin de la Societé d'Archéologie Copte* 34, 85–138.

Zibawi, M. 2003. *Images de l'Égypte chrétienne. Iconologie copte*. Paris.

Index

Abraham (Patriarch of Coptic Church), 100, 112
Abu al-Makarim/Abu Salih (historian), 32, 134, 140, 194
Abu Sayfayn, *see* Mercurius
Agathon (Patriarch of Alexandria), 30
Alexander (Patriarch of Alexandria), 15
altar(s), 60
altar room, 30, 64, 70, 78, 84
    decorations of, 31, 32, 33, 40, 60, 64, 84
    function of, 30
    symbolism of, 30–31
ambon, *see* pulpit
Amun (hermit), 17
Anba Ruways, Abbasiya (Coptic Center), 174, 178
anchorites, 78, 92
angels(s), 34, 78
Anthanasius (Patriarch of Alexandria), 178
Antony (saint), 16–17, 28, 208, 220, 230
Apa Bane (hermit and saint), 242
Apollo (saint), 29
apse, decoration of, 25, 26, 27, 32, 92, 130, 178
archangels, 33, 202
archaeology of early Christian sites, 12, 14, 17, 22, 23, 31, 284
    al-Ashmunayn, 246
    Cliff Churches of Dayr Rifa (Asyut), 256
    Kellia, 23
    Wadi al-Natrun, 23
    Monastery of Abu Fana, 242
architectural sculpture, 33, 34
architecture of Egyptian Churches, 22–29
    building materials, 24, 25, 26, 27, 28, 29, 104, 278, 290
    development and evolution of, 22–24, 27–29
    elements of, 22–29
    financial constraints and considerations, 26, 27
    five-aisled church layout, 24, 25, 27
    influences on, 22, 23, 24, 25, 26, 28, 29, 284
    proximity to pharaonic sites, 23, 24, 25, 27, 246, 254, 266, 300, 308
    uniqueness of, 22–23, 24
Arius, the heresy of, 15
art of Coptic Churches, 29–37
    archaeology of, 31
    images of saints, patriarchs, and bishops, 30, 32
    influences on, 31, 33, 34–35, 70, 150
    instructional function, 33
    preservation of paintings, 35
    symbolism of, 30–31, 32–33, 34, 35
    themes of, 31–33, 34, 35, 58
    uniqueness of, 33
al-Ashmunayn (Hermopolis Magna), 24, 246
Athanasius (saint, Patriarch of Alexandria), 15, 18, 264
Aûr of Naqlun (bishop and saint), 202

Bacchus (saint), 106
baptistery, 22, 23, 24, 26, 146
Barbara (saint), 120
Barsum the Naked (saint), 100
Basil (saint), 100
basilica plan, 23, 24, 25, 26, 27, 28
    churches using, 64, 78, 100, 108, 112, 120, 134, 186, 202, 230, 246, 278, 284, 300
Benjamin (Patriarch of Alexandria), 18, 30, 30

Benjamin II (Patriarch of the Coptic Church), 78, 140
Bigul (saint), 278, 284
borders, 31, 33, 34
Burning Bush, 92
Byzantine rule, 17–18

Catechetical School of Alexandria, 14
Cathedral
    of the Holy Virgin (Port Said), 40–43
    of the Holy Virgin Mary and St. Simeon the Tanner (Muqattam), 188–93
    of St. Mark (Abbasiya), 179
    of St. Mark (Catholic) (Shubra), 146–49
    Old Cathedral of St. Mark (Azbakiya), 174–77
Catherine of Alexandria (saint), 51, 92
Catholics
    churches of, 40
    in Egypt, 20, 166
ceiling(s), painted, 51, 178, 266
Chapel
    of the Burning Bush at St. Catherine's Monastery (Sinai), 96–98
    of the Four Living Creatures in the Church of St. Antony (Red Sea), 208
    of the Martyrs in the Monastery of the Syrians (Wadi al-Natrun), 70
    of St. Anthanasius in Anba Ruways (Abbasiya), 178
Christ
    enthroned, 32, 33, 34, 64, 84
    footprint of, 90
    surrounded by saints, etc., 32
    with angels, 32, 33, 52
    with the four Evangelists, 56
Christians, persecution of, 14–15, 18–21
Christians in Egypt, denominations of, 14, 20
Christodoulus (Patriarch of Coptic Church), 19
church
    function of, 30
    furniture of, 23, 33, 34
    symbolism of, 30
Church
    of Anba Ruways (Abbasyia), 184
    Anglican Church of St. Mark (Alexandria), 56–59
    of St. Antony (Beni Suef), 230–33
    of the Archangel Gabriel (Fayyum), 34, 202–207
    Armenian Cathedral of St. Gregory the Illuminator (Ramses), 130–31
    of St. Athanasius at the Monastery of al-Zawya (Asyut), 262–65
    of St. Barbara (Old Cairo), 120–21
    Basilica of Our Lady (Heliopolis), 170–73
    of Bishop Abraam (Muqattam), 188
    al-Butrusiya *see* Church of St. Peter and St. Paul
    of St. Catherine (Alexandria), 52–55
    of St. Catherine (Sinai), 92
    of the Cave, *see* Church of Sts. Sergius and Bacchus (Old Cairo)
    Cliff Churches of Dayr Rifa, 256–61
    Coptic Evangelical Church (Faggala), 154–55
    Coptic Evangelical Church (Qasr al-Dubara), 128–29
    Coptic Patriarchal Church of St. Mark (Alexandria), 48

of the Cross at the Monastery of the Cross, 290
of St. Cyril Melkite Catholic Church (Heliopolis), 166–69
Franciscan Church of the Assumption (Muski), 130–31
of St. George, (Harat Zuwayla, Muski), 134
of St. George (Naqada), 295–96
Greek Orthodox Church of the Dormition, *see* Sleeping Mary Greek Orthodox Church
Greek Orthodox Church of St. George (Old Cairo), 122–23
Greek Orthodox Cathedral of St. Saba (Alexandria), 60–63
Hanging Church (Old Cairo), 19, 112–15
of Harat al-Rum, 134
on the Hill at the Monastery of Abu Fana (Minya), 242–45
of the Holy Virgin (Maadi), 194–99
of the Holy Virgin Mary (Old Cairo), *see* the Hanging Church (Old Cairo)
of the Holy Virgin Mary and Anba Ruways (Anba Ruways), 183
of the Holy Virgin Mary and St. Pshoi (Anba Ruways), 182
of the Holy Virgin (Zaytun), 156–59
of the Holy Virgin Mary (Sakha), 90–91
of the Holy Virgin at the Monastery of al-Baramus, 34, 35, 64–69
of the Holy Virgin at the Monastery of Durunka (Asyut), 254–55
the Holy Virgin at the Monastery of the Syrians (Wadi al-Natrun), 28, 31, 32, 33, 35, 70–75
Jesuits' Holy Family Church (Faggala), 150
Jesuits' Holy Family Church (Matariya), 160
of St. John at the Monastery of St. George (Naqada), 296–89
of St. Macarius (Wadi al-Natrun), 34, 84
of St. Menas (Fumm al-Khalig), 36, 140–45
of St. Mercurius (Akhmim), 274–77
of St. Mercurius (Old Cairo), 100–105
of St. Mercurius, (Harat Zuwayla, Muski), 134–39
of St. Mercurius (Red Sea), 220–29
in the Monastery of the Blessed Virgin, 256
of the Monastery of St. Hatre, 304
North Church in Bawit, 31
Old Church of St. Antony (Red Sea), 28–29, 31, 33, 34, 35, 208–19, 220
of St. Paul (Muqattam), 188
of St. Paul (Red Sea), 35, 220–29
of St. Peter and St. Paul (Abbasiya), 186–87
of the Pilgrimage Center of St. Dimyana Monastery, 44–47
of St. Pshai (Sohag), 278–83
of St. Pshoi (Wadi al-Natrun), 32, 33, 35, 78–83
of Sts. Sergius and Bacchus (Old Cairo), 108–11, 120
of St. Shenute at the Monastery of the Cross, 292
Sleeping Mary Greek Orthodox Church, 122, 124–27
South Church of Bawit, 31–32, 33
of St. Theodore (Asyut), 256, 261
of St. Theodore (Minya), 234–37
in the Tomb of Khune, 308
of St. Victor at the Monastery of St. Victor (Naqada), 297

of the Virgin (Gabal al-Tayr, Minya), 238–41
of the Virgin (Harat Zuwayla, Muski), 130–31
of the Virgin Mary (Asyut), 256–59
of the Virgin at the Monastery of al-Ganadla (Asyut), 266–73
of the Virgin at the Monastery of al-Muharraq (Asyut), 248–53
churches of Cairo, 34, 35
churches in Luxor Temple and Karnak Temple, 300
churches of the Sohag monasteries, 34
ciboria
in churches of Old Cairo, 37, 112
themes in, 37
wooden, 140, 274
clerestory, 22
clothing, 34
columns, colonnade, 23, 24, 25, 28, 122, 170
painted, 26
conservation and restoration efforts, 26, 32, 33
of specific sites, 64, 70, 78, 100, 108, 112, 120, 132, 134, 140, 156, 166, 202, 208, 248, 266, 290, 292
efforts of Ibrahim and Girgis al-Guhari, 106, 174, 194, 220
Constantine I (emperor), 15, 22
convents
of the Holy Virgin (Harat Zuwayla, Muski), 134
of St. George (Harat Zuwayla, Muski), 134
conversion of temple to church, 27
controversies, theological, 15, 16, 62
Copt/Coptic (term), 14
Coptic Catholic Church, The, 20
Coptic Church, The
development of nationalist sentiment, 16, 17
patriarchal seat, 19
relationship with other churches, 18, 20–21
revival in nineteenth century, 20
theological rift with Church of Rome, 15–16
Coptic language, 15
Coptic Museum, 17, 31
Coptic Synaxarion (Calendar of Saints), 120
corinthian capitals, 24, 48
Council of Chalcedon, 16, 60
Council of Ephesus, 16
Council of Ferrara-Florence, 20
Council of Nicea, 15
cult
of Apa Bane, 242
of St. Catherine, 92
of St. Dimyana, 44
of Menas, 26
Cyril the Great (Patriarch of Alexandria), 15, 16, 166
Cyril IV, the Reformer (Patriarch of Coptic Church), 20, 174
Cyril V (Patriarch of Coptic Church), 174, 194
Cyrus (al-Muqawqas) (Patriarch from Byzantium), 18
Cyrus (medical saint), 120

dating paintings, 35
Decius (emperor), 14, 98
Demetrius (Patriarch of Alexandria), 14
Demetrius II (Patriarch of the Coptic Church), 48, 174
Dimyana (saint), 44
Diocletian (emperor), 15, 44, 297, 300
Dionysius (Patriarch of Alexandria), 14, 15
Dioscorus (Patriarch of Alexandria), 16
dome and ceiling decoration, 34, 156
door(s), decorated, 40, 76, 179
Dormition of the Virgin Mary, 124

Edict of Milan, 15
Entry into Jerusalem, in decoration, 64
Era of the Martyrs, 15

Eusebius (historian), 14
Eutyches (archimandrite), 16

Farouk (King of Egypt), 128
Fatimids, 19
Fayyum, 34
four evangelists, 51, 55
Four Living Creatures, 32, 34
frieze(s), 278, 304
standing saints, 33
Virgin Mary, 33
equestrian saints, 33

Gabriel IV (Patriarch of Alexandria), 18
Gaianite heresy, 6
al-Gawli see Patriarch Peter VII
George (saint), 124
Gregory the Illuminator (saint), 130
al-Guhari, Girgis, 106, 174, 194
al-Guhari, Ibrahim, 20, 106, 174, 220

hall church, 234
domed, 274
Hatre (saint) (also called St. Simeon), 304
al-Hawariya (ancient Marea), 24
Helena (mother of Constantine I), 22
Heraclius (emperor), 18
hermits, 17, 84, 202, 220, 290, 304, 308
Hermopolis Magna see al-Ashmunayn
history of Christianity in Egypt
archeological evidence of, 12, 14, 17, 22, 23, 31
Catholic Missions, 20
development of nationalist identity, 16–17
Islamization of Egypt, 14, 18–21
reconciliation attempts with Rome, 20
spread or growth of in Egypt, 14, 15, 16–18
schism, 20
theological controversies, 15–17
role of Patriarchs of Alexandria in, 15
nature of Christ, 15, 16
nature of the Virgin Mary, 16
Holy Family in Egypt, 10–11, 12, 108, 124, 134, 248, 296
stories and legends about, 11, 90, 122, 164, 194, 238, 246, 254
Holy Family Tree (Matariya), 164
house churches, 22

iconostasis, 48, 60, 90, 120
icons, 11, 36–37, 40, 44, 48, 60, 62, 92, 94, 112, 120, 122, 130, 132, 140, 166, 174, 183, 184, 194, 274
deesis, 36, 208, 284
influences on style 36–37, 48
of Bawit, 36
of Old Cairo, 36
painters of, 28, 36
placement of, 36
production of, 44
restoration, 36
role of, 36
themes, 36, 40, 44, 48, 60
inscriptions in decorations, 32, 33, 70, 208
Iskhirun (equestrian saint), 78

Jerome (saint), 17, 18
Jesuit Christians in Egypt, 150
Joachim (Melkite Patriarch of Alexandria), 122
John (medical saint), 120
Justinian (emperor), 92

Julian the Apostate (emperor), 100
Kellia (the Cells) see monastic communities
khurus, 27, 28, 29, 30 (term), 31, 64, 70, 78, 120, 284
at church of Monastery of St. Jeremiah, 28
covered with wooden doors, 28
decoration of, 32, 33, 34
symbolism of, 31
use of in Wadi al-Natrun, 28

Last Supper, 32, 40, 48
Leo XII (Pope of Rome), 20

Macarius the Great (saint), 17, 64, 84
Macrobius (saint, hermit), 266
Maqar, Anba, see Macarius (saint)
al-Maqrizi (historian), 19, 44, 122, 140, 234, 246, 260, 278, 288
Marcian (emperor), 16
Mark the Evangelist (saint), 14, 179, 184
Mark VIII (Patriarch of Coptic Church), 174
martyr(s), 14, 15, 26, 44, 51, 108, 122, 297
legends of, 100, 120, 184
matyrion, 26, 29
Matthew IV (Patriarch of Coptic Church), 20, 134
Maximinus Daia (emperor), 15
Melkite Christians, 16, 18, 19, 60, 122
Menas (saint), 26, 140
Mercurius (saint), 100
miracle of moving the Muqattam Mountain, 100, 112
missionaries
French, 160
Protestant, 20
Modernization of Egypt, 20
Monastery
of Abu Fana (Minya), 242–45
of St. Andrew (Naqada), 292
of St. Antony (Red Sea), 17, 28, 31, 33, 208–19, 230
of St. Apollo (Bawit), 31
of the Archangel Gabriel (Fayyum), 202–207
of the Archangel Michael (Naqada), 299
of al-Baramus (of the Romans), 17, 28, 34, 64–69
of St. Catherine (Sinai), 92–97, 170
of the Cross (Naqada), 290–92
of the Crosses (Minya), see Monastery of Abu Fana
of St. Dimyana, 44
of Durunka (Asyut), 254–55
at Faw Qibili (Pbow), 24
of al-Ganadla (Asyut), 31, 32, 33, 266–73
of St. George (Naqada), 295–296
of St. Hatre (Aswan), 28, 32, 304–307, 308
of the Holy Virgin, see Monastery of al-Muharraq (Asyut)
of St. Jeremiah (Saqqara), 28, 31
of John the Little (Wadi al-Natrun), 17
of St. Macarius (Wadi al-Natrun), 16, 17, 28, 30, 34, 35 36, 84–89
of St. Macrobius, 266
of the Martyrs, 29
of al-Maymun (Pispir), 17
of al-Muharraq (Asyut), 248–53
of St. Paul (Red Sea), 35, 220–29
of St. Pisentius (Naqada), 296
of St. Pshoi (Wadi al-Natrun), 28, 34, 70, 74–83
at Qubbat al-Hawa (Aswan), 308–309
Red Monastery of St. Pshai (Sohag), 17, 25–26, 31, 32, 266, 278
of al-Sanquriya (Minya), 234–37
of St. Simeon the Tanner (Muqattam), 188–93
of the Sycamore (Beni Suef), 230
of the Syrians (Wadi al-Natrun), 17, 28, 31, 32, 33, 70–77

of St. Victor (Naqada), 297–98

White Monastery of St. Shenute (Sohag), 17, 18, 26–27, 278, 284–89

of al-Zawya (Asyut), 262–65

monastic church at Monastery of St. Jeremiah, 28

monastic communities

Aswan, 28, 304

Fayyum, 202

Nag' Hammadi, 17

Nitria, 17

Kellia, 17–18

Naqada, 290–303

Sohag, 18

Wadi al-Nar, 58

Wadi al-Natrun, 17, 64, 78, 80

monasticism,

history and growth of, 15, 16–18

influence of Egypt on Western monasticism, 15, 17, 18

role in preservation of Christian history, 18

monks, role in Egyptian Church, 18

mosaics

at Armenian Cathedral of St. Gregory the Illuminator (Ramses), 130

at the Church of the Holy Virgin Mary and St. Pshoi (Anba Ruways), 182

at St. Catherine's Monastery (Sinai), 92

Moses of Nisibis (abbot), 70

al-Mu'allaqa Church, *see* Hanging Church

al-Muqawqas (Cyrus), 18

Muslim rule

taxation of Christians, 18, 19, 20

role of Christians in government, 18, 19–20

status of Copts under, 18–20

revolts against, 18

murals, *see* wall paintings

narthex, 22, 24, 25, 26, 27, 28

nave, 22, 23, 24, 25, 28, 60, 70, 84

decoration of, 33, 34, 64

function of, 31

symbolism of, 31

two-aisled design, 23, 24, 25

Nero (emperor), 24

Nestorius (Patriarch of Constantinople), 16

New Testament themes, 84

Ascension of Christ, 32

Communion of the Apostles, 32

scenes from the Book of Revelations, 33

Twenty-four Priests of the Apocalypse, 33

niches, decorative, 25, 26, 28, 64, 262, 266, 278, 284, 304, 308

nimbus, rectangular, 304, 308

Nitria, *see* monastic communities

Old Testament themes, 33, 35

Abraham willing to sacrifice Isaac, 33, 62

Dream of Jacob, 35

Isaiah getting his lips purified, 33

Jephthah sacrificing his daughter, 33

Job, 35

meeting of Abraham and Melchizedek, 33, 62

organ(s), 51, 55

orphanage, 154

Pachomius (saint), 17, 24

Pachomian Rule, 17, 248, 284

paintings, 31–33

paintings on wood, 36

Palladius (monk, bishop, historian), 18

panel(s)

inlaid, 88

painted, 31

sculpted, 76

Paul of Thebes (saint), 220

Peter I (Patriarch of Alexandria), 15

Peter VII (al-Gawli) (Patriarch of the Coptic Church), 48

Photius (Melkite Patriarch of Alexandria), 122

Pichoshe (equestrian saint), 202

Pilgrimage Center of St. Dimyana Monastery (Bilqas), 44

Pilgrimage Center of the Cult of St. Menas, 26

Pisentius (saint), 290, 296

proximity of Christian sites to pharaonic sites, 23, 24, 25, 27, 246, 254, 266, 300, 304

Protestant Church in Egypt, The, 20

Pshai (saint), 278

Pshoi (saint), 78

pulpit, decorated, 25, 51, 56, 60, 112, 174, 234

quarry church

of the Monastery of al-Ganadla, 33

of Wadi Sarga (Middle Egypt), 31–32

Qiddis 'Agib 'Abd al-Mashi (zabbalin), 188

relics, 78, 92, 140, 178, 179, 184

Saba (saint), 58

saints

equestrian, 33, 84, 202

in paintings, 32–33, 40, 51, 56, 64, 78

legends and stories of, 17, 29, 51, 92, 100, 120, 188, 202, 220, 242, 278, 304

medical, 32, 120

military, 100, 108

Samaan (saint), *see* Simeon the Tanner (saint)

sanctuary 22, 23, 24, 25, 26, 27, 28, 40, 48

apsidal, 24

decoration of, 33, 181, 186, 280

trilobed or triconch, 25, 32

tripartite, 27

screens

wooden, 34, 35, 40, 112, 120, 156, 174, 182, 183, 230, 234, 274

inlaid, 140, 234

sculpture, architectural, 31, 33–34, 278

painting of, 31

stone, 33, 130

wooden, 33–34, 51, 130

See of Constantinople, 16

See of Alexandria (See of St. Mark), 16, 18, 60

loss of leading position in Christian Church, 16

removal of Patriarchal Seat, 19

Septimius Severus (emperor), 14

Sergius (saint), 108

Shenouda III, Anba (Patriarch of the Coptic Church), 20–21, 78, 178, 188

Shenute of Atripe (saint), 17, 18, 33, 278, 284

Shrine of St. Mark in Anba Ruways (Abbasiya), 184

Simeon the Tanner (saint), 188

Socrates (church historian), 15

stairs, 25, 60, 134, 174

statues, 40

of Christ, 56, 150

of the Holy Family, 160

of saints, 40, 146

of Virgin Mary, 40

synthronon, 22, 23, 174

tetraconch church layout, 26

theology, 15, 16, 20, 21

Theodosius I (Patriarch of Alexandria), 15, MSH

Theodosius II (Patriarch of Alexandria), 16

Theophilus (Patriarch of Alexandria), 248, 304

Theotokos, 16

Timothy II (Patriarch of Alexandria), 238

tombs,

of Ibrahim and Girgis al-Guhari (Old Cairo), 106

of Boutros Ghali in Church of St. Peter and St. Paul (Abbasiya), 186

of St. Pisentius at Monastery of St. George (Naqada), 295

Three Hebrews in the Fiery Furnace, 33, 78, 84

Three Patriarchs in Paradise, 33

transept, 24, 25, 134

Transfiguration, 92

Tree of Mary, 160, 164

tribelon, three-arched doorway, 24

triconch church, 27

trilobed sanctuary, 32, 278, 284

tripartite sanctuary, 28, 64

Twenty-four Priests of the Apocalypse, 33, 78, 84

Valerians (emperor), 15

vaults and domes, decorations of, 32, 33

Victor (equestrian saint), 297

Virgin Mary, 32

apparitions of, 156

as *orant*, 32

as *Theotokos*, 64

in legends, 202

nursing Christ, 32

statue of, holding a globe, 40

with Christ Child, 32, 33, 34, 64

with prophets, angels, 32

wall paintings, 28, 34–36,

as found in specific sites, 40, 64, 70, 78, 108, 112, 130, 140, 148, 160, 170, 202, 242, 266, 278, 286, 304, 308

dating, 35

in Bawit and Saqqara, 34

depiction of figures, 34

influences on, 34–35

preservation and restoration, 35

styles, 34

themes, 34–35, 62

use of color in, 34

White Monastery Federation of St. Shenute, 25

windows, stained glass, 44, 150, 179, 184

wooden sculpture

doors, 34

in churches of Wadi al-Natrun, 34

in churches of Cairo, 34

influences on style, 34

screens, 34, 35

Zacharius (Patriarch of Coptic Church), 202

Acknowledgments

Ît is impossible to acknowledge the help and support of so many over the past years. My great gratitude goes to the Coptic Orthodox churches especially, along with the monasteries, who opened their doors to make this book possible; to the Supreme Council of Antiquities of Egypt and all the inspectors who personally assisted me on the sites; and to all the wonderful and supportive friends of the American University in Cairo with whom I have been cooperating for so many years, especially Mary Iskander.

I am also immensely gratefully to Gregory Dillon and Jean-Pierre Minardi of Hilton Hotels for their grand hospitality and their wonderful staff; to Mohamed Nazmy of Quest Travel and his staff, for their guidance, along with Janice Brannon of Seven Wonders Travel; to Ehab Gaddis in Luxor; to Farid Fadel, and Mona and Isis Zaki, for guidance in Cairo; to Aaron Katz and Richard Restler and their staff, for their advice and patience; and to family and friends at home, for their caring prayers, especially Sondra Jones, George Wurzel, Pamela Ludwig, Charla Thompson and Susana Funsten in Los Angeles.

Carolyn Ludwig

I want to thank Mansour Borayek and Mohamed Abu Al-Yazeed for their contacts with the Supreme Council of Antiquities and for smoothing the way; Samia Fakhry for her help in the difficult communications and in organizing the thousands of slides taken for this book; Hannah Sonbol, who worked as an assistant photographer, carrying the equipment, and who took the main shot in Port Said Cathedral; Gerd Carlson and Samir Naoum for helping us to reach and work in the more remote churches; Bahaa Sobhy, the inspector in Old Cairo; and Sinout Shenouda for his patience and for arranging appointments with the Church authorities.

Sherif Sonbol